DOCUMENTS
FROM
OLD TESTAMENT
TIMES

Revised January, 1970

ḣarper 🔥 ꭲorcḣbooks

American Studies: General

CARL N. DEGLER: Out of Our Past: *The Forces that Shaped Modern America* CN/2
ROBERT L. HEILBRONER: The Limits of American Capitalism TB/1305
JOHN HIGHAM, Ed.: The Reconstruction of American History TB/1068
JOHN F. KENNEDY: A Nation of Immigrants. *Illus. Revised and Enlarged. Introduction by Robert F. Kennedy* TB/1118
GUNNAR MYRDAL: An American Dilemma: *The Negro Problem and Modern Democracy. Introduction by the Author.*
Vol. I TB/1443; Vol. II TB/1444
GILBERT OSOFSKY, Ed.: The Burden of Race: *A Documentary History of Negro-White Relations in America* TB/1405
ARNOLD ROSE: The Negro in America: *The Condensed Version of Gunnar Mydral's An American Dilemma* TB/3048

American Studies: Colonial

BERNARD BAILYN: The New England Merchants in the Seventeenth Century TB/1149
ROBERT E. BROWN: Middle-Class Democracy and Revolution in Massachusetts, 1691–1780. *New Introduction by Author* TB/1413
JOSEPH CHARLES: The Origins of the American Party System TB/1049

American Studies: The Revolution to 1900

GEORGE M. FREDRICKSON: The Inner Civil War: *Northern Intellectuals and the Crisis of the Union* TB/1358
WILLIAM W. FREEHLING: Prelude to Civil War: *The Nullification Controversy in South Carolina, 1816-1836* TB/1359
HELEN HUNT JACKSON: A Century of Dishonor: *The Early Crusade for Indian Reform.* ‡ *Edited by Andrew F. Rolle* TB/3063
RICHARD B. MORRIS, Ed.: Alexander Hamilton and the Founding of the Nation. *New Introduction by the Editor* TB/1448
RICHARD B. MORRIS: The American Revolution Reconsidered TB/1363
GILBERT OSOFSKY, Ed.: Puttin' On Ole Massa: *The Slave Narratives of Henry Bibb, William Wells Brown, and Solomon Northup* ‡ TB/1432

American Studies: The Twentieth Century

WILLIAM E. LEUCHTENBURG: Franklin D. Roosevelt and the New Deal: 1932-1940. † *Illus.* TB/3025
WILLIAM E. LEUCHTENBURG, Ed.: The New Deal: *A Documentary History* + HR/1354

Asian Studies

WOLFGANG FRANKE: China and the West: *The Cultural Encounter, 13th to 20th Centuries. Trans. by R. A. Wilson* TB/1326
L. CARRINGTON GOODRICH: A Short History of the Chinese People. *Illus.* TB/3015
BENJAMIN I. SCHWARTZ: Chinese Communism and the Rise of Mao TB/1308

Economics & Economic History

PETER F. DRUCKER: The New Society: *The Anatomy of Industrial Order* TB/1082
ROBERT L. HEILBRONER: The Great Ascent: *The Struggle for Economic Development in Our Time* TB/3030
W. ARTHUR LEWIS: The Principles of Economic Planning. *New Introduction by the Author°* TB/1436

Historiography and History of Ideas

J. BRONOWSKI & BRUCE MAZLISH: The Western Intellectual Tradition: *From Leonardo to Hegel* TB/3001
WILHELM DILTHEY: Pattern and Meaning in History: *Thoughts on History and Society.° Edited with an Intro. by H. P. Rickman* TB/1075
J. H. HEXTER: More's Utopia: *The Biography of an Idea. Epilogue by the Author* TB/1195
ARTHUR O. LOVEJOY: The Great Chain of Being: *A Study of the History of an Idea* TB/1009

History: Medieval

F. L. GANSHOF: Feudalism TB/1058
DENYS HAY: The Medieval Centuries ° TB/1192
HENRY CHARLES LEA: A History of the Inquisition of the Middle Ages. ‖ *Introduction by Walter Ullmann* TB/1456

---

† The New American Nation Series, edited by Henry Steele Commager and Richard B. Morris.
‡ American Perspectives series, edited by Bernard Wishy and William E. Leuchtenburg.
a History of Europe series, edited by J. H. Plumb.
§ The Library of Religion and Culture, edited by Benjamin Nelson.
‖ Researches in the Social, Cultural, and Behavioral Sciences, edited by Benjamin Nelson.
⚡ Harper Modern Science Series, edited by James R. Newman.
° Not for sale in Canada.
+ Documentary History of the United States series, edited by Richard B. Morris.
# Documentary History of Western Civilization series, edited by Eugene C. Black and Leonard W. Levy.
A The Economic History of the United States series, edited by Henry David et al.
¶ European Perspectives series, edited by Eugene C. Black.
** Contemporary Essays series, edited by Leonard W Levy.
* The Stratum Series, edited by John Hale.

History: Renaissance & Reformation

JACOB BURCKHARDT: The Civilization of the Renaissance in Italy. *Introduction by Benjamin Nelson and Charles Trinkaus. Illus.* Vol. I TB/40; Vol. II TB/41

JOEL HURSTFIELD: The Elizabethan Nation TB/1312

ALFRED VON MARTIN: Sociology of the Renaissance. ° *Introduction by W. K. Ferguson* TB/1099

J. H. PARRY: The Establishment of the European Hegemony: 1415-1715: *Trade and Exploration in the Age of the Renaissance* TB/1045

History: Modern European

MAX BELOFF: The Age of Absolutism, 1660-1815 TB/1062

ALAN BULLOCK: Hitler, A Study in Tyranny. ° *Revised Edition. Illus.* TB/1123

JOHANN GOTTLIEB FICHTE: Addresses to the German Nation. *Ed. with Intro. by George A. Kelly* ¶ TB/1366

H. STUART HUGHES: The Obstructed Path: *French Social Thought in the Years of Desperation* TB/1451

JOHAN HUIZINGA: Dutch Cviilization in the 17th Century and Other Essays TB/1453

JOHN MCMANNERS: European History, 1789-1914: *Men, Machines and Freedom* TB/1419

FRANZ NEUMANN: Behemoth: *The Structure and Practice of National Socialism, 1933-1944* TB/1289

A. J. P. TAYLOR: From Napoleon to Lenin: *Historical Essays* ° TB/1268

H. R. TREVOR-ROPER: Historical Essays TB/1269

Philosophy

HENRI BERGSON: Time and Free Will: *An Essay on the Immediate Data of Consciousness* ° TB/1021

G. W. F. HEGEL: Phenomenology of Mind. ° || *Introduction by George Lichtheim* TB/1303

H. J. PATON: The Categorical Imperative: *A Study in Kant's Moral Philosophy* TB/1325

MICHAEL POLANYI: Personal Knowledge: *Towards a Post-Critical Philosophy* TB/1158

LUDWIG WITTGENSTEIN: The Blue and Brown Books ° TB/1211

LUDWIG WITTGENSTEIN: Notebooks, 1914-1916 TB/1441

Political Science & Government

C. E. BLACK: The Dynamics of Modernization: *A Study in Comparative History* TB/1321

DENIS W. BROGAN: Politics in America. *New Introduction by the Author* TB/1469

KARL R. POPPER: The Open Society and Its Enemies *Vol. I: The Spell of Plato* TB/1101 *Vol: II: The High Tide of Prophecy: Hegel, Marx, and the Aftermath* TB/1102

CHARLES SCHOTTLAND, Ed.: The Welfare State ** TB/1323

JOSEPH A. SCHUMPETER: Capitalism, Socialism and Democracy TB/3008

PETER WOLL, Ed.: Public Administration and Policy: *Selected Essays* TB/1284

Psychology

LUDWIG BINSWANGER: Being-in-the-World: *Selected Papers.* || *Trans. with Intro. by Jacob Needleman* TB/1365

MIRCEA ELIADE: Cosmos and History: *The Myth of the Eternal Return* § TB/2050

SIGMUND FREUD: On Creativity and the Unconscious: *Papers on the Psychology of Art, Literature, Love, Religion.* § *Intro. by Benjamin Nelson* TB/45

J. GLENN GRAY: The Warriors: *Reflections on Men in Battle. Introduction by Hannah Arendt* TB/1294

WILLIAM JAMES: Psychology: *The Briefer Course. Edited with an Intro. by Gordon Allport* TB/1034

Religion

TOR ANDRAE: Mohammed: *The Man and his Faith* TB/62

KARL BARTH: Church Dogmatics: *A Selection. Intro. by H. Hollwitzer. Ed. by G. W. Bromiley* TB/95

NICOLAS BERDYAEV: The Destiny of Man TB/61

MARTIN BUBER: The Prophetic Faith TB/73

MARTIN BUBER: Two Types of Faith: *Interpenetration of Judaism and Christianity* TB/75

RUDOLF BULTMANN: History and Eschatology: *The Presence of Eternity* TB/91

EDWARD CONZE: Buddhism: *Its Essence and Development. Foreword by Arthur Waley* TB/58

H. G. CREEL: Confucius and the Chinese Way TB/63

FRANKLIN EDGERTON, Trans. & Ed.: The Bhagavad Gita TB/115

M. S. ENSLIN: Christian Beginnings TB/5

M. S. ENSLIN: The Literature of the Christian Movement TB/6

HENRI FRANKFORT: Ancient Egyptian Religion: *An Interpretation* TB/77

IMMANUEL KANT: Religion Within the Limits of Reason Alone. *Introduction by Theodore M. Greene and John Silber* TB/67

GABRIEL MARCEL: Homo Viator: *Introduction to a Metaphysic of Hope* TB/397

H. RICHARD NIEBUHR: Christ and Culture TB/3

H. RICHARD NIEBUHR: The Kingdom of God in America TB/49

SWAMI NIKHILANANDA, Trans. & Ed.: The Upanishads TB/114

F. SCHLEIERMACHER: The Christian Faith. *Introduction by Richard R. Niebuhr.* Vol. I TB/108 Vol. II TB/109

Sociology and Anthropology

KENNETH B. CLARK: Dark Ghetto: *Dilemmas of Social Power. Foreword by Gunnar Myrdal* TB/1317

KENNETH CLARK & JEANNETTE HOPKINS: A Relevant War Against Poverty: *A Study of Community Action Programs and Observable Social Change* TB/1480

GARY T. MARX: Protest and Prejudice: *A Study of Belief in the Black Community* TB/1435

ROBERT K. MERTON, LEONARD BROOM, LEONARD S. COTTRELL, JR., Editors: Sociology Today: *Problems and Prospects* || Vol. I TB/1173; Vol. II TB/1174

GILBERT OSOFSKY: Harlem: The Making of a Ghetto: *Negro New York, 1890-1930* TB/1381

PHILIP RIEFF: The Triumph of the Therapeutic: *Uses of Faith After Freud* TB/1360

GEORGE ROSEN: Madness in Society: *Chapters in the Historical Sociology of Mental Illness.* || *Preface by Benjamin Nelson* TB/1337

DOCUMENTS
FROM
OLD TESTAMENT
TIMES

TRANSLATED WITH INTRODUCTIONS
AND NOTES
BY MEMBERS OF THE OLD SOCIETY FOR
OLD TESTAMENT STUDY
AND EDITED BY

D. WINTON THOMAS

HARPER TORCHBOOKS
HARPER & ROW, PUBLISHERS
NEW YORK

Preface

THE Society for Old Testament Study was founded in January 1917. At a meeting held in January 1956, the Society decided to mark its forty years of existence by the publication of a volume which would be the fourth of a series. *The People and the Book*, edited by A. S. Peake, was published in 1925, *Record and Revelation*, edited by H. Wheeler Robinson in 1938 and *The Old Testament and Modern Study*, edited by H. H. Rowley in 1951. It was the Society's wish that this latest volume should consist of a selection of non-biblical documents illustrative of the Old Testament, designed to meet the needs more particularly of teachers of Scripture in schools, of the clergy, and of others who are not professional scholars. The Society did me the honour of entrusting me with the editorship of the volume, and I was given complete freedom in the planning of it and in the choice of contributors.

The aim throughout the volume has been to relate each document as closely as possible to the Old Testament, and to bring out relevant points of interest touching history, chronology, archæology, religion, literature, geography, and so on, in illustration of the Old Testament. Not all Israel's story is told in the Old Testament. It has to be supplemented by the evidence of ancient documents discovered by archæologists— inscriptions on clay, stone, seals and coins, and writings on potsherds, papyrus and leather. Some part of this story it is the purpose of this volume to tell. Some of the documents here discussed were found in Palestine itself, but mostly they were discovered in countries surrounding Palestine—in Mesopotamia, Egypt, Syria and Moab. While Israel is not without her testimony to herself, it is for the most part the witness of her neighbours which is met with in the pages of this volume. Considerations of length have inevitably imposed a limitation upon the number of selected documents. Some of those included have long been known ; others are of more recent discovery. Common to them all is the contribution which, in greater or lesser degree, they make to the better understanding of the history and of the life and thought of Israel, set as she was amidst the peoples of the ancient Near East.

The contributors have been required to conform to the general plan of the volume but, apart from this, have been allowed to treat the texts assigned to them in their own way, and the views they express are their own. The selected texts, whether presented in full or in extracts, have all been translated afresh from the original documents. Each text, or group of texts, is accompanied by an introduction, notes and bibliography. The bibliographies consist of the main authorities, and are not intended to be exhaustive. As far as possible, works written in English have been selected, but some works in French, German and Italian have also been included. In a few cases, where works in English are few, literature in foreign languages predominates.

While exact uniformity in such a work as this is not easy to attain, every effort has been made to secure as great a degree of it as possible. The text of the Revised Version has been used throughout, and the names of persons and places have been spelled in the forms familiar from it. Egyptian names appear in forms most likely to be familiar to the reader. Hebrew and other Semitic words are transliterated in such a way as to convey to the non-Hebraist an indication of their approximate pronunciation.

It is a pleasure to express thanks to those to whom thanks are due. I am grateful to the Society for Old Testament Study for entrusting me with a task which I have found highly rewarding ; to Dr. P. R. Ackroyd, Lecturer in Divinity in the University of Cambridge, who has kindly given of his time to prepare the indexes ; to Mr. D. J. Wiseman for his valuable assistance in connection with the plates ; and to the publishers, who have throughout shown a keen interest in the volume and have brought to its production high technical skill. I would like to express my thanks also to the contributors to the volume, with whom it has been a pleasure to co-operate. It is their hope, as it is also mine, that they have succeeded in bringing together material which is not readily accessible yet which is of considerable interest to all students of the Old Testament.

D. WINTON THOMAS.

List of Illustrations

Contributors

M. BLACK, D.D., F.B.A., Principal of St Mary's College, Professor of D
and Biblical Criticism, University of St Andrews.

D. DIRINGER, M.A., D.LITT., Lecturer in Semitic Epigraphy, Uni
of Cambridge.

T. FISH, M.A., PH.D., Professor of Mesopotamian Studies, Univers
Manchester.

A. E. GOODMAN, M.A., Lecturer in Aramaic, University of Cambrid

J. GRAY, M.A., B.D., PH.D., Lecturer in Hebrew and Biblical Cri
University of Aberdeen.

J. V. KINNIER WILSON, M.A., Eric Yarrow Lecturer in Assyr
University of Cambridge.

W. G. LAMBERT, M.A., Lecturer in Near Eastern Studies, Univer
Toronto.

W. D. McHARDY, M.A., B.D., D.PHIL., Samuel Davidson Professor
Testament Studies, University of London.

W. J. MARTIN, M.A., PH.D., Rankin Lecturer in Hebrew and A
Semitic Languages, University of Liverpool.

J. MAUCHLINE, M.A., D.D., Principal of Trinity College, Professor
Testament Language and Literature, University of Glasgow.

J. M. PLUMLEY, M.A., Herbert Thompson Professor of Egypt
University of Cambridge.

H. H. ROWLEY, D.D., F.B.A., Professor of Hebrew Language and Liter
University of Manchester.

J. N. SCHOFIELD, M.A., B.D., Lecturer in Divinity, University of Camb

N. H. SNAITH, M.A., D.D., Principal of Wesley College, Headingley,
Tutor in Old Testament Languages and Literature in Wesley Coll

T. W. THACKER, M.A., Professor of Semitic Philology, Univers
Durham.

D. WINTON THOMAS, M.A., Regius Professor of Hebrew, Univers
Cambridge.

E. ULLENDORFF, M.A., D.PHIL., Reader in Semitic Languages, Uni
of St Andrews.

J. WEINGREEN, M.A., Professor of Hebrew, Trinity College, Univer
Dublin.

C. J. MULLO WEIR, M.A., B.D., D.PHIL., Professor of Hebrew and S
Languages, University of Glasgow.

R. J. WILLIAMS, M.A., B.D., PH.D., Professor of Near Eastern St
University of Toronto.

D. J. WISEMAN, M.A., Assistant Keeper in the Department of W
Asiatic Antiquities, British Museum.

Contents

Cuneiform Documents

Egyptian Documents

A Moabite Document

Hebrew Documents

Aramaic Documents

Acknowledgments

THE editor wishes to thank the following for permission to reproduce prints :

Archives Photographiques, Paris—Pl. 10 ; the Trustees of the British Museum—Pls. 1, 3-6, 9, 14 (coins of John Hyrcanus and Alexander Jannaeus) ; Professor M. Dunand and the National Museum, Aleppo—Pl. 15 ; Dr N. Glueck—Pl. 13 (seal and seal impression of Jotham) ; the Hebrew University, Jerusalem—Pls. 13 (seal of Jaazaniah), 14 (Yehūd and Hezekiah coins) ; the Museum of the Ancient Orient, Istanbul—Pl. 11 (Siloam inscription) ; Dr C. F. A. Schaeffer and the British Academy—Pl. 7 ; and the Trustees of the late Sir Henry S. Wellcome—Pls. 10, 13 (seal impression of Gedaliah and weights).

Pl. 11 (Gezer Calendar) has been reproduced from D. Diringer, *Le Iscrizioni Antico-Ebraiche Palestinesi*, Florence 1934 ; Pls. 2, 8 from L. H. Grollenberg, *Atlas of the Bible*, Edinburgh 1956 ; Pl. 13 (seal of Shemaʻ) from A. Reifenberg, *Ancient Hebrew Seals*, London 1950, and Pl. 16 from E. Sachau, *Aramäische Papyrus und Ostraka*, Leipzig 1911.

Abbreviations

A.f.O.	*Archiv für Orientforschung.*
A.J.S.L.	*American Journal of Semitic Languages and Literatures.*
A.J.T.	*The American Journal of Theology.*
A.N.E.T.	J. B. Pritchard (ed. by), *Ancient Near Eastern Texts relating to the Old Testament*, second ed., 1955.
B.A.	*The Biblical Archæologist.*
B.A.S.O.R.	*Bulletin of the American Schools of Oriental Research.*
B.W.A.T.	Beiträge zur Wissenschaft vom Alten Testament.
C.A.H.	*Cambridge Ancient History.*
E.T.	*Expository Times.*
H.J.	*Hibbert Journal.*
I.C.C.	The International Critical Commentary.
J.B.L.	*Journal of Biblical Literature.*
J.E.A.	*Journal of Egyptian Archæology.*
J.P.O.S.	*Journal of the Palestine Oriental Society.*
J.Q.R.	*Jewish Quarterly Review.*
J.T.S.	*Journal of Theological Studies.*
LXX	The Septuagint (The Greek Version of the Old Testament)
M.T.	The Massoretic (Hebrew) Text of the Old Testament.
P.E.F.Q.S.	*Quarterly Statement of the Palestine Exploration Fund.*
P.E.Q.	*Palestine Exploration Quarterly.*
P.S.B.A.	*Proceedings of the Society of Biblical Archæology.*
R.B.	*Revue Biblique.*
W.C.	Westminster Commentaries.
Z.A.	*Zeitschrift für Assyriologie.*
Z.A.W.	*Zeitschrift für die alttestamentliche Wissenschaft.*
Z.D.P.V.	*Zeitschrift des deutschen Palästina Vereins.*

Note on the editing of the text

Words within square brackets represent restorations of the text. Words within round brackets are insertions made for the better understanding of the text. Dots indicate a lacuna in the text.

Introduction

THE documents selected for inclusion in this volume are arranged in five main groups. The first consists of documents written in cuneiform (wedge-shaped writing) and in the Akkadian (Assyrian and Babylonian) and Ugaritic languages, Ugaritic being the language of the texts from Ras Shamra (ancient Ugarit). The second consists of documents written in Egyptian; the third of one document only, written in Moabite; the fourth of documents written in Hebrew, and the fifth of documents written in Aramaic. The documents are thus grouped together on a basis of the script and language in which they are written. They are, however, of different types, and it may be helpful to the reader to provide a brief survey of them, and to give some indication of the way in which they are related to the Old Testament and of their approximate dates. A chronological table is appended.

The following types of document may be distinguished.

(i) *Epics, legends and myths.* The volume opens with extracts from two Babylonian epics, the Epic of Creation (*c.* 1750-1400 B.C.) and the Epic of Gilgamesh (*c.* 2000-1800 B.C.), into the second of which the Babylonian story of the Flood has been written. The extracts from the Epic of Creation are presented on a basis of a new analysis of stanza division, and newly identified texts of the hitherto fragmentary fifth tablet—there are seven in all— are included. The unusual view is advanced that the Epic of Creation has no connection of any kind with the account of the creation in Genesis. The Babylonian story of the Flood, however, contains material closely similar in substance to certain themes in the Flood story as found in Genesis.

The texts from Ras Shamra (*c.* 1400 B.C.), which embody legends and myths, reveal in all its nakedness the type of popular religion in Canaan which the prophets attacked so vehemently. They are important not only for the study of the religion of the Old Testament, but also for the light they throw on Hebrew literary conventions and on the Hebrew language, to which the Semitic dialect of the texts is closely allied. The extracts presented are from the Legend of King Keret, the Legend of Aqhat, Son of Dan'el, and the Baal Myths.

(ii) *A legal text*. It has long been known that the law code of Hammurabi, king of Babylon (*c.* 1792-1750 B.C.), bears many resemblances to ancient Hebrew law. Extracts from the Babylonian code are given and parallels with the Pentateuchal laws noted.

(iii) *Historical texts*. These form the great majority of the texts. The disturbed situation in Palestine *c.* 1400 B.C., to which invaders who are called Habiru (? Hebrews) largely contributed, is described in the letters to the Pharaoh sent by Abdiheba, governor of Jerusalem. These letters were found at Tell el-Amarna, in Egypt. The 'Israel Stele' of Merenptah (*c.* 1223-1211 B.C.) informs us, as the Old Testament does not, of this Pharaoh's Palestinian campaign, and contains references to the plundering of Canaan and the desolation of Israel, the only reference to the name Israel in any Egyptian inscription.

The kings of Assyria, from the ninth to the seventh centuries B.C., have left records of their interventions in the west in which references to Israel and Judah and their kings are frequent. Ahab's defeat at Qarqar in 853 B.C., and the tribute imposed upon Jehu, are recorded by Shalmaneser III (859-824 B.C.). The Old Testament tells us nothing directly of Israel's recognition of Adad-nirari III (810-782 B.C.). This Assyrian king claims, however, to have received tribute from her. Tiglath-pileser III (745-727 B.C.) mentions Menahem, Pekah and Hoshea, kings of Israel, as well as Ahaz, and perhaps too Azariah, both kings of Judah. Tiglath-pileser's son and successor, Shalmaneser V (727-722 B.C.), besieged Samaria for three years. It fell in 722 B.C. to the next king of Assyria, Sargon II (722-705 B.C.), and with its fall the northern kingdom of Israel came to an end. Sennacherib (705-681 B.C.) gives a vivid account of his siege of Jerusalem in 701 B.C. and of the tribute imposed upon King Hezekiah. Sennacherib's attack on Lachish and the obscure circumstances of his death are also recorded. Another Judaean tributary to Assyria, Manasseh, is mentioned by Esarhaddon (681-669 B.C.).

Two royal inscriptions in Aramaic throw welcome light on the long struggle of Israel with Syria. The first, belonging to the middle of the ninth century B.C., is the monument of Bar-Hadad, son of Tab-Rammon, which is dedicated to the god Milqart. This Bar-Hadad is probably Ben-hadad I (1 Kings xv.18). The second inscription, which is to be assigned to the middle of the eighth century B.C., is the inscription of Zakir, king of Hamath and Lu'ash, in commemoration of his victory at Hazrak over Ben-hadad, son of Hazael, king of Syria (2 Kings xiii.24) and his allies.

To the last quarter of the ninth century B.C. belongs the Moabite stone, which preserves the account of the victories of Mesha, king of Moab, over Israel. There is something of a discrepancy between the Old Testament narrative and the record on the stone, for whereas in the Old Testament (2 Kings iii.5ff.) Mesha's revolt against Israel is said to have occurred after Ahab's death, the stone, with the authority of a contemporary document, makes it clear that it took place in the latter years of the Israelite king. The stone has thus important historical links with the Old Testament. It gives much information also about the language and religion of the Hebrew Bible. The language of Moab was closely akin to Hebrew, more akin to it indeed than to any other Semitic language ; and Chemosh was Moab's national god in much the same way as Yahweh was Israel's.

The date of the potsherds from Samaria—invoices or labels sent with oil and wine from crown property to the king of Israel —is uncertain. They could belong to the ninth or the eighth century B.C., more probably perhaps to the latter. Many of the personal names mentioned in them are found in the Old Testament and have considerable significance for the under-standing of Hebrew religious ideas. The Siloam inscription also belongs to the eighth century B.C. It was cut into the rock when the tunnel which connects the Virgin's Spring with the Pool of Siloam was constructed. This tunnel was in all probability made by Hezekiah, king of Judah (2 Kings xx.20), and may have been built between Sargon's capture of Samaria in 722 B.C. and Sennacherib's siege of Jerusalem in 701 B.C.

The age of Jeremiah is illustrated by a number of documents.

Nineveh, over whose impending fate the prophet Nahum rejoiced exultantly, is now known from the Babylonian Chronicle to have fallen to the Babylonians and their Median and Scythian allies in 612 B.C., and not, as previously thought, in 606 B.C. A papyrus from Saqqarah, in Egypt, contains a letter to the Pharaoh (c. 603 B.C., or perhaps somewhat later), written in Aramaic, from Adon, king of some Semitic kingdom, possibly Ashkelon. It asks the help of the Pharaoh against the advancing troops of the Babylonian king, Nebuchadrezzar (605-562 B.C.), in much the same way as Abdiheba, governor of Jerusalem, had sought help from Egypt eight centuries earlier, in the Amarna age. Several of the documents relate to Nebuchadrezzar. There is the record of his expedition to Syria and of his liberation of the district and people of Lebanon ; of his crushing defeat of the Egyptian army at Carchemish in 605 B.C., a victory which may have influenced Jeremiah in his policy of submission to Babylon ; and of his capture of Jerusalem in 597 B.C. The exact date of the last event is now known for the first time— the city fell on 16 March of that year. Jehoiachin, king of Judah, was taken to Babylon, and from tablets discovered there, dated 595-570 B.C., we learn of the rations supplied to him and his five sons during their captivity—a highly interesting sequel to the narrative in 2 Kings xxiv.11ff. Jehoiachin was restored to favour by Evil-Merodach, king of Babylon (562-560 B.C.), as we are informed by Jer. lii.31ff.—'And for his allowance, there was a continual allowance given him of the king of Babylon, every day a portion until the day of his death, all the days of his life' (verse 34 ; cp. 2 Kings xxv.27f.).

Two further documents relate to the period of Jeremiah. The Babylonian Chronicle throws light on the conflict of Pharaoh Necho II with Judah which resulted in the death of Josiah on the battle-field of Megiddo in 609 B.C. (cp. 2 Chr. xxxv.20ff. ; Jer. xxii.10). The letters from Lachish (c. 590 B.C.) reflect the historical situation in Palestine just prior to the end of the southern kingdom in 587 B.C., when Zedekiah was on the throne of Judah (cp. Jer. xxxiv.7). They contribute to Old Testament study in a variety of ways. On the use of the Tetragrammaton (YHWH = Yahweh), the operation of fire signals, the kind of script used by Judaeans in the time of Jeremiah, the textual criticism of the Hebrew Bible, the historical development of the Hebrew language and Hebrew proper names—on all these, and on other matters the letters have much to teach.

From the period of the Babylonian Exile there are texts relating to Nabonidus, king of Babylon (556-539 B.C.), and to Cyrus, king of Persia (558-530 B.C.). In 539 B.C. Cyrus took Babylon, and by his edict of 538 B.C. (Ezra i.2ff.) the Jews were enabled to return home to Palestine from exile in Babylon. A few details concerning the fall of Babylon are supplied by the Nabonidus Chronicle. The Cyrus Cylinder, however, gives a fuller account of it.

Two sets of documents belong to the fifth century B.C. First, there are the papyri, written in Aramaic, from Elephantine, an island in the Nile. The dated texts cover almost the whole of the century. While they bear upon the history of the Old Testament—for example, upon the much debated question of the relative order of Nehemiah and Ezra—it is rather for the history of Hebrew religion that they are significant. The four texts presented in this volume relate to the religious practice of the Jewish colony in the island, a practice which reflects the popular pre-exilic religion of Canaan. They inform us that the temple there, dedicated to Yahu, was destroyed by the mob at the instigation of the Egyptian priests, and that the community made efforts to secure authority to rebuild it. The existence of this temple at Elephantine raises difficult problems when considered in connection with the law of the central sanctuary in Deut. xii.5ff. It is of rather special interest that the so-called Passover Papyrus was sent to the Jewish community by the king of Persia himself, Darius II, in 419 B.C.

The second set of documents from the fifth century are the Murashu tablets, written between 455 and 403 B.C. They were found at Nippur, south-east of Babylon, and belonged to a business house owned by the Murashu family. Some of the personal names found in them occur also in the books of Ezra, Nehemiah and Chronicles. While the tablets clearly show that there were Jews in central and southern Babylonia in the fifth century B.C., Murashu and his sons appear not themselves to have been Jews.

(iv) *Wisdom texts*. The Old Testament itself recognises that

Israel had no exclusive possession of Wisdom literature (1 Kings iv.30f. ; Jer. xlix.7 ; Obad. 8). Recent years have seen the discovery of a number of Sumerian, Babylonian and Egyptian works which testify to the existence of this extra-Israelite Wisdom and to the similarity of many of its main characteristics to those of Israelite Wisdom literature. The Babylonian 'Counsels of Wisdom' (c. 1500-1000 B.C. or earlier) in many respects resembles the book of Proverbs. 'The Babylonian Theodicy' (c. 1400-1000 B.C.), which is concerned with the suffering of the righteous, falls into the same category as the book of Job, and the Babylonian 'Shamash Hymn' (c. 1000 B.C.) reflects the sun-god's interest in moral conduct. 'The Instruction for King Meri-ka-re' (c. 2150-2080 B.C.), the work of an Egyptian sage, is likewise concerned with morality and just dealing, and contains many parallels to the language of the eighth century prophets and other Old Testament passages. Some kind of relationship may exist between the Egyptian work, 'A Dispute over Suicide' (c. 2280-2000 B.C.), and the book of Job. While no direct relationship can be claimed between any of these works and the Old Testament writings which they resemble, the case is remarkably different when another Egyptian work, 'The Teaching of Amenemope' (c. 1300 B.C.), is compared with the book of Proverbs. That a part of the book of Proverbs (xxii.17-xxiv.22) betrays literary dependence upon this Egyptian work is no longer open to doubt, and the text of the book of Proverbs can frequently be restored by reference to it.

The widely current cycle of Assyrian folk-lore and wisdom, known as 'The Words of Ahikar', may go back in origin to about the middle of the seventh century B.C. It is preserved in a fragmentary Aramaic version of the fifth century B.C., written on papyrus, from Elephantine, but is here translated in the main from a seventeenth-century Syriac manuscript, in which the text can be more fully studied than in the older fragmentary version. The work shows similarities, amounting sometimes to identity, with the books of Psalms, Proverbs and Ecclesiastes.

(v) *Hymns and Prayers*. The Babylonian 'Hymn to Shamash' has already been mentioned. In it the Mesopotamian sun-god, whose all-seeing eyes rove the universe, is praised as the giver of light and for the care he bestows upon all creatures. The

Babylonian 'Prayer to any God' (*c.* 700 B.C.) contains features which are found in the penitential psalms of the Old Testament, such as confession of sin and a plea for pardon ; and a certain resemblance to Old Testament penitential psalms is observable in the Egyptian 'Penitential Psalm' (*c.* 1290-1220). From the religious point of view, however, these Babylonian and Egyptian compositions show none of the noblest features of their Old Testament counterparts. The Egyptian 'Hymn to Aten' (*c.* 1370 B.C.) has much in common with Psalm civ, and a direct relationship between the two compositions has indeed been claimed.

(vi) *Letters.* The Old Testament contains but few examples of letter writing. The letters in Akkadian from Tell el-Amarna, in Hebrew from Lachish, and in Aramaic from Elephantine, add significantly to the material now available for the study of the epistolary style prevalent throughout the ancient Near East.

(vii) *Love songs.* The extracts from collections of Egyptian love songs, belonging to the period of the later Egyptian Empire (*c.* 1300-1100 B.C.), offer interesting parallels to the Song of Songs.

(viii) *A tale.* The Egyptian story 'The Tale of the Two Brothers' (*c.* 1210 B.C.) has often been compared with the story of Joseph and Potiphar's wife in Gen. xxxix. The claim that the Egyptian story is the origin of the incident described in Genesis scarcely seems tenable. Markedly absent in the Egyptian story is the religious element with which the Old Testament story is informed.

(ix) *An agricultural calendar.* A small tablet discovered at Gezer bears what is probably the most ancient inscription known in Early Hebrew script—it may be as old as the age of Saul or David (*c.* 1000 B.C.). The agricultural operations which it catalogues are of much interest in connection with Old Testament agricultural matters.

(x) *Seals.* Seals and seal impressions, with inscriptions in Early Hebrew characters, date from the ninth century B.C. and onwards, and are important for the contribution they make to the study of Hebrew palæography, proper names, and representational art. Familiar names are met with, such as Jeroboam, Gedaliah, Eliakim, Jotham and Hananiah, but their identification with persons known from the Old Testament is a matter of much uncertainty.

(xi) *Weights*. A number of weights, belonging to the sixth century B.C. and onwards, with their denomination inscribed upon them in Early Hebrew characters, have been unearthed in Palestine. One of them bears doubtfully the word *shekel*, some are inscribed with the word *netseph* 'half' (perhaps of the 'heavy' shekel), and others with the word *beqaʿ* 'half-shekel'. The most interesting, however, are those found at Lachish and inscribed with the word *pim*, for they enable a long-standing difficulty in the text of I Sam. xiii.21 to be satisfactorily cleared up.

(xii) *Coins*. Coins do not appear in the Old Testament until post-exilic times. The Persian gold daric is mentioned in Ezra ii.69 and Neh. vii.70ff. Especially important are coins of the fourth century B.C. with the word *Yehūd*, i.e. Judah, inscribed upon them, for they make it possible to carry investigation further into the organisation of the Jewish state in post-exilic times under Persian rule. Later (135-37 B.C.) come the coins struck during the Maccabaean period, with Jewish emblems impressed upon them in addition to inscriptions in Early Hebrew script. They have a special value as testifying to the religious and nationalistic spirit of the age.

The chronological table which follows is intended to be no more than a useful appendix to the present survey. The dates of the documents which are given are mostly based upon those which are to be found in the introductions to the documents or in the notes. In a few cases, where a date has not been mentioned elsewhere in the volume, it has been supplied in the table. Since on many points of Old Testament and ancient Near Eastern chronology scholars have not yet reached general agreement and the dates they propose frequently differ, sometimes within wide limits, the dates which are here given must for the most part be regarded as approximate only. It will be observed that they do not always correspond exactly to the dates given by the contributors to this volume.

D. WINTON THOMAS

A CHRONOLOGICAL TABLE

Circa
B.C.

2280-2000	Dispute over Suicide		
2150-2080	Instruction for King Meri-ka-re		
2000-1800	Story of the Flood		
		1800-1500	Age of the Patriarchs
1792-1750	Law Code of Hammurabi		
1750-1400	Epic of Creation		
1500-1000	Counsels of Wisdom		
1400	Texts from Ras Shamra		
1400-1360	Letters from Tell El-Amarna		
1400-1000	Babylonian Theodicy		
1370	Hymn to Aten		
1300-1100	Love Songs		
1300	Teaching of Amenemope		
1290-1220	Penitential Psalm		
1220-1210	'Israel Stele' of Merenptah		
1210	Tale of the Two Brothers		
1000	Gezer Calendar	Saul. David.	
	Shamash Hymn		
900-	Hebrew Seals		
		876-869	Omri
859-824	Shalmaneser III		
		869-850	Ahab
		853	Battle of Qarqar
850	Milqart Stele		
842-744	Potsherds from Samaria		
		842-815	Jehu
		814-798	Jehoahaz
		784-744	Jeroboam II
830	Moabite Stone		
810-782	Adad-nirari III		
755	Zakir Stele		
745-727	Tiglath-pileser III		
		783-742	Uzziah
		745-738	Menahem
		737-732	Pekah
		735-715	Ahaz
		732-724	Hoshea
727-722	Shalmaneser V		
722-705	Sargon II		
720-701	Siloam Inscription	722	Fall of Samaria
705-681	Sennacherib	715-687	Hezekiah
700	Prayer to Any God	701	Siege of Jerusalem
		687-642	Manasseh
681-669	Esarhaddon		

Circa
B.C.

650	Words of Ahikar		
		626-587	Age of Jeremiah
626-539	Babylonian Chronicle		
		621	Josiah's Reform
612	Fall of Nineveh		
		609	Death of Josiah
605-562	Nebuchadrezzar		
605	Battle of Carchemish		
603	Letter from Saqqarah		
600-	Hebrew Weights		
		598-587	Zedekiah
597	Fall of Jerusalem (16 March) ; the first Exile		
595-570	Jehoiachin Tablets		
		562-560	Evil-Merodach
590	Letters from Lachish		
		587-538	Babylonian Exile
558-530	Cyrus		
556-539	Nabonidus		
539	Fall of Babylon Cyrus Cylinder		
495-400	Papyri from Elephantine		
455-403	Murashu Tablets		
423-404	Darius II		
400-300	*Yehūd* Coins		
135-37	Maccabaean Coins	135-104	John Hyrcanus
		103-76	Alexander Jannaeus

Cuneiform Documents

The Epic of Creation
The Story of the Flood
The Law Code of Hammurabi
Letters from Tell El-Amarna
Historical Records of Assyria and Babylonia
The Jehoiachin Tablets
Nebuchadrezzar's Expedition to Syria
Texts relating to Nabonidus
The Cyrus Cylinder
The Murashu Tablets
The Babylonian Theodicy
Babylonian Moral Teachings
Prayer to any God
Texts from Ras Shamra

The Epic of Creation

THE Babylonian Epic of Creation, annually recited on the fourth day of the New Year's festival and anciently called *Enuma elish* after the opening words of the poem, is presented on seven tablets, each of an average length of one hundred and fifty lines, and has been known to Assyriology since 1876 when a pioneer edition of the first pieces was published by GEORGE SMITH in *The Chaldean Account of Genesis*. At the present time, and with the inclusion of newly identified texts of the hitherto fragmentary fifth tablet, some nine-tenths of the original work can be reconstructed.

The story of the birth of the gods, the battle between Marduk and Tiamat, and the creation of man in a god-ordered universe form the leading motifs of the epic, making it at once a Theogony and a 'Genesis'. Yet here, even more essentially, is the official statement of the Enthronement of Marduk, a composition entirely dependent upon the rise of Babylon in the middle of the Old Babylonian period. At the beginning of this period Marduk was the (comparatively unknown) city-god of Babylon, one of many other city-gods. In the epic he has become 'the King of the gods of heaven and earth, the King of all the gods' (VI.28). No doubt the Babylonians themselves could have argued that, if Babylon was destined to become the world's leading city, then Marduk had also been destined to become the world's leading god, so that there could be nothing amiss in advancing him to the rank of Creator, or in assigning him to the Hero's rôle of what is probably an older story. But at all events *Enuma elish* must be seen as a carefully composed document, precious for the light it throws on early Mesopotamian concepts of the beginning of things, yet scarcely less fascinating because of its witness to religious history in the making.

To set the central theme of Marduk's kingship in true perspective, however, some account must be given here of the system of government which recent research has shown was in force in early times in Mesopotamia. At this time political authority was not invested in a single ruler, but in an Assembly of the freemen of the city-state, who normally surrendered executive power to a smaller council of elders. In times of crisis, however, the Assembly could, if necessary, appoint a king; but this appointment stood for the emergency only, so that democratic government would normally revert to the larger bodies on the return of peaceful conditions. Government by this system, although older than the epic itself, was that used by the gods at the time in which the action is set. The crisis is staged when Tiamat and the rebel gods, together with her army of monsters and their rebel commander, Kingu, prepare for total war against the great gods; it is raised to quite alarming proportions when first Ea and then Anu, two of the most powerful of the great gods, are sent against Tiamat but yet forced to retire; and then, with total destruction imminent, the divine Assembly is called and the young Marduk proclaimed king for the emergency. By his hand Tiamat is slain, her host captured, and the rebel gods forced into servitude in the employ of their masters. But here is not, as has been stated, a dramatic height such that all that follows is anticlimax. For when the wonders of Marduk's creation are completed and the divine Assembly once again convened, it is not to revoke the crisis appointment which they had earlier made. Marduk is confirmed in his position as king; he is proclaimed king for ever. Thus the final scene of the epic is the most significant of all.

One other aspect of the epic calls for special mention. The action of the poem takes place in the Universe, and we may usefully consider this as the 'stage'. But the gods of the drama are not only personalities who walk the stage; they are also personifications of it. Thus Apsu and Tiamat, who speak and move about, fight or are fought, even as we may read it in the epic, are otherwise two great Seas, who existed in the beginning when all was water. With them at that time was a third being, Mummu, who is seen as the minister or 'Counsellor' of Apsu, one who even casts his vote for him at a crucial point in the story, and yet who in another function is also some aspect of water, whether clouds, mists or ice. Again, in their capacity as Seas, Apsu and Tiamat give birth to the gods (I.9), and all these take active part, according to their personalities, in the great battle against Tiamat. But such gods we would today call 'matter', for there are born the Silts (?) (Lahmu, Lahamu) and the Horizons (Anshar, Kishar) and in subsequent generations the Sky (Anu) and the Earth (Ea). These are hard concepts for modern reading, but no appreciation of the complex religious thought of the epic is possible without at least some awareness of them. As to the question of the religious affinities of the epic, and the problem of whether or not it has connections, as has often been affirmed, with the Hebrew account of Genesis, the decision has been taken to defer this issue to the notes so that the reader may first have a direct acquaintance with the poem.

The following extracts from the epic are presented on the basis of a new analysis of stanza division.

Text

I. 1 When the heaven(-gods) above were as yet uncreated,
The earth(-gods) below not yet brought into being,
Alone there existed primordial Apsu who engendered them,
Only Mummu, and Tiamat who brought all of them forth.

5 Their waters could mix together in a single stream,
Unrestricted by reed-beds, unimpeded by marsh :
For, since none of the gods had at this time appeared,
These had not yet been formed, or been with destinies decreed.

9 In the depths of their waters the gods were created :
There appeared Lahmu and Lahamu, they (first) were given
name ;
But only to an appointed size did they grow and become large,
And Anshar and Kishar were born bigger than they.

13 As lengthened the days and there multiplied the years,
Anshar in like size produced Anu, his firstborn :
And as Anu, their son, was the equal of his parents,
So did Anu beget Ea in the likeness of himself.

17 But Ea, Nudimmud, was else the master of his parents,
More intelligent, wiser, mightier in strength :
More powerful he was than his grandfather, Anshar,
Nor had he a rival amongst the (many) gods, his brothers.

*The swift action of the epic begins with these 'brothers', the noise of whose
continuous dancing and revelling now becomes, in a most human situation,*

a source of great disturbance to the first parents. Apsu seizes the initia-
tive. He summons his servant Mummu and takes the matter to court with
Tiamat. Speaking first, he declares he can neither rest by day nor sleep
by night because of the noise, and advocates the total destruction of the gods.

41 But Tiamat on hearing this
Was furious, and cried out against her husband,
Cried in bitterness of spirit . . .,
Broke into an evil storm of temper :
'How can we thus destroy what we have borne !
Their ways, for all they are abhorrent, it is our duty to abide.'

47 There spoke in turn Mummu, deciding for Apsu,
For in no [wise] acceptable was the counsel of his mother :
'Destroy, O my father, these perverted ways,
That by day you may find rest, that by night you may sleep !'

51 Apsu rejoiced at him, his face grew bright with joy,
For the fatal vote was cast against the gods, his sons :
He threw out his arms and Mummu embraced,
Who sat upon his knees, him kissed he many times.

55 What decision they had voted in this their legal court
Was then (officially) told unto the gods, their sons :
The gods when they heard moved aimlessly about,
They lapsed into silence, sat in speechless despair.

59 But now the most wise, the accomplished and all-able,
All-knowing Ea did foil their fell intent :
He drew a faithful map of the (pristine) Universe,
Skilfully composed for it *Shuturu*, his most masterly incantation.

63 He recited this, setting it against the waters (of the map) :
The spell poured sleep into it, and the map fell sound asleep.
Transmitting the sleep it then made Apsu sleep,—
And for Counsellor Mummu, but short was his sleeplessness.

67 Ea . . . his . . ., tore off his royal head-dress,
Removed his aura-cloak, put it on himself :
He bound him, even Apsu, and did kill him,
While Mummu he close confined, laid him crosswise over him.

In this initial victory over the would-be Sleepers of the Beginning of things, sympathy necessarily rests with the new forces of life and energy. But the scene changes. An embassy of gods, whom we shall know here-after as the rebel gods, has approached Tiamat and succeeded in persuading her to avenge the death of Apsu. It is a very changed Tiamat who now prepares for battle.

133 Then Mother Hubur, who cast every mould of life,
    Unleashed the Irresistible Weapon, bore monster-serpents :
    Sharp was their tooth and pitiless their fang,
    With poison in stead of blood she filled their bodies.

137 Next, snarling *ushumgalle* she clothed with terror,
    Charged them with aura-rays, made them like gods :
    'All who shall look thereon they shall dismay !
    With bodies reared ne'er turned shall be their breast !'

141 She formed besides the Serpent, Dragon, Drake,
    The Lion, the Uridimmu, Scorpion-Man :
    The Driving Storm, Kulili, Kusariqqu,
    Bearers of weapons unsparing, fearless in battle.

145 So powerful were her decrees they were unopposable,
    As thus eleven species did she bring forth :
    And now from the gods, her sons, who formed [her army],
    (As a twelfth) she exalted Kingu, made him chief among them.

149 To march in the van of the host and to captain the army,
    To raise the weapon signalling 'Assault' and launch the attack,
    The high command during battle,
    She entrusted to his hand, seating him in Council :

153 'I have cast thee a spell, made thee all-great in the gods' Assembly,
    The sceptres of all the gods given into thy hand :
    Yea, supremely great shalt thou be, thou my only husband !
    And greater thy titles than those of all the Anunnaki.'

Receiving intelligence of this array, Ea informs his grandfather, Anshar. For a time the latter is too horrified to act, but eventually he sends first Ea and then his own son, Anu, against Tiamat. According to their natures, the one is directed to use Magic, the other Authority, against her ; but both are forced to draw back, seemingly before their powers can operate, and it is clear that Tiamat must be fought with weapons. Earlier we had been told of the birth of the eventual Champion.

79 In the Chamber of Destinies, in *Atman usurati*,
   A god then engendered the strongest, the 'Sage of the gods' :
   In the depths of the Apsu the god Marduk was born,
   In the depths of the Pure Apsu Marduk was born.

83 He that begot him was Ea, his father,
   Damkina, his mother, was she that did bear him. . . .
   He looked on him, Ea, his father who begot him,
   He rejoiced and was glad, his heart filled with joy.

91 Double he made him, twofold divinity imparted to him,
   Exceeding tall he was, rising much above them :
   But too intricate are his two parts for man to understand,
   They are not suited for thinking on, too difficult to contemplate.

But Marduk, for all his size and strength, is yet young as a god ; and when he is approached by Anshar to champion the cause of the gods against Tiamat, he accepts only on the condition that he be legally accorded that supreme authority which his new responsibility demands. Lahmu and Lahamu convene the Assembly, and, after a great feast of food and wine, the gods appoint Marduk as King.

IV. 1 On the throne-dais *Rubutum* which they had placed in position
   He sat, facing his fathers, for the ceremony of Kingship :
   'Hereby art thou enrolled within the number of the great gods,
   Thine appointment has no equal, thine authority is absolute.
   Marduk, thou art enrolled within the number of the great gods,
   Thine appointment has no equal, thine authority is absolute.

7 'For unspecified time shall thy word stand inviolate,
   To promote and to abase lie both in thy power :
   Thine utterance shall be law, thy command uncontrovertible,
   None among the gods shall dispute thy decree. . . .

13 'Hereby thou, Marduk, art appointed our avenger,
   Thus we give thee the Sceptre of Kingship, *Kishat-kal-gimreti* :
   When thou sittest in this Assembly thy word shall be paramount,
   (On the battlefield) thy weapons . . . shall bring low thy foes :
   Spare thou the life of the god who trusts in thee,
   Pour out the life of the god who conceiveth ill.'

19 In the midst of their circle then a garment they placed,
   And thus spake the gods unto Marduk, their son :
   'If thine authority, O Lord, is indeed foremost amongst gods,
   Command destruction and re-existence to come respectively to
        pass.
   Speak thou a word and let the garment be destroyed,
   Command thou again and let the garment be whole !'

25 He spoke, and at his word was the garment destroyed :
   Again he commanded, and the garment was remade.
   And as the (great) gods, his fathers, saw the power of his word,
   In glad acclaim they gave the blessing, crying, 'Marduk is King !'

*Immediately after the ceremony Marduk arms himself for the fight with
bow, arrows, mace and a net held by the four winds.   Then—*

49 His great weapon *Abubu* the lord raised (signalling 'Assault'),
   Mounted his fearful chariot, *Umu-la-mahru* :
   Hitched to it four teams-of-two, reined them to his side,
   'Destroyer' and 'Pitiless', 'Trampler' and 'Swift'—

53 'Open of lips', whose teeth carried poison,
   'Who knoweth not weariness', trained to destroy :
   While he placed to his right 'Fierce Battle and Resistance',
   To his left 'Relentless Warfare subduing all Bands'.

57 He wore (as armour) his *nahlaptum*, *Apluhti-pulhati*,
   His aura-helmet *Rashubbatum* was attached to his head :
   And he drove off, the lord, moving fast on his road,
   Set his course toward the sounds of Tiamat enraged. . . .

93 So they came together—Tiamat, and Marduk, Sage of the gods :
   They advanced into conflict, they joined forces in battle.
   He spread wide his net, the lord, and enveloped her,
   The Evil Wind, the rearmost, unleashed in her face.

97 As she opened her mouth, Tiamat to devour him,
He made the Evil Wind to enter that she closed not her lips :
The Storm Winds, the furious, then filling her belly,
Her inwards became distended, she opened fully wide her mouth.

101 He shot therethrough an arrow, it pierced her stomach,
Clave through her bowels, tore into her womb :
Thereat he strangled her, made her life-breath ebb away,
Cast her body to the ground, standing over it (in triumph).

There follows the inevitable account of the defeat and capture by Marduk of Tiamat's army and their commander, Kingu. His mission thus accomplished, Marduk's task, like that of many another ruler after a revolution, is now one of reform. As he returns to the fallen body of Tiamat, he conceives the idea of giving concrete form to the new law by first creating a new heaven.

135 He rested, the lord, examining her body :
Would divide up the monster, create a wonder of wonders !
He slit her in two like a fish of the drying yards,
The one half he positioned and secured as the sky. . . .

V. 1 (Therein) traced he lines for the mighty gods,
Stars, star-groups and constellations he appointed for them :
He determined the year, marked out its divisions,
For each of the twelve months appointed three rising stars.

5 Having established the rules for the (astronomical) seasons,
He laid down the Crossing-line to make known their limits :
And that none should make mistake or in any way lose speed
He appointed, conjointly with it, the Enlil- and Ea-lines.

9 The great (Sun-)gates he opened in both sides of her ribs,
Made strong the lock-fastening to left and right :
In the depths of her belly he laid down the *elati*.
He made the moon to shine forth, entrusted to him the night.

Two further stanzas, devoted to the phases of the moon, continue the theme of the establishment of the calendar and the regulation of time. A break in continuity follows, but new texts presently resume the narrative and Marduk is then seen reshaping the earth out of the lower half of Tiamat's body. Thus in one act of creation

53 He placed her head in position, heaped [the mountai]ns upon
    it . . .
    Made the Euphr[ates] and Tigris to flow through her eyes,—

*and broken contexts subsequently feature Tiamat's nostrils, breasts and
huge tail. Thereafter Marduk finally disposes of her eleven monsters.*

73 The eleven monster(-species) which Tiamat had created,
    Whose [weapo]ns he had broken, binding them at his feet,
    He made of them (stellar) images to wat[ch over] the Apsu,
    That as signs (of the Zodiac) the group should ne'er be forgotten.

77 As there saw them [the gods], so their hearts filled with joy,
    Even Lahmu and Lahamu and all of his fathers :
    Anshar turned to him and hailed him with a royal address,
    Anu, Enlil and Ea presented him with gifts.

*The rebel gods also do obeisance and acknowledge Marduk as King.
But now, as King, Marduk needs a house, and in an important speech
he imparts his plans for such a building, to be built on the Earth immediately above the subsoil waters of the Apsu. In one of its* kummu*s, or
'inner chambers', Marduk will set up his sceptre of kingship, and there will
be places for the gods to pass the night before their annual Assembly at
the New Year. There will also be permanent dwellings for the great gods,
—and this great complex of buildings is to have a name, the exalted name
of Bab-ili, 'the city-quarter of the gods', the home of Marduk and his
family. But the plans cannot at once proceed, for the rebel gods, charged
with the building of this Babylon, appeal to Marduk. The text is
fragmentary at this point, but to judge from what follows, their fear is
that they will subsequently be compelled to provide unending service for
the great gods in the maintenance and running of their new households,
so that the future can hold for them neither prospect of relief nor hope
of rest from labour.*

As Marduk acknowledged this appeal of the gods,
He decided to create another wonder of wonders :
Opening his mouth, he spake forth to Ea,
Invited him to comment on the theory he proposed.

5 'Blood will I compose, bring a skeleton into being,
Produce a lowly, primitive creature, "Man" shall be his name :
I will create *lullu-amelu*—an earthly, "puppet"-man.
To him be charged the service that the gods may then have
    rest . . .'

11 Ea gave answer, spake forth a word to him,
Relating to him a counter plan for the relief of the gods :
'Nay, let one of their own number be surrendered to me,
Let him be put to death and peoples cast from the mould ;
And if the guilty one be surrendered in a great gods' Assembly,
The rebels can be legally re-established (as gods).'

17 So Marduk called in session the mighty gods,
Giving instruction in how properly to chair an Assembly :
To the conduct of his speech did the gods pay attention
While the King to the Anunnaki made formal address :

21 'By saying, "We declare unto you that the evidence is true",
Swear now by me that you will testify to the truth.
Who was it among you that started this conflict,
That urged Tiamat to revolt and the battle staged ?
If he that started the conflict be surrendered to me,
I will lay the punishment on him—be you still set on relief.'

27 The great gods, the Six-hundred, gave answer unto him,
Even to Lugal-dimmer-an-ki-a, 'the king of all the gods' :
'Verily it was Kingu that started the conflict,
Who made Tiamat to revolt and the battle staged.'

31 They (formally) bound him, held him fast before Ea,
Laid the (total) crime upon him, cutting into his blood :
Thereupon from his blood [he cre]ated mankind,
Imposed the service upon him, released the gods who must else
    have served.

*The rebel gods,—and so to describe them for the last time,—are now
assigned to new and responsible tasks in heaven and the underworld. But
first they must build Marduk's Babylon, and out of gratitude for their
deliverance they seek permission to alter radically the original plans. Let*

Babylon, they cry, be not only Marduk's home, but a parakku, *a sanctuary, a great religious centre for gods and men. Delighted approval is given, and allowed also to choose their own designs, the gods commence building* (VI.59). *They build the great temple Esangila, Marduk's dwelling place called a* paramahhu *where he might also receive his family and guests, dwellings for the great gods, and finally their own abodes for the annual gathering at the New Year. In Esangila the final scene of the epic is set. Here the 'destinies'—the eternal, unchangeable states of things—are determined, and in a long ceremony, which ends with the reciting of his fifty names, the destiny or status of Marduk himself is determined, and thus also, in full Assembly of gods, he is confirmed for ever in his appointment as King. At a point where we may briefly join this great ceremony, Anu has just determined the destiny of Marduk's bow, according it an eternal permanence in three forms : Weapon, [Rainbow ?], and Bow-star.*

92 After Anu had determined the (three) existence-states of 'bow',
   He set in place the Throne of Kingship, *Mahar-ili-shaqat* :
   Anu seated him thereon in the Assembly of the gods . . .
   Who [proceeded] to affirm Marduk's eternal rank (as King).

97 Curses they severally pronounced upon themselves,
   Swore with water and oil, bled their throats (in treaty-oath)' :
   So yielded him the power to ever rule them as King,
   Confirmed him legally as overlord of the gods of heaven and
       earth.

101 Then Anshar did extol, did proclaim his name 'Asalluhi' :
    'At the using of this name let us bow down in reverence ;
    Upon the opening of his mouth be all other gods silent,
    His command shall be pre-eminent above and below.

105 'Be exalted our Son, even he who avenged us,
    Let his authority be supreme, be it second to none :
    And let him act as the shepherd of mankind, his creatures,
    Who, unforgetting, to later ages shall ever tell of his deeds.'

Notes

I. Line 3. *Apsu* was the great 'male' ocean, the source of lakes—especially a large tidal lake which anciently surrounded the city of Eridu in Southern Babylonia—of marshes, and the waters of the subsoil. The word comes from the Sumerian *Abzu*, the first element being *ab* 'sea' ; it appears in Greek as *abussos* (the 'bottomless pit' mentioned in Rev. ix.1f., 11, etc., is a familiar translation of it), and the word still survives in the English 'abyss'. It has also been thought to lie behind the Hebrew *'ephes*, meaning in the plural 'ends, extremities' (of the earth ; cp. Ps. lix.14, etc.).

Line 4. *Tiamat*. The theory that the Hebrew Genesis is genetically related to the Babylonian has long been held (see, e.g. S. R. DRIVER), and has relied to a large extent on the much publicised equation of Tiamat with the Hebrew *tehōm* 'the deep' (e.g. Gen. i.2). It is now, however, recognised that, since the two words have different meanings—for they cannot be used interchangeably —it is of no importance whether they are etymologically connected or not. As to the only other serious proposition that has been made in favour of a relationship between the two accounts, namely, that both works follow a common sequence for the acts of creation or other events which they describe, we believe the comparison to be partly artificial, partly explainable in terms of coincidence. Thus it seems very probable that the epic has no connections of any kind or at any point with Genesis, and that each is *sui generis*. The many and obvious differences, due in large part to the fact that the essential religious concepts underlying the epic are those of the Sumerians—the non-Semitic predecessors in Mesopotamia of the third millennium Akkadians and later Babylonians and Assyrians—weigh heavily in support of this opinion. Quite another situation is presented by the Babylonian story of the Flood which does contain material closely similar in substance to certain themes of the O.T. story. But the two issues are not the same, and neither should be allowed to influence the other.

Lines 13-16. The statement *Anshar in like size produced Anu* means that the heaven-horizon was the same size as the sky. Similarly, *So did Anu beget Ea in the likeness of himself* means that the sky was the same size as the earth. The same remark in Hesiod's *Theogony*—'And Earth first bare the starry Heaven, of equal stature to herself'—is an example of the possibility of 'coincidence' in creation stories mentioned under line 4 above. Hesiod's work is full of interest as comparative material, but whereas there Earth bears the Sea (Pontos) and 'in the bed of Heaven the deep-eddying Okeanos', in the epic the situation is reversed and Heaven and Earth are born after the Seas (Apsu and Tiamat). As a general observation, it may be noted that, in polytheistic Theogonies which accept the male and female principle as present from the beginning, creation is quite naturally expressed in terms of begetting and birth. In the Hebrew Genesis the coming into being of the universe is expressed as acts of creation on the part of one God ; only thereafter is it said : 'male and female created He them' (Gen. i.27).

Line 48. *of his mother*. This translation rests upon an emendation of the text.

Line 57. *The gods . . . moved aimlessly about.* There was no appeal, for Apsu's authority to destroy the gods was secured by decision of a *puhrum* or legal court (line 55)—despite the fact that this 'court' was hardly properly constituted either by modern or even Hammurabi standards.

Lines 61-6. This passage, long recognised as having a basis in magic—Ea was above all the god of magic—has been variously interpreted in detail. The present translation supposes that it constitutes an example of sympathetic magic involving the use of a model. Normally this model took the form of an image of the person against whom the magic was ultimately to be directed. One can readily appreciate, however, why a slight departure from practice was required in the case of a 'sea' such as Apsu.

Line 70. *laid him crosswise over him*—that is, it may be supposed, laid Mummu crosswise as ice (?) over Apsu (cp. Introduction).

Line 134. *the Irresistible Weapon.* Possibly the flood, but this 'weapon' is not certainly identified.

Line 156. *Anunnaki.* A group designation of the gods standing outside the direct Lahmu-Marduk lineage, and one of the many synonyms for the 'rebel gods' of the epic.

IV. Line 51. *reined them to his side.* Probably to his waist, thus allowing the hands free for the use of weapons. This practice for one-man chariots may be seen on several Egyptian reliefs depicting Rameses III riding into action.

Lines 57f. *Apluhti-pulhati . . . Rashubbatum.* The naming of weapons (as also sceptres and thrones) was common in Sumerian and Akkadian times. The present examples, meaning something like 'Armour of terror' (with a clever play on words) and 'Awfulness' (Marduk's helmet), recall the Almighty's breastplate 'Righteousness' and helmet 'Salvation' in Is. lix.17 (cp. Eph. vi.13ff.).

Line 93. *So they came together . . .* Comparative mythology knows many 'Cosmic Battles'. The fight of the Saxon Beowulf with the Firedrake, and of Indra with Rudra sung in the Rig-Veda ; the Greek battle of Zeus against the Titans, and of Apollo against the Dragoness, related in the Homeric Hymns ; even the victory of the Almighty over Leviathan or Rahab referred to in the O.T. (Ps. lxxiv.14, Is. li.9)—these and many others will be familiar. How we should interpret any one of them is still a completely open question, though a bold attempt to treat them collectively has recently been made (see H. S. BELLAMY).

Lines 101-4. A remarkably fast stanza. The eight verbs, one verb to each half-line, know only one temporal conjunction between them. The dramatic description of the death of Sisera recorded in Jud. v.26f. is something similar.

V. Lines 5-8. *the Enlil- and Ea-lines* were two imaginary lines lying astride and parallel to the celestial equator such that they divided the Sun's annual march along the *Crossing-line* (the Ecliptic) into seasonal periods of three months. The ecliptic was represented at night by the line of Marduk's own Crossing 'star', Jupiter, and it is a remarkable commentary on this identification, actually false, that the inclination of the orbit of Jupiter to the plane of the ecliptic is in fact only just over one degree. It may be noted that Marduk's heaven was very scientifically conceived (contrast that of the O.T.), a point in no way surprising, for Babylonia was one of the great centres of observational astronomy in ancient time.

Line 11. For *elati* there is no certain identification at present.

VI. Line 33. [*he cre*]*ated mankind*. He, that is, Ea. One text reads 'they created', but the plan to create man is best stated as conceived by Marduk, executed by his father Ea, supervised and directed by Marduk. There were, however, other traditions of the birth of man prevalent in ancient Mesopotamia. For the comparative cuneiform material, see A. HEIDEL, ch. ii.

Line 59. *the gods commence building*. That the epic could promulgate the doctrine that the buildings involved, still to be seen in the ruins of ancient Babylon, were built by gods and not by men is perhaps owed to the circumstance that there was no strong tradition of their real origins at the time the epic was composed. There could, however, be no objection to such a theory. The Babylonians, like the Sumerians before them, believed in the divine origin of all the arts of civilisation. Man might copy, man might develop, but the gods invented—indeed it was unthinkable that man should have any knowledge which was not possessed also by the gods, which did not in fact derive immediately from them. Thus only the gods could have invented building, and must surely have provided examples of such work whence man was first able to learn the art.

Bibliography

BELLAMY, H. S.   *Moons, Myths and Man : a Reinterpretation*, second ed., 1949.

DRIVER, S. R.   *The Book of Genesis* (*WC*), 1904, 19-33.

HEIDEL, A.   *The Babylonian Genesis*, second ed., 1954.

JACOBSEN, THORKILD, in *The Intellectual Adventure of Ancient Man*, ed. H. FRANKFORT, 1946, chs. v-vii (republished in Pelican Books under the title *Before Philosophy*, 1949).

LABAT, R.   *Le poème babylonien de la création*, 1935.

SKINNER, J.   *A Critical and Exegetical Commentary on Genesis* (*ICC*), 1912, 41-50.

SPEISER, E. A., in *A.N.E.T.*, 60-72.

J. V. KINNIER WILSON

The Story of the Flood

THE Epic of Gilgamesh, into which the Babylonian story of the Flood has been written, is a composition altogether different from the Epic of Creation. With Gilgamesh, legendary ruler of the ancient city-state of Uruk, we are in what has been aptly called 'The Age of Heroes'—for there were giants in the land in those days. Gilgamesh was 'two-thirds god and one-third man' so that, with his sworn friend Enkidu, he could overcome the monster Huwawa of the Cedar Forest, or brazenly refuse the approaches of the goddess Ishtar who sought his love, and kill the Great Bull of Heaven which, in her anger, she sent to destroy him. But the divine attributes of even this greatest of Heroes must not be taken to imply divine nature. And when, after the death of Enkidu, his long quest for immortality ends in the Plant of Youth being snatched from him by the Serpent as he bathed, we are sure that the third of him that was man was the ultimate controlling factor of his destiny.

The story of the Flood, known specifically as 'the Great Flood of Enlil' after one of the greatest names of the Sumerian and Akkadian pantheon, is told on the eleventh of the twelve tablets which make up the Epic of Gilgamesh (Plate 1). In its Babylonian form, this story is intricately woven into a deeper, yet unsolved, problem of life and death which gives the whole epic its essential meaning and unity. Thus in fairness to the ancient writer, it should be recognised that our excerpt is taken a little hurtfully from its context. At the same time such a move is yet of service in that it can draw attention to the fundamental difference between the Babylonian account and its O.T. counterpart. Whereas in the latter the Flood story is told as a straight narrative and is for all to know, in the epic it is told to Gilgamesh alone, and is in reality the story of how Utnapishti the Far Distant obtained everlasting life. Utnapishti was the Hero of the Flood—the Babylonian Noah—and it is he and his boatman, Puzur-Amurri, who will be steering us through the tumult of those seven days. But if we be true to the larger context of the story, the real significance of those days is for Gilgamesh and his horror of death.

And for him at the end of the story the message of Utnapishti is clear : to have everlasting life, to dwell in the Far Distance 'at the mouth of the Rivers', is a gift bestowed only by the gods.

The name Gilgamesh is Sumerian and, in its origins, the epic is in fact based on a number of older Sumerian stories, texts of which have independently survived in varying degrees of completeness. A Sumerian Flood-tablet (not belonging to the Gilgamesh cycle) is also known, and this document stands in some part as a forerunner to the Babylonian version, although unfortunately it is not well preserved. It would be wrong, however, to overstress the Sumerian connection, present though it is, for in the epic the earlier themes have been completely reworked, indeed recreated, while the motif of the death of Enkidu has given an altogether new direction to the whole narrative. What all this means more particularly is that the Epic of Gilgamesh is a story, an artificial composition created by an artist who was a master of the art of story-telling and whose work is now one of the world's classics. It is as a story that the account of the Flood is here presented, and while it can be, and has been, intellectualised to provide material for legitimate historical, theological and scientific interests, it may well be felt that it is on its worth as a story that, in the final analysis, the work must be judged.

Let us then follow Gilgamesh in his lonely travels. Enkidu, his beloved friend, has died at the decree of the gods, and the Hero's broken spirit knows no comfort, his mind now obsessed by the awful reality that he also must die. But he has heard of one who, he knows not how, has yet been able to escape the common fate of mankind. Gilgamesh sets forth to find him and learn his secret. He crosses the great mountains where the sun sets and the Scorpion-men live. They tell him his quest is in vain, but Gilgamesh must go on. In a journey of utter darkness, when he can see neither what lies ahead nor yet behind him, he travels the long road of the night sun. By the shore of a great sea he meets Siduri, the divine Ale-wife who provides beer for the sea's travellers. If his quest is in vain, yet must he go on. And with the help of Urshanabi, the boatman, he crosses the sea, crosses even the Waters of Death at its farther limit, to stand at last in the Far Distance before Utnapishti,—Utnapishti, son of Ubar-Tutu, one-time ruler of Shuruppak, the only mortal to have obtained everlasting life.

Text

X. iv Utnapishti the Far Distant spake unto him, unto Gilgamesh :
    'Why are thy cheeks wasted, is sunken thy face, is thy mind
45 distraught and thy countenance fallen? Why is there grief
in thine heart, and the look of thee that of a man who has gone a
far journey? Why are thy features ravaged by cold and heat?
And wherefore hast thou been seeking the domain of the wind,
roaming desert ways?'

50   Gilgamesh spake unto him, unto Utnapishti the Far Distant :
v   'How could my cheeks be not wasted, not sunken my face,
my mind not distraught and my countenance not fallen? How
could there not be grief in my heart, and the look of me not as of a
man who has gone a far journey? Should my features not be
5 ravaged by cold and heat? Or should I seek not the domain
of the wind, roaming desert ways? For my friend, the driven
mule, the wild ass of the open country, yea, the panther of the
steppe, even Enkidu, the driven mule, the wild ass of the open
country,—we who stood together, who, climbing the mountain,
10 did seize and slay the Bull of Heaven, who overthrew Huwawa
that dwelled in the Cedar Forest,—oh, my friend whom I so
dearly loved, who walked beside me through all adventures :
Enkidu, my friend whom I so dearly loved, who walked beside me
through all adventures,—him has the fate of mankind overtaken.

15   'For six days and seven nights I bewailed him, aye, until
a maggot dropped from the nose of him. And I became frightened,
became afeared of death, began roaming the desert. The matter
of my friend rested heavy upon me and I roamed the long road
of the desert : the matter of Enkidu, my friend, rested heavy
20 upon me and I roamed the long road of the desert. How can
I be silent? How can I be still? My friend, whom I loved,
has returned to clay. And I, must I not as him lay me down, to
rise not again for ever and ever?' . . .

vi   Utnapishti the Far Distant spake unto him, unto Gilgamesh :
    'O Gilgamesh . . ., is it "forever" that we build an house,
is it "forever" that we seal a document? Is it "forever" that
brothers divide an inheritance? "Forever" will enmity persist
in the land? "Forever" stands the river in spate, does the flood
sweep away? (It is said) :

30   "Kulili, the dragon-fly, [knows] the cocoon,
    And her face may ever look on the face of the Sun."
And indeed in ancient time there was no [death]. . . . But when
36 the great gods, the Anunnaki, were gathered in Assembly,
with them to determine man's destinies was Mammetum,
Creatress of Death.   Then it was they decreed death and life,
death-days having not previously been appointed.'

XI   Gilgamesh spake unto him, unto Utnapishti the Far Distant :
'But Utnapishti, as I look upon thee, thy appearance is not
different : thou art like unto me.   Thou art no different : thou
5 art like unto me.   Spent for thee, too, is the thrill of doing battle,
[and thy bow] has been cast aside from upon thy back.   Then tell
me how thou didst stand in the gods' Assembly and find life
everlasting.'
    Utnapishti spake unto him, unto Gilgamesh :
10   'Gilgamesh, I will reveal unto thee a hidden thing and a
secret of the gods will I tell thee.   Shuruppak, a city that thou
knowest and which now lies [in ruins on the bank] of the
Euphrates,—when that city was old and there were yet gods
within it, the great gods decided to bring on a deluge.
15   '[Took their seats in the Council] their father, Anu ; warrior
Enlil, their adviser ; their minister, Ninurta ; and their irrigator,
Ennugi.   But Nin-igi-ku, even Ea, sat (invisibly) with them,
20 and repeated their words to the reed brick-bond (of the Council
room), saying : "Brick-bond, brick-bond, wall, wall !   Brick-
bond hearken, wall remember ! (Echo this message unto Utnapishti) :   Lord of Shuruppak, son of Ubar-Tutu, destroy thy
25 house and build a vessel !   Abandoning riches, do thou seek
out livingkind :   despising possessions, preserve what has life :
thus load in the vessel the seed of all creatures.   And the vessel
30 thou buildest, be her measurements measured, let her length
and breadth be equal, and do thou Apsu-wise enroof her."
    'And I, for I knew I was speaking unto Ea, my lord, said :
"But my lord, were I to honour and do what thou thus com-
35 mandest, what should I say to the city assembly and the elders ? "
    'Ea opened his mouth and spake unto me, his servant, saying :
"Thus (in a double message) thou shalt speak unto them : . . .
40 Enlil hates me and I can no longer dwell among you, can no
longer set my footsteps on the soil that is Enlil's ; but if I go down
into the Apsu, dwelling with my lord Ea, then will Enlil send

you showerfuls, raining down abundance on you. . . . [The
45 land will know] its richest harvest (and this is its sign) : *Who
sendeth the bran, on the previous evening will pour down the grain.*"

'When something of morning had dawned, I commanded that
the land be assembled . . . [(For four days were gathered the
55 parts of the vessel)]—the boys fetching pitch, while the stronger
brought (timber-)materials.

'On the fifth day I erected her framework. One *iku* in area
was her flooring, ten times twelve cubits were the uprights of
her walls, and ten times twelve cubits was the measure of each
edge of the top of her. I filled in the shape of her sides and
60 did join her together. Six decks I laid into her, did thus seven-
fold divide her, cut her beam again ninefold. I drave water-
plugs into her, chose out quant-poles and laid by what were
needed. And as for the pitching, when already ten thousand
65 baskets of pitch I had poured into the oven, ten thousand again
did I pour in behind them, and ten thousand the more did the
basket-carriers bring me,—besides one *sar* of oil which the
(wood-)seasoning consumed, and two *sar* of oil which the boatman
bestowed (for the journey). . . . So the vessel was finished. . . .

80 'All that I had I now loaded aboard her. All I had of silver
I loaded aboard her, all I had of gold did I load aboard her ;
yea, of the species of all living creatures, all that I had did I
load aboard her. I made enter the vessel all my family and
85 kindred ; beasts wild and domestic and all of the craftsmen I
made enter the vessel.

'It was Shamash (the Sun-god) who the set time appointed :
"*Who sendeth the bane, on the previous evening will pour down the rain :*
then enter the vessel and close down thy doorway."

90 'Came the set time appointed : who was sending the bane,
on the previous evening did pour down the rain. I gazed up
at the look of the weather ; it was fearful to behold, and I
entered the vessel and did close down my doorway. And on
95 caulking the vessel, to the boatman, to Puzur-Amurri, I assigned
the great house and its contents.

'When something of morning had dawned, there arose a
black cloud from the horizon. While Adad (the Storm-god)
was thundering within it, there went on ahead (the gods) Shullat
100 and Hanish, went forth (his) lieutenants across mountain and
plain. (Where irrigation dams they found) Nergal tore out

the dam-stays : came Ninurta behind, made the weirs overflow.
Already the Anunnaki had taken up their torches that per-
chance with their brightness they might illumine the land.
105 But as the Horror-(cloud) of Adad passed over the heavens,
it turned aught that had light into uttermost darkness. . . .
Swift blew the storm . . ., it passed over the land like a battle.
110 No man could make out his brother, nor could people be seen
from the heavens.   Even the gods were afeared at the deluge,
115 took to flight and went up to the heaven of Anu, cowered they
like dogs and crouched down at the outer defences. . . .

'For six days and [seven] nights the wind blew, and the flood
and the storm swept the land.   But the seventh day arriving
130 did the rainstorm subside and the flood which had heaved like
a woman in travail ; there quieted the sea, and the storm-wind
stood still, the flood stayed her flowing.   I opened a vent and the
fresh air moved over my cheek-bones.   And I looked at the sea ;
135 there was silence, the tide-way lay flat as a roof-top—but the
whole of mankind had returned unto clay.   I bowed low : I
sat and I wept : o'er my cheek-bones my tears kept on
running.

'When I looked out again in the directions, across the expanse
of the sea, mountain ranges had emerged in twelve places and
140 on Mount Nisir the vessel had grounded.   Mount Nisir held
the vessel fast nor allowed any movement.   For a first day and
a second, fast Mount Nisir held the vessel nor allowed of any
movement.   For a third day and a fourth day, fast Mount Nisir
held the vessel nor allowed of any movement.   For a fifth day and
a sixth day, held Mount Nisir fast the vessel nor allowed of
any movement.

145 'On the seventh day's arriving, I freed a dove and did release
him.   Forth went the dove but came back to me : there was
not yet a resting-place and he came returning.   Then I set
free a swallow and did release him.   Forth went the swallow
150 but came back to me : there was not yet a resting-place and he
came returning.   So I set free a raven and did release him.   Forth
went the raven—and he saw again the natural flowing of the
waters, and he ate and he flew about and he croaked, and came not
returning.

155 'So all set I free to the four winds of heaven, and I poured
a libation, and scattered a food-offering, on the height of the

Plate 1 The Babylonian Story of the Flood: Epic of Gilgamesh,
Tablet XI

mountain. Seven and seven did I lay the vessels, heaped into
their incense-basins sweet-cane, cedarwood and myrtle.   And
160 the gods smelled the savour, the gods smelled the sweet savour,
the gods gathered like flies about the priest of the offering.

'Then, as soon as the Mother-goddess arrived, she lifted
up the great jewels which, (in childhood, her father) Anu had
made as a plaything for her : "O ye gods here present, as I still
165 do not forget these lapis stones of my neck, so shall I remember
these days—shall not forever forget them !   If it please now
the gods to come here to the offering, never shall Enlil come
here to the offering, for without any discrimination he brought
on the deluge, even (the whole of) my people consigned to
destruction."

170 'But as soon as Enlil arrived, he saw only the vessel—and
furious was Enlil, he was filled with anger against the (heaven-)
gods, the Igigi : " Has aught of livingkind escaped ?   Not a
man should have survived the destruction !"

'Ninurta opened his mouth and spake unto warrior Enlil :
175 "Who except Ea could have designed such a craft ?   For Ea
doth know every skill of invention."

'Then Ea opened his mouth and spake unto warrior Enlil :
"O warrior, thou wisest among gods, how thus indiscriminately
couldst thou bring about this deluge ?   (Had thou counselled) :
180 On the sinner lay his sin, on the transgressor lay his transgression :
loosen (the rope) that his life be not cut off, yet pull tight (on
the rope) that he do not [escape] : then instead of thy sending
a Flood would that the lion had come and diminished mankind : instead of thy sending a Flood would that the wolf had
come and diminished mankind ; instead of thy sending a Flood
would that a famine had occurred and impoverished mankind ;
185 instead of thy sending a Flood would that a pestilence had
come and smitten mankind.   And I, since I could not oppose
the decision of the great gods, did reveal unto the Exceeding-
Wise a (magic) dream, and thus did he hear the gods' decision.
Wherefore now take thee counsel concerning him."

190 'Thereupon Enlil went up into the vessel : he took hold of
my hand and made me go aboard, he bade my wife go aboard
and made her kneel at my side. Standing between us, he touched
our foreheads and did bless us, saying : "Hitherto Utnapishti has
been but a man ; but now Utnapishti and his wife shall be as

195 gods like ourselves.   In the Far Distance, at the mouth of the Rivers, Utnapishti shall dwell."

'So they took me and did make me to dwell in the Far Distance, at the mouth of the Rivers. . . .'

Notes

X. v. Line 22. *has returned to clay.* The idea that man was fashioned out of clay existed in Mesopotamia independently of the very different account of the birth of man given in the Epic of Creation (VI.33). In the O.T. cp. Job iv.19, xxxiii.6 ; Is. lxiv.8, etc., also several passages in the new Scroll of Hymns from the Dead Sea.

XI. Line 11. *Shuruppak.* This ancient city, the modern Fara, has been excavated, and since its upper level belongs to an archæological period known as Early Dynastic, it would indeed have been uninhabited and in ruins at the time the epic was written. A consideration of the much publicised flood deposits of varying depth and of certainly two dates, discovered at Ur, Kish, Uruk(?) and Shuruppak, and submitted as evidence by those who follow the hypothesis that the unborrowed Flood myths of the world are mythopœically exaggerated expressions of local phenomena, must be deemed to lie outside the scope of the present notes.

Line 14. *the great gods decided.* Both innocent and guilty appear to have perished in the Flood (see note to line 168). The destruction of man was not, however, caused essentially by any sin of man (contrast Gen. vi.5). The reason given takes the form of a self-confession by the goddess Ishtar (conceived in the epic as the Mother-goddess of the lost race) who had 'spoken evil' —whatever this may mean exactly—'in the Assembly of the gods' (lines 118-21, not included in the translation). Similarly the destruction of Ur at the end of its Third Dynasty was ascribed at the time to the fact that Nanna, the god of Ur, had aroused the wrath of his father Enlil. That the destruction of mankind could be assigned to a crime committed by their Mother-goddess, or the destruction of a city to an offence committed by its city-god, are hard concepts for the lay reader to appreciate ; but previous comment which could only explain the Flood in terms of 'the caprice of the gods' misunderstands the complex theocentric approach to history of Sumerian times.

Line 21. *Brick-bond.* Babylonian builders customarily interposed mats made of reeds between the layers of brick at intervals of four or five feet.

Line 24. *and build a vessel.* This line introduces the first of the O.T. parallels (Gen. vi.14ff.). Others include the loading of the vessel with all species of animals (Gen. vi.19ff.), the coming of a Flood of such proportions that the mountains were covered (Gen. vii.19), the grounding of the vessel on a mountain (Gen. viii.4), the sending forth of the birds (Gen. viii.7ff., with slight differences), and the mountain sacrifice (Gen. viii.20). These similarities have been explained by supposing, either that the Babylonian story travelled westward, preferably in oral form, into the lands of the Bible, or that the O.T. and Babylonian accounts are independently derived from a more original version which antedates both. The issue appears to be quite open.

Line 31. *Apsu-wise.* See note on line 57.

Line 35. *what should I say to the city assembly?* Although Utnapishti was the ruler of Shuruppak, in the democratic times of the story he would hold such position only by virtue of the confidence the city assembly placed in him. He might only hope to keep that confidence, and so be able to recruit the community for the building of his vessel, if his action was capable of being shown to lie to the advantage of the community itself. Ea's cryptic reply (lines 43-7) overcomes this problem in that seemingly the men of Shuruppak are to be told that forthcoming plenty will attend Utnapishti's departure. But the message contains two words which have double significance ; and the context of line 87 demands that they there be taken in their far more ominous meanings.

Line 57. *One iku,* an area representing the square of 120 cubits. Since the 'walls' were also of 120 cubits, the vessel was conceived and built as a cube, and it is probable that the 'Apsu-wise' of line 31 represented Ea's command that it should be this shape. In this connection it may be noted that an Ea-designed craft *had* to be different, otherwise it could not have been characterised as the work of Ea.

Line 64. *ten thousand baskets.* An approximation. The text actually gives the number as 3 *sar,* that is $3 \times 3,600$.

Line 68. *(wood-)seasoning* is an uncertain translation.

Line 103. *had taken up their torches* has been variously interpreted. We would propose it to mean that the sky grew so dark that the stars came out temporarily in advance of the storm-cloud.

Line 160. *sweet savour.* Different in kind from the 'sweet savour' of Gen. viii.21, since the Hebrew word there used indicates that Noah's sacrifice was wholly burnt.

Lines 168, 179. *without any discrimination, indiscriminately.* Much hinges on these words, but if they correctly translate the original the sense is clear. Ea, rallying to the side of Ishtar—a truly pathetic figure in the story—supports her accusation against Enlil that the Flood was directed against the *whole* of mankind without distinction. If it had to come (cp. note to line 14) it should have been directed against sinners only. The sentence beginning *loosen (the rope),* line 181, is unfortunately of uncertain meaning, but could be proverbial from an original instruction to soldiers on the handling of captured prisoners.

Line 186. *oppose.* The translation is based on a new reading.

Line 187. *the Exceeding-Wise* is a translation of the proper name Atrahasis, another name for Utnapishti, known also from the fragmentary Epic of Atrahasis.

Bibliography

FRAZER, J. G.   *Folk-Lore in the Old Testament*, I, 1919, 104-361.

HEIDEL, A.   *The Gilgamesh Epic and Old Testament Parallels*, second ed., 1954.

KRAMER, S. N.   *From the Tablets of Sumer* (ch. 18.   'A Flood : the First Noah'), 1956 (republished with the title *History Begins at Sumer*, 1958).

PARROT, A.   'The Flood and Noah's Ark', *Studies in Biblical Archæology*, No. 1, 1955.

SKINNER, J.   *A Critical and Exegetical Commentary on Genesis* (*ICC*), 1912, 174-81.

SPEISER, E. A., in *A.N.E.T.*, 72-99, 104-06 (Atrahasis Epic).

J. V. KINNIER WILSON

The Law Code of Hammurabi

THE stele of Hammurabi (*c.* 1792-1750 B.C.) inscribed with his famous law code (Plate 2) was discovered between December and January 1901-2 by V. SCHEIL at Susa, one-time capital of the Elamites. It is in the form of a boundary stone and stands about eight feet high. The upper part has a relief depicting Hammurabi receiving sceptre and ring from Shamash, the sun-god. The rest of the surface is taken up with the code ; the direction of writing is from top to bottom. Seven columns have been deleted, presumably to make way for a memorial to its captor, most probably Shutruk-Nahhunte, who raided and pillaged Sippar in the early part of the twelfth century. One would have expected such an important stele to have been erected in the capital, Babylon, but it may well be that more than one copy existed.

The language of the Code is already grammatically fully organised and classical in form. The choice of the Akkadian language rather than of the Sumerian may indicate that Hammurabi's reforming activities extended to language as well as to jurisprudence. He must have embarked early on his work of reform, for in the Chronological Lists the designation of his second regnal year is—'He established justice in the land'. The reference is probably to the promulgation of the Code, but this copy must have been made much later, as certain events referred to in the prologue belong to the latter part of his reign. Although his father and grandfather bore Semitic names, his own harks back to his Amorite origin. In racial matters, however, his policy seems to have been one of compromise, even down to the matter of dress : he adopted the Sumerian long cloak and head-dress, but continued to wear his hair long in Semitic fashion. The compilation of his laws may have been carried out in this same spirit of compromise. In the prologue his avowed purpose is to ameliorate the condition of the weak, presumably including vassals and serfs. There are earlier collections of legal maxims, such as that of Bilalama (?) of Eshnunna. These laws date probably from about a century before Hammurabi. Despite some agreement in terminology, there is no ground for supposing that this or any other collection was utilised by Hammurabi. Responsible as he was for a kingdom composed of former independent states, he could hardly have afforded not to acquaint himself with the contents of their various legislative systems, and the knowledge thus acquired would have brought home to him the need of something approaching universal law. It would be the task, and not the sources, that dictated, if at all, the composite character of his work. One extraordinary fact is that, great as was his prestige as a ruler and his achievement in formulating the laws, the Code seems to have remained merely an ideal lacking practical application. There is no evidence in the contemporary legal documents that the provisions of the Hammurabi Code were ever carried out, and to all intents and purposes it might not have existed for them.

The laws of Hammurabi touch on many matters which are dealt with also in the legal parts of the Pentateuch. Despite many resemblances, there is no ground for assuming any direct borrowing by the Hebrew from the Babylonian. Even where the two sets of laws differ little in the letter, they differ much in the spirit, for instance, in the Babylonian regard for the status of litigants. The explanation of the similarities is obvious : the limitation in the variety of crimes and in the possible forms of punishment. How much both owed to a *jus gentium* would be hard to determine. But perhaps both owe more to a *jus naturale*. In the Babylonian Code punishments are always stated, whereas in the Hebrew there occurs, as is inevitable in the rules of a theocratic community, the 'absolute imperative'. Any theory which fails to take into account this and the resulting division of statements of principle from statements of specific provisions, has little to commend it. Perhaps the most remarkable feature of the Hammurabi Code is that such specific provisions should have been formulated in a fully organised legal language as early as the eighteenth century B.C.

In the extracts here presented, the numbers refer to the paragraphs of the Code.

Text

1. If a citizen has accused a citizen and has indicted him for a murder and has not substantiated the charge, his accuser shall be put to death.

2. If a citizen has indicted a citizen for sorcery and does not substantiate the charge, the one who is indicted for sorcery shall go to the river and shall throw himself in. If the river overwhelms him, (then) his indicter shall take away his house. If the river exculpates that citizen and he is preserved, the one who indicted him for sorcery shall die, (and) the one who threw himself into the river shall take away his house.

3. If a citizen in a case has borne false witness, and does not substantiate the statement which he has made, (and) if that case is one warranting the death-penalty, that citizen shall be put to death.

4. If he comes forward to witness concerning wheat or money, he shall bear the penalty appropriate to that case.

5. If a judge has given a judgement and has passed a sentence and has drawn up a sealed document, and afterwards revises his findings, they shall convict that judge of revising his findings; he shall give the prescribed indemnity which follows from that case twelve-fold, and they shall eject him from the council, from the seat of his judicature ; he shall not return and he shall not sit with the judges in judgement.

6. If a citizen has stolen property of the temple or of the crown, that man shall die, and whosoever receives the stolen goods from his hand shall die.

7. If a citizen has purchased or has accepted for safe custody silver, or gold, or serf, or bondmaid, or ox, or sheep, or ass, or whatsoever it may be, from the hand of the son of a citizen, or from the serf of a citizen, without witnesses or contracts, that man is a thief, (and) he shall die.

8. If a citizen has stolen an ox, or a sheep, or an ass, or a pig, or a boat, if it is the property of the temple or of the crown, he shall give thirty-fold, but, if it is the property of a vassal, he shall restore ten-fold, whereas if the thief has nothing to give, he shall die.

14. If a citizen steals the child of a citizen, he shall die.

22. If a citizen has committed a robbery and is caught, that man shall die.

117. If a debt renders a citizen distrainable, and he has sold for money his wife, or son, or daughter, or if anyone is sold for service in lieu of debt, they shall work for three years in the house of their purchaser or their distrainer. In the fourth year they shall attain their freedom.

118. If a serf or bondmaid has been sold, and should the merchant proceed to (re-sell) and either is sold for money, they cannot be reclaimed.

119. If a debt renders a citizen distrainable, and he sells for money his bondmaid who has borne him children, the master of the bondmaid may repay the sum and redeem his bondmaid.

122. If a citizen gives to a citizen for custody silver, or gold, or anything whatsoever, he shall show to witnesses all that is deposited. He shall furnish the contracts, and (then) he shall hand the goods over for safe custody.

123. If he has given into custody without witnesses and contracts, and those to whom he gave it deny the transaction, no claim can lie in such a case.

124. If a citizen has given another citizen silver, or gold, or anything whatsoever for safe custody in the presence of witnesses and he denies it, they shall convict that citizen, and in spite of his denial, he shall restore it twofold.

125. If a citizen has handed over anything of his whatsoever for safe custody, and if the place where it is deposited (is entered)

either by breaking in or by (climbing a) ladder, and his property and that of the owner of the house is lost, the householder, who has been negligent, shall make restitution of what was given him for safe custody and was lost, and shall compensate the owner ; the householder shall further search for what was lost and recover it from the thief.

127. If a citizen has pointed a finger at a priestess, or the wife of a citizen, and does not substantiate his imputation, they shall charge that citizen before the judge and they shall shave his front hair.

128. If a citizen has taken a wife but has not deposited her contracts, that woman is not a (legal) wife.

129. If the wife of a citizen is taken cohabiting with another male, they shall both be bound and cast into the water ; if the husband of the wife reprieves his wife, then the king may reprieve his servant.

130. If a citizen has forced a citizen's wife, who has not known a man, and has lain in her bosom, and they seize him, that man shall be put to death ; that wife shall go free.

131. If the wife of a citizen is accused by her husband, but she has not been caught lying with another male, she shall take an oath of the god and return to her house.

132. If the finger is pointed at the wife of a citizen on account of another man, but she has not been caught lying with another man, for her husband's sake she shall throw herself into the river.

133a. If a citizen has been carried away captive, and there is sustenance in his house, his wife . . . shall guard her property and shall not enter the household of another.

133b. If that wife does not guard her property but enters into the household of another, they shall convict this wife and cast her into the water.

134. If a citizen has been carried away captive, and there is no sustenance in his house, his wife may enter into another household, and no crime may be imputed to this woman.

135. If a citizen is carried away captive, and there is no sustenance in his house, (and) before his re-appearance his wife has entered the household of another, and borne children, (and if) subsequently her husband returns and comes to his city, that woman shall return to this her former husband, but the children shall follow their (natural) father.

144. If a citizen has taken a priestess-wife, and that priestess has given a bondmaid to her husband and she has borne children, if that man plan to take a votaress (as concubine), they shall not give that citizen permission, a votaress he may not take.

145. If a citizen has taken a priestess-wife, and she has not presented him with children, and if he plans to take a votaress (as concubine), that citizen may take a votaress, and bring her into his house ; but this votaress shall not make herself equal with the priestess-wife.

146. If a citizen has taken a priestess-wife, and she has given a bondmaid to her husband, and she has borne children, and if afterwards that bondmaid has made herself equal with her mistress, her mistress may not sell her for money, since she has borne children ; she may, however, impose on her the badge of serfdom and reckon her among the bondmaids.

147. If she has not borne children she may sell her for money.

148. If a citizen has taken a wife, and intermittent fever attacks her, and if he plans to take another wife, he may do so. He may not forsake his wife who is attacked by the intermittent fever, but she shall dwell in a house which he has prepared, and he shall support her for life.

153. If the wife of a citizen through association with another male has caused the death of her husband, they shall impale that woman.

154. If a citizen has known his daughter, they shall cause that citizen to leave the city.

155. If a citizen has chosen a bride for his son, and his son has known her, and he himself (the father) lies in her bosom, they shall seize that citizen and bind him and cast him into the water.

156. If a citizen has chosen a bride for his son, and his son has not known her, and he himself lies in her bosom, he shall pay her a half-mina of silver, and he shall refund to her whatsoever she brought from her father's house. She may take a husband according to her heart.

157. If a citizen after (the death of) his father lies in the bosom of his mother, they shall burn them both.

158. If a citizen after (the death of) his father is seized in the bosom of his foster-mother who has borne children, that man shall be turned out of his father's house.

170. If a citizen, whose wife has borne him children and (also) his bondmaid has borne him children, (and) the father during his lifetime has said to the bondmaid's children, which she has borne him, 'My children'; he has added them to the children of the wife. After the father goes to his fate, the children of the wife shall divide the property of the father's house equally with the sons of the bondmaid ; the son and heir, the son of the wife, shall choose a share (first) and take it.

195. If a son has struck his father, they shall cut off his hand.

196. If a citizen has destroyed the eye of one of citizen status, they shall destroy his eye.

197. If he has broken the bone of a citizen, his bone shall they break.

198. If he has destroyed the eye, or has broken the bone, of a vassal, he shall pay one mina of silver.

199. If he has destroyed the eye of a slave of a citizen, or has broken the bone of a serf, he shall pay half of his market-value.

200. If a citizen has knocked out the tooth of one of equal status, they shall knock out his tooth.

201. If he has knocked out the tooth of a vassal, he shall pay a third of a mina of silver.

202. If a citizen has struck the cheek of his superior, he shall receive in the council sixty strokes with a thong.

203. If one of citizen status has struck the cheek of his equal, he shall pay one mina of silver.

204. If a vassal has struck the cheek of a fellow vassal, he shall pay ten shekels of silver.

205. If the serf of a citizen has struck the cheek of one of citizen status, they shall cut off his ear.

206. If a citizen has struck a citizen in a quarrel, and has inflicted on him a wound, that citizen shall swear 'I struck him un-wittingly', and he shall pay the doctor.

207. If he has died as a consequence of his attack, he shall swear, and, if he was of citizen stock, he shall pay a half-mina of silver.

208. If he belonged to the vassal class, he shall pay a third of a mina of silver.

209. If a citizen has struck the daughter of a citizen, and she miscarries, he shall pay ten shekels of silver for her miscarriage.

210. If that woman dies as a result, they shall put his daughter to death.

211. If the blow has caused the daughter of a vassal to miscarry, he shall pay five shekels of silver.

212. If that woman dies as a result, he shall pay a half-mina of silver.

213. If he has struck the bondmaid of a citizen and has caused her to miscarry, he shall pay two shekels of silver.

214. If that bondmaid dies as a result, he shall pay a third of a mina of silver.

250. If an ox has gored a citizen, while going along the road, and has occasioned his death, there shall be no penalty attached to this case.

251. If the offending ox belonged to a citizen who has been notified by the authorities of its propensity to gore, and he has not removed its horns, or has not tethered the ox, and that ox gored a man of citizen status occasioning his death, he shall pay a half-mina of silver.

252. If he was the serf of a citizen, he shall pay a third of a mina of silver.

280. If a citizen has bought in a foreign country a serf or a bondmaid of a man, and when he came home, a (former) owner of the serf or bondmaid recognises either his serf or his bondmaid, if the serf and bondmaid are natives of the land, their emancipation shall be asserted without money.

281. If they are natives of another land, the buyer shall declare before the god the sum he paid, and the owner of the serf or bondmaid shall reimburse the merchant for the (whatever) money he expended, and shall redeem his serf or bondmaid.

282. If a serf has declared to his master—'Thou art not my master', his master shall confirm him (to be) his serf and shall cut off his ear.

Notes

Paragraphs 1-4 deal with false witness in specific cases, while Deut. xix.1ff. lays down general principles. In both the principle of commensurate retaliation is invoked.

Paragraph 5 refers rather obscurely to the malpractice of a judge in rescinding a legal decision. The purpose behind this enactment would seem to be to prevent anyone from bringing improper influence to bear on a judge following a case, possibly by means of a bribe. The Pentateuchal passages dealing with the conduct of a judge are in this respect much more explicit Exod. xxiii.6-9 ; Lev. xix.15 ; Deut. xvi.18-20, xxvii.19).

The death-penalty not only for theft but also for the receiving of stolen goods (paras. 6 and 22) stands in sharp contrast to the terms of reparation laid down in Exod. xxii.1ff. for deliberate theft, and in Lev. vi.2ff. to those in the case of goods obtained accidentally but retained dishonestly.

Paragraphs 7, 122, 123, 124, 125 deal with deposits. The penalty for dereliction is restoration of double the value. In Exod. xxii.7, if the goods are stolen by a third party, the thief restores twofold. The penalty to be imposed on the depositary in the case of goods is a matter for the court (verse 8), but in the case of cattle, if stolen, he must make restitution. In Lev. vi.4f. the voluntarily imposed penalty, where obviously the owner had refrained from bringing an action, was the restoration of the full value plus one-fifth.

In both the Code (para. 14) and in Exod. xxi.16 and Deut. xxiv.7 kidnapping is punishable by death. The Deuteronomic passage, like that of the Code, has a particular class of people in view.

The debtor's lot under the Code (paras. 117-19) is severe indeed compared with that of his counterpart in Exod. xxii.25ff.

In the matter of slander (para. 127) the Code takes a particular instance, whereas a general application is made in Exod. xxiii.1.

The Babylonian marriage contract would seem to have been much more highly legalised than the Hebrew one, the main part of which seems to have been the payment of a dowry by the husband (Exod. xxii.16f.).

Proved adultery with a married woman (para. 129) incurred the death-penalty for the participants (Deut. xxii.22). The penalty for rape (para. 130) is the death of the man (Deut. xxii.25). Both the Code (paras. 131f.) and Num. v.13ff. legislate for alleged adultery on the part of the wife.

The situation arising from the capture of a husband is dealt with in great detail (paras. 133a-5), whereas the O.T. is content by implication alone to ensure that such a situation will not occur during the first year of marriage (Deut. xxiv.5, xx.7).

The control of concubinage and of the concubine (paras. 144-7 and 170) throws light on some instances of the practice in the O.T., such as in the case of Abram (Gen. xvi.1ff.).

The Code lays down that the sickly wife must be retained (para. 148), while according to Deut. xxiv.1 the husband may divorce her.

One misses in the Code a statement dealing with homicide in general and its penalty. From the particular case cited (para. 153) we may infer that, in common with the O.T., it involved the death-penalty.

The attitude of the Code to incest (paras. 154-8) differs little in severity from that of Lev. xx.11f. and xviii.6ff.

The right of primogeniture (para. 170) obtains also in Deut. xxi.15ff.

Violence on the part of a son towards his father is punished by maiming (para. 195), but in Exod. xxi.15 by death.

The *lex talionis* (paras. 196ff.) appears in both the Code and in Exod. xxi.23ff., Lev. xxiv.17ff. and Deut. xix.21. The Code, however, observes class distinctions.

The Code knows the distinction in its simplest terms between deed and intent (para. 206), but it evidently does not assign to this principle the importance attached to it in Exod. xxi.13 and Num. xxxv.11ff.

The law dealing with injury inflicted on a pregnant woman (paras. 209-14) is similar in general to that of Exod. xxi.22f.

The menace of a goring ox (paras. 250ff.) is familiar to both the Code and Exod. xxi.28-32.

There is considerable contrast between the Code (paras. 280ff.) and the O.T. in the matter of slavery. In the former emancipation would seem to have been exceptional (para. 280 ; cp. Exod. xxi.2ff. ; Deut. xv.12ff.).

Bibliography

ALT, A. *Kleine Schriften*, 1953, 278ff.

BERGMANN, E. *Codex Hammurabi*, 1953.

COOK, S. A. *The Laws of Moses and the Code of Hammurabi*, 1903.

DRIVER, G. R., and MILES, J. C. *The Babylonian Laws*, I, 1952 ; II, 1955.

EILERS, W. *Die Gesetzesstele Chammurabis*, 1932.

HARPER, R. F. *The Code of Hammurabi*, 1904.

MEEK, T. J., in *A.N.E.T.*, 163ff.

MENDENHALL, G. E. *Law and Covenant in Israel and the Ancient Near East*, 1955 (reprinted from *B.A.* xvii (1954) 26-46, 49-76).

PINCHES, T. G. *The Old Testament*, 1903, 487ff.

POHL, A. and FOLLET, R. *Codex Hammurabi*, 1950.

RAPAPORT, J. 'The Origins of Hebrew Law', *P.E.Q.*, 1941, 158ff.

W. J. MARTIN

Letters from Tell El-Amarna

THE following letters, written in Akkadian with a few Canaanite glosses, were found at Tell el-Amarna in Egypt, and form part of the diplomatic correspondence and dispatches sent from rulers and officials in Western Asia to the Pharaohs Amenhotep III and Amenhotep IV (Akhenaton), c. 1400-1360 B.C. Those from Palestine and Syria, including the six from Abdiheba, governor of Jerusalem, describe a Palestine nominally under a weakening Egyptian suzerainty, but gravely disturbed by Habiru invaders and by the mutual feuds of virtually independent city governors, who appeal to the Pharaoh for help against the Habiru and against each other, making mutual accusations of disloyalty. The situation is vaguely reminiscent of parts of Joshua and Judges, but, although O.T. place names are mentioned, the associated personal names are different (cp. the names of the kings of Jerusalem, Lachish and Gezer in Josh. x.3, 33) and the O.T. gives no inkling of an Egyptian occupation. The peaceful conditions in Genesis (except chs. xiv and xxxiv) are quite dissimilar, and the period is evidently one between Joseph and the Exodus on which the O.T. is silent. The Letters give the Canaanite point of view and evidence a widespread use of writing and a closeness of international connections not hinted at in the O.T. The complicated question of the relation between Habiru and Israelites has been much discussed recently (see MEEK and ROWLEY). The Israelites, who, like the Hebrew patriarchs, were Habiru in Canaanite eyes, seem gradually to have amalgamated with other Habiru groups (cp. 1 Sam. xxix.3), although some of the latter remained distinct as late as Saul's reign (cp. 1 Sam. xiii.6f., xiv.21).

The rapid changes from one subject to another and back again recall the irregular style of St Paul's letters in the N.T. Like Paul (cp. Rom. xvi.22), the writer was dictating to a professional scribe.

Other large collections of Akkadian letters and reports survive from the reigns of Zimrilim of Mari (c. 1730-1700 B.C.), Hammurabi of Babylon (c. 1792-1750 B.C.) and Esarhaddon of Assyria (680-669 B.C.). Hebrew dispatches form the major part

38

Plate 2 Hammurabi receiving his laws from the sun-god Shamash,
the god of justice

of the Lachish ostraca (*c.* 590 B.C.). The Elephantine papyri
(495-400 B.C.) include Aramaic letters from Egyptian Jews to
Jerusalem. The O.T. often mentions, and sometimes quotes
from, letters (e.g. 2 Sam. xi.15 ; 1 Kings xxi.8ff. ; Jer. xxix.1ff. ;
Ezra vii.11ff.).

Text

LETTER NO. 287

[To the kin]g, my lord, [say : Thus says] Abdiheba, thy
servant. [At] the feet of my lord seven t[imes and seven times I
fall. I have heard a]ll the words the king, my lord, (5) has sent
in to me concerning (?) . . . [Behold,] the deed which [the
Habiru(?) have] done . . . of bronze . . . the word . . . (10)
. . . brought in to [Keila]h(?). Let the [kin]g know that all
the lands are at peace but there is hostility against me ; so let
the king take thought about his land. Behold, the land of [G]ezer,
the land of Ashkelon and (15) Lachish (?) have given them food,
oil and all their needs ; so let the king take thought about
archers ; let him send archers against the men who are com-
mitting a crime against the king, my lord. (20) If this year there
are archers, then the lands [and] the regent will belong to the
king, my lord, [but] if there are no archers, the lands and the
regents will not belong to the king. (25) Behold, this land of
Jerusalem, neither my father nor my mother gave it to me ; the
mighty arm [of the king] gave it to me. Behold, this deed is the
deed of Milkilu (30) and the deed of the sons of Labaya who have
given the land of the king to the Habiru. Behold, O king, my
lord, I am in the right. As for the Cushites, let the king ask
the commissioners if the house is (really) very strong ; (35) for
they attempted a grave and serious crime ; they took their
implements and broke through the . . . of the roof . . . sent
into the land . . . came up (?) with . . . (40) servants. Let the
king take thought about them . . . gone forth (?) . . . the
lands into their hand, [so] let the king demand (satisfaction)
from them—abundance of food, abundance of oil and abundance of clothing, (45) until Pauru, the commissioner of the king,
comes up to the land of Jerusalem. Addaya has left with the
men of the warden's garrison [which] the king gave me. Let
the king know. Addaya said to me : (50) 'Behold, I am leaving,

but thou shalt not abandon it'. This [year] send me a garrison [and] send me a commissioner of the king. Even as we are (?), I sent [gift]s (?) to the king, [my] lord, . . . captives, five thousand [shekels of silver (?) (55) and (?)] eight (?) bearers (in) caravans for the king, but they were captured in the open country at Aijalon. Let the king, my lord, know. I am not able to send a caravan to the king, my lord,—that thou mayest know. (60) Behold, the king has set his name in the land of Jerusalem for ever, so he cannot abandon the lands of Jerusalem.

To the scribe of the king, my lord, (65) say: Thus says Abdiheba, thy servant. At the feet I fall; thy servant am I. Take in clear words to the king, my lord. I am a warden of the king. (70) I am subordinate to thee.

But they did a wicked deed against me, the Cushites. I was almost killed by the hand of the Cushites (75) in the midst of my house. Let the king [demand (satisfaction)] from them. [Seven] times and seven times [I fall at the feet of the king,] my lord. I am [in the right].

Notes

This, and the following letter, is numbered in accordance with the edition of J. A. KNUDTZON.

SUMMARY. Lines 1-5, introduction; lines 6-46, reports of attacks on Abdiheba's lands by Milkilu, the sons of Labaya, Habiru and the Cushites, with appeals to the Pharaoh for help; lines 47-63, local news and renewed appeal for help; lines 64-70, conclusion; lines 71-8, postscript.

Lines 1-10. *To the king* (Akhenaton of Egypt, *c.* 1377-1360 B.C.); cp. Ezra v.7. *my lord.* Cp. 1 Sam. xxiv.8, etc. *say.* The person addressed is the Egyptian scribe (cp. line 64). *Abdiheba* was 'king' of Jerusalem, and governor appointed by the Pharaoh. Heba is a Hittite or Hurrian goddess, and the whole name may be read as Hurrian, namely, 'Putiheba', 'servant of Heba'. *Abdi* is Canaanite, meaning 'servant (or worshipper) of'. Cp. the O.T. names Obadiah ('servant of Yah', i.e. of Yahweh), Obed-edom (2 Sam. vi.10), Obed (Ruth iv.17), Ebed (Jud. ix.26) and Ebed-melech (Jer. xxxviii.7). Abdiheba was probably of Hittite origin; one of the idioms in this letter is Hittite (cp. note on line 14). The O.T. lists Hittites among the early inhabitants of Palestine (e.g. Josh. iii.10), and preserves the memory of an early Hittite element in the Jerusalem population (Ezek. xvi.3). Cp. the Palestinian Hittites—all with Semitic names—Ephron (Gen. xxiii.10), Ahimelech (1 Sam. xxvi.6), and Uriah (2 Sam. xi.6). *thy servant* (or 'thy slave') is the usual O.T. phrase in addressing kings and other superiors (1 Kings ii.38; 2 Kings iv.1). [*At*] *the feet . . . I fall.* This normal O.T. act of obeisance (1 Sam. xxv.24;

2 Kings iv.37) is here used metaphorically ; cp. Letter No. 288, lines 4, 64. *seven times and seven times*, i.e. many times. Seven and its multiples are often so used in the Bible, e.g. Gen. iv.15 ; Matt. xviii.22. The restoration of lines 4-11 is doubtful. *Habiru.* Cp. line 31. *Keilah*, or perhaps 'Rubute'. Keilah was a Judaean hill town later frequented by David's outlaws (1 Sam. xxiii.1ff.) ; Rubute has been doubtfully identified with Rabbith (Josh. xix.20), or with Rabbah (Josh. xv.60), or even with Kiriath-arba, i.e. Hebron (Josh. xv.13). *Let the [king] know.* This phrase is repeated in lines 48 and 57 ; cp. Ezra iv.12f., v.8 ; Dan. iii.18.

Lines 11-20. *all the lands are at peace*, i.e. the king's other territories have come to terms with the invading Habiru ; cp. lines 29-31 and Letter No. 288, lines 27f. and 44. But it is possible to translate—'all the lands are united (against me)'. *hostility.* Cp. note on Letter No. 288, line 31. *his land*, i.e. Palestine, especially Jerusalem and its environs. *land of.* Literally, 'land of the city of', a Hittite idiom, found also in lines 25 and 46. *Gezer, Ashkelon and Lachish* (cp. Letter No. 288, line 43) were important cities in the plain south and south-west of Jerusalem (Josh. x.33 ; Jud. i.18), owing allegiance to the Pharaoh. Later, Ashkelon became a Philistine city, and Lachish figured largely in the history of Southern Israel. *them.* Presumably the Habiru are meant. *food, oil.* Cp. line 44. Olive oil was used for food (1 Kings xvii.12 ; 1 Chr. xii.40) and in lamps (Exod. xxv.6). *archers* is evidently a general term for Egyptian foot-soldiers.

Lines 21-30. *regent.* He was a high official, administering a province from headquarters in a city. Subordinate to him was the *commissioner* (cp. lines 34 and 45), who was apparently a travelling deputy in charge of troops. Lower still was the *warden*, or town governor, like Abdiheba (cp. line 69). *regents.* As an afterthought Abdiheba uses the plural. *will not belong*, i.e. will no longer belong ; cp. Ezra iv.16. *Jerusalem*, not at this time a very important town, is mentioned in the Letters only by Abdiheba ; the alternative name, Jebus, never occurs, and may be later. The Israelites did not conquer the town until David's reign (2 Sam. v.6f. ; cp. Josh. xv.63 ; Jud. i.21). *arm.* Cp. Deut. ix.29 ; Josh. xxiv.12 ; Ps. xliv.3. The statement is not to be taken too literally ; cp. note on Letter No. 288, line 15. *this deed.* Cp. line 6. *Milkilu* was a regent. The name may mean 'Milk is god' ; cp. Molech (1 Kings xi.7). More probably, however, it means 'El (or 'God') is king' ; cp. Malchiel (associated in Gen. xlvi.17, etc. with Heber, as Milkilu is with the Habiru), Malchijah (Neh. iii.14), and Elimelech (Ruth i.3). *Labaya* was a ruler in South Palestine. He and his sons are, like Milkilu and others, often accused in the Letters, by Abdiheba and others, of disloyalty to the Pharaoh, and he and Milkilu, with others, make countercharges in letters to him. If the name is Semitic, it means 'lion'. Cp., with the same meaning, the names Laish (1 Sam. xxv.44) and Arieh (2 Kings xv.25). O.T. personages are often named after animals ; cp. Rachel 'ewe', Leah 'cow', Achbor 'mouse'.

Lines 31-40. *Habiru* (in Egyptian, 'Apiru') was a derogatory name given at this time to nomadic and semi-nomadic invaders—Semites and non-Semites— infiltrating into Palestine from the north. The O.T. name 'Hebrew', used for the Israelites (only rarely, and chiefly by foreigners), may be derived from it, but Habiru is not primarily an ethnic term, and it was used in Mesopotamia of loosely organised and unorganised immigrants for centuries before it reached Palestine and Egypt. *in the right*, i.e. innocent of charges of disloyalty and of the annexation of land levelled against him. *Cushites* (cp. line 74). Literally, 'men of Kashi', the O.T. Cush (Gen. ii.13) or 'Ethiopia' (Is. xviii.1 ; Ps. lxviii.31), i.e. Nubia ; cp. note on Letter No. 288, line 36. They were presumably Egyptian mercenary troops, either attached to Milkilu or to the sons of Labaya, or resident in Jerusalem as a garrison. The O.T. name Cushi (Jer. xxxvi.14 ; Zeph. i.1) shows that their descendants survived in Israel into the late period of the monarchy ; cp. also 'the Cushite' of 2 Sam. xviii.21ff. *commissioners*. See note on line 22. *the house*, i.e. Abdiheba's fortified palace in Jerusalem ; cp. line 75. *implements*, presumably of bronze ; cp. line 7. Iron was still scarce in Palestine at this time, the Late Bronze Age (cp. 1 Sam. xvii.5ff.). *the roof*, i.e. of the palace-fortress. The meaning of lines 38-40 is obscure ; they seem to describe a raid. *servants*. Either slaves or armed retainers.

Lines 41-50. *into* (or 'in') *their hand*, i.e. apparently to the Habiru ; cp. line 31 and Letter No. 288, line 44. *demand (satisfaction)* (cp. line 76), i.e. exact punishment ; cp. the O.T. idiom 'require at the hand of' (1 Sam. xx.16). *food, oil*. Cp. line 16. *Pauru* probably succeeded Addaya (line 47) in Jerusalem as commissioner. Eventually, like Addaya, he left with his troops for Gaza. *comes up*. Jerusalem lies high among the hills ; cp. 1 Kings xii.28. *Addaya* was Egyptian commissioner in Jerusalem and perhaps elsewhere in South Palestine. The name is perhaps Hurrian ; it can scarcely be connected with the O.T. Adaiah 'Yah has adorned' (2 Kings xxii.1). *has left*—for Gaza on the Palestine coast, south-west of Jerusalem. *warden's garrison* was evidently a bodyguard for Abdiheba. Presumably Addaya retired to Gaza as a safer place, taking the bodyguard as escort. *abandon it*, i.e. Jerusalem.

Lines 51-60. *a commissioner*, i.e. Pauru ; cp. line 45. *bearers*, i.e. porters. *caravans*—of tribute, gifts and prisoners. These were regularly expected by the Pharaoh, but the letters sometimes mention the impossibility of sending them owing to attacks of bandits or of disloyal local rulers. *open country*. Literally, 'fields', of Aijalon (cp. 'valley of Aijalon', Josh. x.12). Aijalon was a town west of Jerusalem, near Gezer.

Lines 61-70. *for ever*. Cp. Josh. xiv.9, etc. *he cannot*, or, 'I cannot'. *scribe*, i.e. secretary, who dealt with the king's correspondence. Royal scribes, Israelite and other, are often mentioned in the O.T. ; cp. 2 Kings xii.10 ; Esth. iii.12. *the feet*, i.e. thy feet. *clear*, or perhaps 'eloquent' ; literally 'bright'. The scribe would translate the message and report it to the king in his own words. *warden*. See note on line 22. *subordinate to thee*, i.e. thy humble servant, equivalent to 'Yours obediently'. The interpretation 'much (beholden) to thee', the equivalent of 'Thanking you in anticipation', is dubious.

Lines 71-8. *Cushites*. Cp. lines 33ff. *almost*. Literally 'by a finger', i.e. but for a finger's breadth ; cp. Ps. xxxix.5, 'as hand-breadths'. *demand (satisfaction)*. Cp. line 43. *times*. Cp. line 3. *in the right*. Cp. line 32.

Text

LETTER NO. 288

To the king, my lord, my Sun-god, say : Thus says Abdiheba, thy servant. At the feet of the king, my lord, seven times and seven times I fall. (5) Behold, the king, my lord, has set his name at the rising of the sun and at the setting of the sun. It is outrageous what they have committed against me. Behold, I am not a regent, (10) but I am a warden to the king, my lord. Behold, I am a shepherd of the king, and a tribute-bringer of the king am I. Neither my father nor my mother but the mighty arm of the king (15) set [me] in the house of [my] father. . . . [Behold,] . . . came to me . . . I gave ten servants [into his h]and. Shuta, the commissioner of the king, came (20) to me. Twenty-one maidens [and eigh]ty (male) captives I gave into the hand of Shuta as a gift to the king, my lord. Let the king take counsel for his land. The land of the king is lost ; all of it (25) is taken away from me. There is hostility against me as far as the lands of Seir and as far as Gath-carmel. There is peace to all the regents, but there is hostility against me. I am treated like a Habiru, (30) and I do not see the eyes of the king, my lord, for there is hostility against me. I am made like a ship in the midst of the sea. The mighty arm of the king may take (35) Naharaim and Cush, but now the Habiru have taken the cities of the king. No regent is left (40) to the king, my lord ; all are lost. Behold, Turbazu has been killed in the city-gate of Zilu, yet the king holds back. Behold, Zimrida at Lachish—his servants have smitten him and have made themselves over to the Habiru. (45) Yaptihadda has been killed in the city-gate of Zilu, yet [the king] holds back and does not demand (satisfaction) from them. [So] let the king take thought [about his land and] let the king give his attention to (50) (sending) archers for his (?) land. [For] if there are no archers this year all the lands of the king, my lord, will be lost. They are not reporting in the presence of the king, my lord, (55) that the land of the king, my lord, is lost and that all the regents are lost. If there are no archers this year, let the king send a commissioner, and let him take me (60) to himself with my brothers, and we shall die beside the king, our lord. [To] the scribe of the king, my lord, [thus]

says Abdiheba, the servant.   At the feet I fall.   Take in (65)
very (?) clear words to the king, [my lord.   Thy] servant [and]
thy son am I.

Notes

SUMMARY.   Lines 1-7, introduction ;   lines 8-15, complaint of an attack ;
lines 16-22, protestations of loyalty ;   lines 23-38, appeal for help against
Habiru ;   lines 39-61, local news and appeal for help ;   lines 62-6, conclusion.

Lines 1-10. *Sun-god.* Egyptian kings claimed to be divine and sons of the
sun-god, Re or Amon, the supreme god of Egypt.   Some O.T. passages use
very similar language of Israelite kings, e.g. 2 Sam. vii.14 ;   Pss. ii.7, xlv.6,
lxxxix.26f. ;   cp. also Is. ix.6.   The Letters often address the Pharaoh as
'sun-god' and 'god'.   Akhenaton had instituted a new form of sun-worship,
that of the solar disc, Aton (Aten), personified as supreme or only god. *set his
name,* i.e. extended his rule to the eastern and western limits of the world—
a flattering exaggeration, since Babylonia, Assyria, Mitanni and the Hittites
were powerful independent kingdoms ;   cp. Pss. lxxii.8, cxiii.3 ;   Mal. i.11.
what they have committed.   The reference is to attacks on his lands. *regent,
warden.*   See note on Letter No. 287, line 22.

Lines 11-20. *shepherd,* i.e. ruler ;   cp. Is. xliv.28 ;   Ezek. xxxiv.2ff. *tribute-
bringer,* i.e. a punctual remitter of the Pharaoh's dues. *the house of my father,*
i.e. the palace in Jerusalem ;   the phrase indicates that Abdiheba was a
hereditary ruler, confirmed in his position by the Pharaoh. *gave,* as tribute
or as a free gift, thus demonstrating his loyalty. *Shuta* was an Egyptian
commissioner in Palestine. *maidens.*   Literally 'daughters'.

Lines 21-30. *take counsel* is a different phrase from 'take thought' in line 48
and in Letter No. 287, lines 13, 17 and 40. *taken from me,* by Habiru, with the
connivance or inactivity of disloyal Egyptian vassals ;   cp. Letter No. 287,
lines 29ff. *hostility.*   Cp. note on line 31 and Letter No. 287, line 12. *Seir*
i.e. Edom (cp. Gen. xxxii.3), or part of it.   Its centre lay south-east of the
Dead Sea. *Gath-carmel.*   The name means 'winepress of Carmel' ;   cp. Gath-
rimmon (Josh. xxi.25), Gath (1 Sam. v.8) and Gath-hepher (2 Kings xiv.25).
The O.T. mentions two Carmels, one on the north-west coast (Jer. xlvi.18),
usually called 'mount Carmel' (1 Kings xviii.19), the other in Judah (1 Sam.
xxv.2).   Perhaps the latter is meant, but, as a contrast to Seir, a region to the
north-west is likely. *peace.*   See note on Letter No. 287, line 12. *treated
like a Habiru,* i.e. misrepresented to the Pharaoh as an enemy annexing Egyptian
lands.   Cp. note on Letter No. 287, line 31. *see the eyes of the king,* i.e. appear
before him in person to defend himself against calumniators.   Cp. 2 Sam.
xiv.24, 28, 32.

Lines 31-40. *hostility.* Attacks on his lands and slanders to the Pharaoh are
included. *like a ship,* isolated from help and surrounded by dangers. *Naharaim,*
Upper Mesopotamia, the land between 'the two rivers' ;   cp. Aram-naharaim
(Ps. lx, title), 'Syria between the two rivers', i.e. Mesopotamian Syria.   One
river is the Euphrates, the other is either a tributary or the Tigris.   Egypt had

invaded the area but it was now ruled by the powerful kingdom of Mitanni. *Cush*, i.e. Nubia, the Nile valley region just south of Egypt, partly under Egyptian suzerainty. Cp. note on Letter No. 287, line 33. Naharaim and Cush represent the northern and southern limits of Egyptian rule. *Habiru.* Cp. Letter No. 287, line 31.

Lines 41-50. *Turbazu.* The name is perhaps Egyptian, and he may have been a regent (cp. line 39) ; probably Yaptihadda (line 45) was his successor or his junior officer. *Zilu.* A town near the Egyptian frontier. *Zimrida* was apparently a regent or subordinate official at Lachish and probably a Semite ; cp. the O.T. names Zimri (Num. xxv.14 ; 1 Kings xvi.9) and Zimran (Gen. xxv.2). He is the author of a letter professing loyalty to the Pharaoh, but another letter accuses him of treachery. *Lachish.* See note on Letter No. 287, line 14. *Yaptihadda.* Cp. note on line 41. The name, meaning 'Adda opens (the womb)', is Semitic, Yaptih being identical with Jephthah (Hebrew *Yiphtach*, Jud. xi.1ff.). Cp. Pethahiah (Neh. ix.5), meaning 'Yah has opened'. Adda is the same as Adad or Hadad, a west-Semitic storm-god, who was also called Rimmon ; cp. Hadadrimmon (Zech. xii.11), Hadadezer (2 Sam. viii.3), Hadad (1 Kings xi.14), and the variants Hadarezer (2 Sam. x.16) and Hadar (Gen. xxxvi.39). *demand (satisfaction).* Cp. Letter No. 287, lines 42 and 76. *his attention.* Literally 'his face'. Cp. Dan. xi.17f. *Archers.* Cp. note on Letter No. 287, line 17.

Lines 51-60. *are not reporting*, i.e. the Pharaoh's officials, in Palestine and perhaps also at the Egyptian court, are concealing the truth from him. *in the presence of* is a ceremonious phrase, used especially of gods and kings ; cp. Gen. xli.46 ; 2 Sam. xvi.19 ; Ps. c.2 ; Dan. ii.27. *commissioner.* Cp. Letter No. 287, line 52. *himself.* The text has erroneously 'myself'.

Lines 61-6. *die*, i.e. live out their lives in safety. *scribe.* Cp. Letter No. 287, line 64. *the servant*, or 'the slave' ; cp. note on Letter No. 287, line 2. *I fall*, Cp. note on Letter No. 287, line 3. *clear.* Cp. note on Letter No. 287, line 67. *Thy servant and thy son.* Cp. 2 Kings xvi.7.

Bibliography

ALBRIGHT, W. F., in *A.N.E.T.*, 488f.

COOK, S. A., in *C.A.H.*, II, 1924, 296-351.

KNUDTZON, J. A. *Die El-Amarna Tafeln*, 1907-15.

MEEK, T. J. *Hebrew Origins*, revised ed., 1950.

MERCER, S. A. B. *The Tell el-Amarna Tablets*, 1939.

OLMSTEAD, A. T. *History of Palestine and Syria*, 1931.

ROWLEY, H. H. *From Joseph to Joshua* (Schweich Lectures, 1948), 1950.

C. J. MULLO WEIR

Historical Records
of Assyria and Babylonia

THE kings of Assyria, like their precursors the Old Babylonians and Sumerians, kept written records of their military and building operations. With the expansion of the Assyrian Empire westwards during the ninth to seventh centuries B.C., increasing reference is made in these texts to Syria and, eventually, to the smaller and more distant city-states of Israel and Judah. These historical contacts are of considerable interest, since the information given by the Assyrian and O.T. sources is often complementary. The brevity of the references, however, sometimes raises difficulties of interpretation which cannot easily be solved from existing sources, as is well illustrated by the brief extracts here presented. The Assyrian annals have been found to be generally reliable, though given to exaggeration in time of victory or silence on the rarer occasion of defeat. The detail given varies according to the version of an event, those written contemporaneously being fuller records which are condensed in subsequent editions. For the Neo-Babylonian period, an unusually objective and reliable source is provided by the 'Babylonian Chronicle'.

These historical texts were written on clay tablets, prisms and cylinders, or inscribed on stone obelisks, stelæ or even rock faces. The majority were found in the royal capitals of Nineveh, Nimrud (Calah of Gen. x.10f.), Ashur and Babylon, from which military expeditions set out for Syria and Palestine.

I SHALMANESER III's OPERATIONS AGAINST THE ARAMÆANS (853-841 B.C.)

The Assyrians entered one of their most vigorous periods of influence with the reign of Ashurnasirpal II (883-859 B.C.). In a series of well conducted military campaigns he reopened the Assyrian trade-routes to the Mediterranean, and sought to make the smaller city-states of Syria vassals, imposing on them the payment of annual tribute. Shalmaneser III (859-824 B.C.) continued his father's policy against stiffening opposition led by Irhuleni, king of Hamath, who headed a coalition of twelve kings, including Ahab of Israel (Text *a*). At the battle of Qarqar in 853 B.C. Shalmaneser claimed the victory, but the outcome was sufficiently adverse for the Assyrians not to appear again in the west for at least three years, when a further series of operations, still directed against Hadadezer of Damascus and Irhuleni, were undertaken from 849 to 845 B.C. By 841 B.C., the eighteenth year of Shalmaneser's reign, that alliance had broken up and Hazael, who now ruled Aram from his capital Damascus, in the place of the murdered Irhuleni, had to face the Assyrian army alone. Hazael checked the Assyrian advance and was able to ward off a close siege of that city, so that Shalmaneser moved off westwards *via* the Hauran to the Mediterranean, where he received tribute brought by Jehu of Israel (Texts *b* and *c*).

Text

(*a*) I departed from Aleppo and drew near to the two towns of Irhuleni of Hamath, Adennu and Barga. I captured the town of Argana, his royal residence, and took out fine booty, the movable and immovable goods of his palaces. I set fire to his palaces. I departed from Argana and drew near to Qarqar, and then demolished, destroyed and burned down Qarqar, his royal residence. 1,200 chariots, 1,200 cavalry horses, 20,000 men belonging to Adad-'idri of Damascus, 700 chariots, 700 cavalry, 10,000 men of Irhuleni the Hamathite, 200 chariots and 10,000 men of Ahab the Israelite, 500 men from Cilicia, 1,000 men of Musru, 10 chariots, 10,000 men of Uqanata, 200 men of Matinu-ba'ali the Arvadite, 200 men of Usantu, 30 chariots, 10,000 men of Adunu-ba'ali of Shizana, 1,000 camels of Gindibu' of Arabia, . . ., 000 men of Ba'asa, son of Ruhubi of Ammon—these were the twelve kings who came to help him. They came directly toward me in close battle, (but) with the superior aid which Ashur the lord had given, and with the mighty weapons which Nergal, my leader, had gifted me, I fought with them. From Qarqar to Gilzau I defeated them. I smote 14,000 of their men with weapons, falling upon them like Adad pouring down a hailstorm. I flung their bodies about, filling the plain with their scattered soldiery.

Kurkh Stele, ii.87-98

(b) In my eighteenth regnal year I crossed the River Euphrates for the sixteenth time. Hazael of Aram put his trust in the numerical strength of his army and called out his army in great numbers. He made Sanir, a mountain-peak which stands out in front of the Lebanon, his strong position, (but) I fought with him and defeated him, smiting with weapons 16,000 of his experienced troops. I snatched away from him 1,121 of his chariots and 470 of his cavalry-horses together with his baggage train. He went off to save his life, (but) I followed after him and surrounded him in Damascus, his capital city. I cut down his plantations (and then) marched as far as the mountains of the Hauran. I destroyed, tore down, and burnt with fire numberless villages, carrying away innumerable spoil from them. I marched as far as the mountains of Ba'ali-ra'si, a headland by the sea, and put up on it a representation of my royal person. At that time I received the tribute of the people of Tyre, Sidon, and of Jehu, son of Omri.

Black Obelisk

(c) The tribute of Jehu, son of Omri. Silver, gold, a golden bowl, a golden vase, golden cups, golden buckets, tin, a staff for the royal hand (?), *puruhati*-fruits.

Black Obelisk—Superscription

Notes

(a) The Kurkh Stele is now in the British Museum (No. 118884). This extract is taken from an account of the events in the year dated by the eponym Daian-Ashur ; the sixth regnal year of Shalmaneser III, i.e. 853 B.C., in which year the stele was erected.

Adad-'idri, or Hadadezer, who may have succeeded Benhadad, was the opponent of Ahab, *c.* 860 B.C. (1 Kings xx), as king of Damascus. After the battle of Aphek in the following year, Ahab was at peace with Aram for two years. It has been suggested that Ahab was a wise enough statesman to come to terms with the vigorous Hadadezer and ally Israel with him in face of the common danger from Assyria. Adad-'idri may be the unnamed 'king of Aram' in fighting whom Ahab met his death at Ramoth-gilead (1 Kings xxii.29-36).

his royal residence. The text has erroneously *my*.

Ahab the Israelite (Ahabbu (mat)Sir'ilaia), i.e. the Ahab of 1 Kings xvi.29, xx.34, xxii.1-37.

From Qarqar to Gilzau I defeated them. This implies only a partial victory, for the withdrawal to Gilzau on the Orontes River probably enabled the allies to reform their ranks. Had Shalmaneser been completely victorious, he would have advanced on Hamath and not have failed to follow up his success during the next two years, after which he had once more to attack Damascus.

I smote 14,000 . . . *men.* This figure includes the wounded. It may well be an exaggeration. Cp. the figures of 20,500 (Annals), 25,000 (Bull Inscription) and 29,000 (Ashur Statue) given for the casualties in later accounts.

(b) *In my eighteenth regnal year,* that is 841-840 B.C.

Sanir (Saniru) seems to be the Assyrian name of the range of hills leading north-west from Mount Hermon (called Senir (A. V. Shenir) in Deut. iii.9), which stood out from the main Lebanon massif, i.e. The Anti-Lebanon.

his strong position was athwart the road north-west of Damascus, down which the Assyrians had to advance.

I cut down his plantations, or cultivated fields, thus precluding any further prolonged opposition. Note that the Assyrian makes no claim to the capture of the city.

Ba'ali-ra'si, the headland by the Nahr-el-Kelb (Dog River), north of Beirut, where inscriptions and stelæ of Shalmaneser III and later kings have been discovered cut in the rock face of the pass.

Jehu, son of Omri (Iaua mar Humri òr, on *c, (m)Humri).* The Assyrian designation for northern Israel from the ninth to the seventh century B.C. was 'the house (or land) of Omri', the term being used both for the dynastic line of Ahab and, as more probably here since Jehu was a usurper, for the territory governed from Samaria as the city founded by Omri (1 Kings xvi.24). 'Son' in both Hebrew and Assyrian texts may, however, be used loosely for any subordinate relationship, and thus 'son of Omri' might denote little more than 'Israelite'.

Although there is no direct reference in the O.T. to this submission of Jehu to Shalmaneser, it is possible that his motive in bringing tribute was to seek the support of Assyria against Hazael who continually raided northern Israelite territory (2 Kings x.31f.). If this was his aim, it proved unsuccessful (2 Kings xxi.3,22f.).

(c) The same submission of Jehu to Shalmaneser III is depicted on an obelisk set up by the Assyrian king in the main square at Nimrud and discovered by A. H. LAYARD in 1846 (Plate 3). This black limestone obelisk is now in the British Museum. The figure who is shown bowing before Shalmaneser is, according to the superscription, 'Jehu, son of Omri'. This is thus the only contemporary representation of any Israelite king. Jehu is bearded and wears a sleeveless mantle over a long fringed and girdled tunic. He is followed by thirteen men, whose facial characteristics show them to be Hebrews, bearing the objects described in the accompanying text. Since the gifts were not large, this act would seem to have been only a token submission.

puruhati-fruits. The meaning is unknown, but the representation of them, borne on a tray carried on the head of the last of Jehu's attendants, is clear on the black obelisk.

Bibliography

GADD, C. J.   *The Stones of Assyria*, 1936, 48.

JEPSEN, A.   'Israel und Damaskus', *A.f.O.* xiv (1942) 153-8.

KRAELING, E. G. H.   *Aram and Israel*, 1918, 65-82.

LAYARD, A. H.   *Nineveh and the Remains*, i, 1849, 346-8.

OPPENHEIM, A. L., in *A.N.E.T.*, 278-81.

II   ADAD-NIRARI'S EXPEDITION TO SYRIA AND PALESTINE *c.* 803 B.C.

For the first five years of the reign of Adad-nirari III (810-782 B.C.) his powerful mother Sammuramat, probably the original of the Semiramis of later Greek legend, acted on his behalf until he came of age to rule.   The main weight of the military effort throughout his reign had to be directed against the tribes to the north and east of Assyria.   Although sixteen campaigns were needed there to follow the policy of his predecessors in keeping the trade-routes open, Assyrian prestige had also weakened in the west since the days of Shalmaneser III, where the rules of the city-states of Syria had rebelled against his son Shamshi-Adad V, the father of Adad-nirari.   According to the notices appended to the Assyrian eponym list for the years 805-802 B.C., the young Adad-nirari sought to remedy this state of affairs by campaigning in support of the pro-Assyrian city of Hamath.   The main attack fell on Damascus, where the death of Ben-hadad II had left the defence to his son Hazael (*c.* 844-801 B.C.), whose attention was thus drawn away from operations against Philistia and the south (cp. 2 Kings xii.17f. ; 2 Chr. xxiv.19).

The claim of Adad-nirari to have received tribute from Tyre, Sidon, Israel (Samaria), Edom and Philistia need only imply that these places brought gifts and homage to him in recognition of his new power and of his aid against Damascus.   There is no direct allusion to this submission in the O.T., but the Israelite successes against Aram in the reign of J(eh)oash (797-781 B.C.) were probably made possible only by the renewed Assyrian advances into Syria in 797 B.C. which further weakened Damascus. Joash recovered towns on his northern border which his father had lost to Hazael (2 Kings xiii.25 ; cp. 1 Kings xx.34), and his successor Jeroboam II (*c.* 781-753 B.C.) was able to extend the boundaries of Israel as far as 'the entering in of Hamath', again doubtless helped by the further Assyrian attacks under Shalmaneser IV (781-772 B.C.) against Damascus (2 Kings xiv.25-8).

Texts

(a) Building by Adad-nirari the great king, the mighty king, king of the world, king of Assyria, the king whom Ashur, king of the gods of the Upper World, chose while still in his youth and granted him an unrivalled princeship. He whose shepherding they made (to be) as good for the people of Assyria as (is) the plant of life and whose throne they founded securely ; the holy priest, unceasing preserver of the Esharra-temple, who fulfils the ritual of the temple, who moves about by the support of Ashur his lord, making to submit at his feet the princes of the four world-regio. ; conqueror from Mount Siluna in the East, the countries Saban(?), Ellipi, Harhar, Araziash, Mesu, Media, Gilzilbunda in its whole area, Munna, Parsua (Persia), Allabria, Apdadana, Nairi in its whole district, Andiu whose location is far off, a mountain fastness in its whole district, overlooking the great Sea of the Rising Sun, from (the districts) above the Euphrates, Hatti-land, Amorite-land in its border (regions), Tyre, Sidon, Israel, Edom, Philistia, as far as the great Sea of the Setting Sun (Mediterranean), I made to bow at my feet (and) I imposed a heavy tribute upon them. I marched to Aram and shut up Mari', king of Aram, in Damascus his capital city. The awful splendour of the god Ashur his lord overwhelmed him and he seized my feet, expressing submission. 2,300 talents of silver, 20 talents of gold, 300 talents of copper, 5,000 talents of iron, embroidered linen garments, an ivory bed, a couch embossed and inlaid with ivory, countless of his goods and possessions I received in his own palace at Damascus, his capital city. All the individual rulers of Kaldu-land expressed their submission, so I imposed heavy tribute upon them (which was inscribed) in tablets. . . .

Nimrud Slab Inscription

(b) In the fifth year I sat upon my royal throne as an adult and called out the country (to war). I gave the word for the vast army of Assyria to march to the land of Philistia. I crossed the Euphrates while it was in flood. The numerous hostile kings who had rebelled against Shamshi-Adad, my father and . . . [withheld their tribute payable] at the command of Ashur, Sin, Shamash, Adad and Ishtar, the gods in whom I trust, [the awful splendour of] Ashur . . . overwhelmed them and they kissed my feet. I received the heavy tribute . . . which they brought to Assyria. I then gave the word to march to Aram (where) I surrounded Mari' in Damascus [and he submitted to me]. 100 talents of gold, 1000 talents of silver, 60 talents of . . . [I received as his tribute].

Saba'a Stele, 11-20

Notes

(a) *Hatti-land* at this time designated the country west of the Euphrates and Syria as far as the 'Amq plain, and south to Hamath.

Amorite-land (*mat amurri*) lay on the desert borders of Hatti and Damascus (see *Aram* below).

Israel is here called *mat humri* 'the territory of Omri', i.e. the area governed from its capital Samaria, elsewhere named 'the house of Omri', see p. 49, (*b*).

Philistia (*Palashtu*), hence the later 'Palestine', lay on the Mediterranean coast between Gaza and Acre and included the cities of Ashkelon, Ashdod and Gath.

Aram. The district here called *sha-imerishu* or *imerishu*. The problem of the definition of these terms, which were apparently interchangeable with Damascus, is unsolved. The rendering *Aram* is adopted here for the whole area for the sake of the O.T. parallels where the king of Damascus is designated 'king of Aram (Syria)' (e.g. 2 Kings xii.17f., xiii.3 ; 2 Chr. xxii.5f.).

Mari'. The Assyrians use the Aramaic title *mari* 'my lord' for the personal name of the king of Damascus who was at this time probably Hazael rather than his successor Ben-hadad III.

Kaldu-land is the Assyrian form of 'Chaldaea' (South Babylonia), of which the Hebrew *kasdīm*, following the Babylonian form *kashdu*, occurs frequently in the O.T.

(b) *In the fifth year.* See p. 50 above.

Bibliography

Texts

UNGER, E. *Relief Stele Adadniraris III aus Saba'a und Semiramis*, 1916.

General

JEPSEN, A. 'Israel und Damaskus', *A.f.O.* xiv (1942) 153-72.

KRAELING, E. G. H. *Aram and Israel*, 1918, 81-4.

OPPENHEIM, A. L., in *A.N.E.T.*, 281f.

III INTERVENTIONS OF TIGLATH-PILESER III IN SYRIA AND PALESTINE (743-732 B.C.)

The historical records of Tiglath-pileser III, king of Assyria (745-727 B.C.), are fragmentary, being known mainly from broken and mutilated stone slabs giving part of the royal annals, and from inscribed clay tablets originally set up in the temple of Nabu (Nebo), at Nimrud. The latter give a summary account of the conquests of Tiglath-pileser arranged in a geographical sequence. However, the Assyrian Eponym Canon lists the principal episode for each year of his reign and thus enables the main events to be followed with certainty. The chronological order of the details recorded in the extracts from the texts translated below is still uncertain, but they are of particular interest for their direct reference to several kings of Israel and of Judah.

In 743 B.C. Tiglath-pileser began a series of campaigns against the Syrian state of Arpad during which he received tribute from Rezin of Damascus and neighbouring rulers. While away on the Armenian frontier during the next year, he was forced to move west again to quell a revolt of a group of North Syrian states apparently instigated by Azariah of Judah (see *Azriau of Yaudi* below). During further Assyrian operations against Arpad, which ended successfully in 739 B.C., Menahem of Israel joined Rezin in bringing tribute to the Assyrian king. In 734 B.C. Tiglath-pileser marched past the 'borders of Israel' down the Phœnician and Philistian coasts to capture Gaza. These moves seem to have been in response to a call from Judah whose king (Jeho)Ahaz, it is claimed, paid tribute. By 732 B.C. Damascus had been defeated and the country bordering on Israel incorporated into the Assyrian provincial system of government. Letters passing between the local Palestinian governors and the Assyrian capital, discovered at Nimrud in 1952, show that their control, though not always effective, was primarily economic in purpose. Tiglath-pileser also claims to have replaced Pekah on the throne of Israel by Hoshea. For all these events cp. 2 Kings xv.17-30, xvi.7-18, and the notes below.

Texts

(a) . . . in the course of my expedition (I received) the tribute of
. . . [Az]riau of Yaudi like . . . [A]zriau of Yaudi in . . .
without number, reaching to the sky, ex[ceedingly great] . . .
with eyes like those which (look) from heaven . . . by infantry
attack . . . he heard of [the approaching] massed [forces] of
Ashur and was afraid. . . . I smashed down, destroyed and
[burned with fire] . . . they had taken away [for Azri]au and
strengthened it . . . very difficult . . . was barred and high
. . . was situated and its exit . . . I deepened . . . I surrounded his trusty troops, to . . . [his soldie]rs I made to do
forced labourers' work and . . . his great . . . like a pot [I
shattered . . . (*break of several lines*) . . . liaia . . .] Azria[u.]
. . . as my royal palace . . . tribute like that which . . . the
city Kul[lani?] his ally . . . the cities Usnu, Siannu, Simirra,
[and Ka]shpuna which are by the sea, together with the cities
up to Mount Saue, a mountain which abuts on the Lebanon
range : Mount Ba'al-Sapuna as far as the Amanus mountains,
the mountain of the *tashkarinu*-tree ; the whole of the Saue
territory, the districts of Kar-Addu, the town of Hatarikka, the
district of the town of Nuqudina, Mount Hasu together with towns
around it, the town of Ara and the villages on both sides of them,
together with the villages round about them. Mount Sarbua,
the whole of the hill-country, the towns of Ashani, Iadabi,
Mount Iaraqu (and) the whole of its hilly territory, the towns
[. . .]-ri, Ellitarbi, Zitanu, as far as Attini, [. . .]ha(?),
Bumame : 19 areas belonging to Hamath, together with the
villages around them which are on the coast of the Western
Sea (Mediterranean), which they had by sin and folly snatched
away from Azriau, I restored to the territory of Assyria. I set
my own official as district-governor over them. 30,300
persons [I removed] from their cities and settled in the district
of Ku[. . .] ; 1,223 persons I settled in the district of Ulluba.
. . . the tribute of Kushtashpi of Kummuh (Commagene),
Rezin of Damascus, Menahem of Samaria, [Hiram] of Tyre,
Sibitti-bi'ili of Byblos, Urikki of Cilicia, Pisiris of Carchemish,
I'ni-ilu of Hamath, Panammu of Sam'al, Tarhulara of Gurgum,
Sulumal of Melidda, Dadi-ilu of Kaska, Uassurme of Tabal,

Plate 3 The Black Obelisk of Shalmaneser III : Jehu, son of Omri,
is seen in the second panel prostrating himself before the
Assyrian king

Ushhitti of Tuna, Urballa of Tuhana, Tuhamme of Ishtunda, Urimme of Hurikna, Zabibe, queen of Arabia ; gold, silver, tin, iron, elephant-hide, ivory, embroidered garments, linen garments, blue-dyed cloth, purple-dyed cloth, ebony, walnut-wood, everything precious, treasure (fit for) royalty, prepared sheep-[skins] whose wool was dyed purple, wild birds whose outspread wings were dyed purple, horses, mules, large and small cattle, male camels, female camels with their foals I received.

Annals, 103-33, 150-7

(*b*) The town of Hatarikka as far as Mount Saue . . . the towns Gebal (Byblos), Simirra, Arga, Zimarra . . . Usnu, [Siannu], Ri'raba, Ri'sisu . . . towns of the Upper [Sea] I brought [under my control], six of my officials . . . I set [as district-governors over] them ; the town of Kashpuna on the coast of the Upper Sea . . . [the towns . . .]nite, Gal'za, Abilakka which are on the border of Israel [the widespread territory of Damascus (*Bit-Haza'i*]*li*) in its whole extent I restored to the border of Assyria. My [official] I set [over them] as district-governor. As for Hanunu of Gaza who had fled before my weapons and run off to Egypt, the town of Gaza [I conquered, his . . . and] his possessions, his gods [I carried off and an image of the god Ashur], my lord, and an image of my own royal person [. . . I set up] within his palace and reckoned them as the gods of their country. I imposed upon them [a heavy tribute . . . silver] I tore out, like a bird . . . he fled [back from Egypt ?]. I restored him to his place and [imposed a heavy tribute upon him ; gold], silver, linen garments with embroidery . . . great, . . . I received. Israel (*Bit-Humria*) . . . the total of its inhabitants [together with their possessions] I led off to Assyria. Pekah their king they deposed and Hoshea I set [as king] over them. I received from them as their [tribute ?] 10 talents of gold and [*x*] talents of silver and brought [them to Assyria]. As for Samsi, queen of Arabia. . . .

Nimrud Tablet (in ROST, 78-81, lines 1-19)

(*c*) I set Idibi'il as guardian (doorkeeper) over the land of Musri. In every country where . . . The tribute of Kushtashpi of the land of Kummuh (Commagene), Urik of the land of Qu'e (eastern Cilicia), Sibitti-Bi'il of [the city of Byblos . . .], Eni-il of Hamath, Panammu of Sam'al, Tarhulara of Gurgum, Su[lumal of Melidda . . .], Uassurme of Tabal, Ushhitti of Tuna, Urballa of Tuhana, Tuham[me of Ushtunda . . .] [M]atani-bi'il of Armad, Sanipu of Beth-Ammon, Salamanu of Moab, . . . [M]itinti of Ashkelon, Jehoahaz of Judah, Qaush-malaka of Edom, Mus[ri . . .], Hanunu of Gaza ; gold, silver, tin, iron, antimony, embroidered linen garments, purple woollen garments of his country . . . everything precious, the product of sea and land, the desirable things of their countries, royal treasures, horses, mules, trained to the yoke. . . . As my representative I sent the *rab-shaqu* to the city of Tyre [to receive the tribute] of Metenna of Tyre, 150 talents of gold [. . .].

Nimrud, South-east Palace, Slab Inscription (rev. 6-16)

Notes

(a) *Azriau of Yaudi* (written *Az-ri-a-u (mat)ia-u-da-a*). Unfortunately, this name occurs only in very broken passages, and two views of the identity of this person and his kingdom have been put forward. According to the widely accepted view, this Azriau (Azariah) was a usurper, ruling a small independent state in North Syria, who succeeded in rousing the districts round Hamath to turn against their Assyrian overlord in a rebellion which was quelled in 742 B.C. This state of Y'di (pronounciation unknown) is known only from an Aramaic inscription from Sam'al (Sinjirli) under whose control it came later. Y'di is therefore located in North Syria and thought to have been independent at this time (*c.* 739 B.C.), even if originally founded by Judaeans from the South. Tiglath-pileser transported captives from Yaudi to Ulluba on the southern Armenian frontier. On the other hand, it would seem an unusual coincidence that a king of this district should bear the same name as his well-known contemporary in historical Judah, a state of which the name is written in an identical way (see *Jehoahaz* below). Azariah (Uzziah) was renowned as a soldier and statesman (2 Chr. xxvi.6-15), and possessed great influence in the Israelite territories won by Jeroboam II, where the ruling house was now weakened by usurpers. As the context of each reference to Azriau is obscure, the older identification with Azariah of the O.T. is not impossible and is still worthy of serious consideration.

Mount Saue lay on the Mediterranean coast, and is probably to be distinguished from a mountain, Jabal Zawi, *c.* 60 km. south-west of Qinnesrin mentioned in Text *c*, line 12 (J. LEWY, *Orientalia* xxi (1952) 418 ff.).

tashkarinu-wood appears to be either box or walnut.

Hatarikka was situated near Qinnesrin, *c.* 25 km. south of Aleppo. It has long been equated with the O.T. Hadrach (Zech. ix.1) and was the seat of an Assyrian district-governor.

Rezin of Damascus (Assyrian *Rahiannu*), Hebrew *Rezin* or *Rezon*, was the king of Aram mentioned in 2 Kings xv.37, xvi.5-9 ; Is. vii.1ff., ix.11.

Menahem of Samaria (written *me-nu-hi-im-me (al)Sa-me-ri-na-a*) paid tribute as is clearly stated in 2 Kings xv.19f. It is likely that the thousand talents of silver paid to Tiglath-pileser, whose native name Pul(u) is used in Babylonian sources (cp. 1 Chr. v.26), was given in response to an Assyrian demand for assurances of goodwill following the conquest of the area north of Damascus. Menahem's action would have prevented the actual entry of Assyrian troops into Israel, and represented the sum of fifty shekels *per capita* levied on the wealthy citizens. This was their worth as a slave at current Assyrian prices (*Iraq* xv (1953) 135, *n.* 1). Despite various attempts, the precise date of Menahem's tribute is not ascertainable from the present text. It would seem to have been shortly before his death in 742/1 B.C. (2 Kings xvi.22), and was probably rendered to Tiglath-pileser during the attack on Arpad (743-740 B.C.), when Rezin of Damascus also sent gifts.

(*b*) *Gal'za, Abilakka* are unknown. Some read Gallil (Galilea), and others assume that in the break further cities are named. It is likely that these are places on the northern and western *border of Israel* (*Bit humri*), of which other towns are named in 2 Kings xv.29. It is known from the excavations of Hazor, undertaken in 1955-7, that that fortified citadel was destroyed at this time.

the widespread territory of Damascus. This reading is restored from a new fragment of Tiglath-pileser's annals found at Nimrud in 1955. It shows that, in addition to the use of *Dimashqi* and *Sha-imerishu* as names for Damascus and its territories, (*mat*) *bit-(m)haza'ili* 'The land of the house of Hazael' was used. Thus the former conjecture of [Napta]li is shown to be wrong. For this form of name, cp. *Bit-humri* 'House of Omri' used of Israel. See above and p. 49, (*b*).

Pekah (*Paqaha*) foolishly allied himself with Rezin and thus became an excuse for Assyrian intervention in Israel. It is likely that the Assyrians instigated the removal of this anti-Assyrian ruler by murder. Pekah himself had gained the throne by murdering Pekhahiah, successor of Menahem (2 Kings xv.29f.). *Hoshea* (*Ausi'*) was the Assyrian nominee. Israel was not ruled by Assyria directly until after the fall of Samaria in 722 B.C.

(*c*) *Jehoahaz of Judah* (*Ia-u-ha-zi* (*mat*)*ia-u-da-a-a*), whose tribute is listed with that of other neighbouring states including Ammon, Moab, Ashkelon, Edom and Gaza is almost certainly the O.T. Ahaz, an abbreviated name of which the full form is (Jeho)ahaz, the despatch of whose tribute is recorded in 2 Kings xvi.8. The Assyrian help was given in response to an appeal for aid against Rezin of Damascus and his ally Pekah of Israel (2 Kings xvi.5-8). Such aid was, however, only given in return for a measure of political subservience locally attested by the introduction of Assyrian symbols. The royal statues or stelæ erected by Tiglath-pileser III at Turushpa (Van), Gaza, and Nahalmusur ('The River of Egypt'), or the cult symbols imported by Ahaz (2 Kings xvi.10-16), are examples of this.

rab-shaqu is the title of an Assyrian state official of high rank. He was the governor of the province east of Harran and was sometimes employed in negotiations with foreign rulers (cp. 2 Kings xviii.17-37 ; Is. xxxvi.2 ; Hebrew *rabshakeh*).

Bibliography

Texts and translations

OPPENHEIM, A. L., in *A.N.E.T.*, 282-4.

ROST, P.   *Die Keilschrifttexte Tiglat-pilesers III*, I, 1893.

WISEMAN, D. J.   'Fragment of the Annals of Tiglath-pileser III', *Iraq* xiii
    (1951) 21-4.

—— 'A Fragmentary Inscription of Tiglath-pileser III from Nimrud', *Iraq*
    xvii (1955) 126-54.

General

ANSPACHER, A.   *Tiglath-pileser III*, 1912.

JEPSEN, A.   'Israel und Damaskus', *A.f.O.* xiv (1942) 153-72.

SAGGS, H. W. F.   *The Nimrud Letters, 1952—Part II* ('Relations with the West'),
    Iraq xvii (1955) 144-54.

SMITH, S., in *C.A.H.*, III, 1925, 32-42.

IV   SARGON'S CAPTURE OF SAMARIA
(722 B.C.)

Shalmaneser V (727-722 B.C.), son and successor of Tiglath-
pileser III, continued the military operations against the West,
besieging both Tyre and Samaria.   No annals of this king have
survived, but, according to the broken Assyrian Eponym List,
the three years in which he besieged Samaria, as a reprisal for the
failure of Hoshea to pay tribute to Assyria, would seem to be
725-723 B.C., that is, from the sixth to the ninth year of the
Israelite king (2 Kings xvii.3ff.).   The Babylonian Chronicle,
which is the only major record for this reign, states that Shalmaneser 'broke (the resistance of) the city of Shamara'in',
which may be Samaria ; others, however, read the city name
Shabara'in and see in it the Sibraim of Ezek. xlvii.16.   The
narrative of 2 Kings xvii.6 states that Samaria fell to 'the king of
Assyria', and since it introduces no new name, it may be assumed
that it means Shalmaneser V, the subject of verses 3ff.   On the
other hand, Sargon II, his successor as king of Assyria (722-705 B.C.),
claims to be 'the conqueror of Samaria' in his accession year
(723/2 B.C.).   Although he does not make this claim in any
of his earlier historical records from Assur, Calah, or Nineveh,
but only in the ambitiously worded final edition of his Annals
from Khorsabad, this circumstance need not necessarily be taken
to support the view that Samaria was taken by Shalmaneser,
not by Sargon.   It might be that the unnamed 'king of Assyria'

of 2 Kings xvii.6 was Sargon, or even that there was joint participation in the capture of the city covered by the statement 'at the
end of three years they took it' (2 Kings xviii.10).

It is certain, however, from the extracts of his inscriptions given
below, that when the citizens of Samaria, incited by Iau-bi'di
of Hamath, refused to pay the recently imposed tribute, Sargon
marched to the city in 721 B.C. 2 Kings xvii.4 may refer to this
later action. Sargon claims to have taken captive men of Samaria
whose numbers vary between 27,270 and 27,290 according to
the date of the version. When he had restored order in Hamath
and Israel, Sargon marched against Hanunu of Gaza, who had
fled when Tiglath-pileser captured the city in 734 B.C., but had
now returned to support the coalition of states led by Ilu(Iau)-bi'di
of Hamath. In this he was aided by Sib'e, the commander-in-
chief of Egypt. In a battle on the Egyptian border near Rapihu
they were defeated, but Sargon had again to intervene in 715 B.C.
against Ashdod and Gath which, instigated by Egypt, sought to
include Palestine, Judah, Edom and Moab in an anti-Assyrian
league (Text *f*). In defeating Ashdod, Sargon may have
claimed that the victory was effective over all these countries,
for, though he claims to have been the 'subjugator of the land of
Judah' (Text *i*), neither this statement nor the O.T. imply that
Assyrian forces entered Judah itself at this time. The failure of this
coalition led Shilkanni, king of Egypt, to bring a token gift
acknowledging the unrivalled power of Assyria (Text *h*). Egypt,
so far as Palestine was concerned, was but a broken reed.

Texts

(*a*) At the beginning [of my rule . . . the city of the Sa]marians I
[besieged and conquered . . .] who let me achieve my victory
. . . carried off prisoner [27,290 of the people who dwelt in it ;
from among them I equipped 50 chariots for my royal army
units . . . the city of Samaria] I restored and made it more
habitable than before. [I brought into it] people of the countries
conquered by my own hands. [My official I set over them as
district-governor and] imposed upon them tribute as on an
Assyrian (city) . . . I made to mix with each other ; the
market price . . .

Annals, 10-18

(b) [The governor of Sa]maria who had consorted with the king who opposed me not to do service and not to bring tribute . . . and they did battle. I clashed with them in the power of the great gods, my lords, and counted as spoil [2]7,280 people together with their chariots . . . and the gods in whom they trusted. From among them I equipped 200 chariots for my royal army units, while the rest of them I made to take (up their lot) within Assyria. I restored the city of Samaria and made (it) more habitable than before. I brought into it people from the countries conquered by my own hands. My official I set over them as district-governor and reckoned them as people of Assyria itself.

Nimrud Prism, iv.25-41

(c) I surrounded and captured the city of Samaria ; 27,290 of the people who dwelt in it I took away as prisoners. From among them I equipped 50 chariots and made the rest of them take up [their allotted] positions. I set over them my official and imposed on them tribute of (i.e. as paid to) the former king. Hanunu, king of Gaza, and Sib'e, the commander-in-chief of Egypt, advanced to Rapihu to make a direct attack and to battle with me. I defeated them. Sib'e fled, taking fright on hearing the din of my weapons, and disappeared. I personally captured Hanunu, king of Gaza. I received tribute from Pir'u of Musuru, Samsi, queen of Arabia, and from It'amar the Sabaean ; gold dust, horses and camels.

Display Inscription

(d) Palace of Sargon . . . king of Assyria . . . [*here follow the titles and a summary of his conquests, continuing*] : conqueror of Samaria and of the whole of the land of Israel, who despoiled the cities of Ashdod (and) Shinuhti, who caught the Greeks who (dwell) in the midst of the sea, like fishes, who uprooted Kasku, the whole of Tabal and Hilakku (north-east of Cilicia), who pursued Mita (Midas), king of Muski ; who defeated Egypt at Rapihu and counted Hanunu, king of Gaza, as a prisoner, who subdued seven rulers of Ia', a district of Iatnana (Cyprus), whose dwelling is situated in the midst of the sea, a journey of seven days.

Khorsabad Pavement Inscription

(e) In the second year of my reign, Ilub[i'di of Hamath] . . . a vast [army] he collected in the town of Qarqar and the oath [of fidelity he forgot . . . and made Arpad, Simirra] Damas[cus and Sa]maria [to revolt against me . . . (*long break*)]. He made [an agreement] and Sib'e called out his [army], being his ally, and advanced to make a direct and close battle with me. By decree of the god Ashur, my lord, I inflicted a defeat upon them (Hanunu and Sib'e) and Sib'e, like a shepherd robbed of his sheep, fled alone and disappeared. I seized on Hanunu with my own hand and brought him in fetters to my city of Ashur. [The city of Rapi]hu I destroyed, demolished and burned. I took away 9,033 people together with their numerous possessions.

Annals, 23-57

f) In my . . . th year of rule [. . . Aziru, king] of Ashdod . . . Ahimiti . . . his younger brother over [them . . .] I made more prominent . . . heavy tribute . . . like that (imposed by) former kings, I imposed upon them . . . evil by . . . not to bear tribute they thought and rebellion against their ruler . . . drove him out . . . Yamani ('Greek'), a commoner . . . they sat [on the throne of] their lord as king over them and . . . their city . . . (*break of three lines*) . . . its extent, a moat which reached 2[0+ *x*] cubits in depth [they dug], underground water to . . . As for the (rulers) of Palestine, Judah, Edo[m,] Moab, and those dwelling in (islands of) the sea, who bring tribute and gifts for the god Ashur, my lord, he spoke innumerable wicked lies to make (them) oppose me and then sent goodwill gifts to Pir'u, king of Musru, a ruler unable to deliver them, asking him for an alliance. I, Sargon, true ruler, respectful of the pronouncements of Nabu and Marduk, guarding the utterance of Ashur, I made my special troops cross the rivers Tigris and Euphrates in full flood as if (they were) dry land. That Yamani, their king, who had confidence in his own power and did not bow to my overlordship, heard afar off of the progress of my expedition, and the splendour of the god Ashur my lord overwhelmed him, so that . . . he fled. . . .

Broken Prism

g) Yamani of Ashdod was terrified of my weapons and, abandoning his wife, sons and daughters, he fled to the frontier of Egypt where he stayed like a thief. I set my official as district-governor over the whole of his broad territory and of its happy peoples, and (thus) enlarged that which belongs to the god Ashur, the king of the gods, as regards its boundaries. As for the king of Meluhha, awe at the splendour of the god Ashur, my lord, overwhelmed him and he threw him (Yamani), hands and feet, into fetters and he sent him to me within Assyria. I conquered and despoiled the towns of Shinuhtu, Samaria, and the whole of Israel. As for Yamani, who (dwells) amid the Western Sea, I caught (him) like a fish.

Annals Khorsabad (Room XIV), 11-5

(*h*) . . . on the border of the town of Nahal-m[usur] I made [march] westward . . . the sheikh of the town Laban . . . Shilkanni, king of Egypt whom . . . the fearful splendour of the god Ashur, my lord, overwhelmed so that he brought as a submission gift large Egyptian horses which are unequalled in (this) country.

Broken Prism from Assur

(*i*) Palace of Sargon, (*titles and summary of conquests follow, then :*) subjugator of the land of Judah which is far off, uprooter of Hamath whose ruler, Iaubi'di, his own hands captured.

Nimrud Building Inscription

Notes

(*a*) *At the beginning* [*of my rule*]. This technical phrase refers to the period between his accession on 12th Tebet (Dec./Jan.) 723/2 B.C. and the beginning of his first regnal year in Nisan (Mar./Apr.) 722 B.C.

carried off prisoner and settled the captives in Assyria itself in their *allotted positions* (Text *c*), in Halah, the Khabur area, Gozan or Guzana (modern Tell Halaf), and in the cities on the Median frontier (2 Kings xvii.6).

[*I brought into it*] *people of the countries conquered. . . . I made to mix.* So 2 Kings xvii.24-34, xviii.11. The replacement population included Babylonians and people from Hamath, which was conquered in 721 B.C., as the principal instigator of subversion in Syria.

(*b*) *the king who opposed* Sargon was Ilubi'di (also called Iau-bi'di) of Hamath (See Text *e*).

(*c*) *the gods in whom they trusted* is interesting evidence of polytheism in Israel at this time (See 2 Kings xvii.7, 16 f.).

Sib'e, the commander-in-chief of Egypt. There has been much discussion on the identity of Sib'e. He is here described as the *turtan* (Hebrew *tartān*, 2 Kings xviii.7 ; Is. xx.1), a high military and administrative official second in rank to the king, but elsewhere (e.g. Text *g*) without qualification. Most identify him with Sewe, or So, the *king* of Egypt, to whom Hoshea sent messengers (2 Kings xvii.4), but since no such king is known from Egyptian sources, he is supposed to be one of the many dynasts in Lower Egypt, possibly Shabaka, an Ethiopian prince, who later became the founder of the XXVth Dynasty of Egypt, who was perhaps at this time in control of the Delta.

Rapihu is the modern Raphia, a town on the Egyptian border with Palestine near Nahal-musur (See Text *h*) 'the River (Wady) of Egypt' of the O.T. (Num. xxxiv.5 ; Josh. xv.4 ; 2 Kings xxiv.7, etc.) ; the modern El 'Arish.

Pir'u, the Pharaoh of Egypt (*per'o*), was probably Bocchoris, a vassal of Pi'ankhi the Ethiopian.

(*d*) *Israel*, or more exactly Samaria, was called *Bit-Humria* 'The House of Omri' throughout this period (see pp. 49, (*b*) ; 52, (*a*).
Ashdod was besieged by Sargon's commander-in-chief (Is. xx.1).

(*f*) *Palestine* (*Pilishte*), i.e. Philistia proper.
Judah (*Iaudi*). Cp. above p. 56, (*a*). Judah is claimed as a tributary, for the term used in the text does not necessarily imply invasion.

(*h*) *Shilkanni, king of Egypt* (Musru), i.e. Uselkan (Osorkon III or IV) in the last year of his reign (715 B.C.). His capital was Bubastis *c.* 140 miles from El 'Arish, where his tribute was probably received by Sargon's *turtan*.

Bibliography

ALBRIGHT, W. F. 'Further Light on Synchronisms between Egypt and Assyria in the period 935-685 B.C.', *B.A.S.O.R.* No. 141 (1956) 23-5.

GADD, C. J. 'Inscribed Prisms of Sargon II from Nimrud', *Iraq* xvi (1954) 173-201.

LIE, A. G. *The Inscriptions of Sargon II, King of Assyria*, 1929.

OLMSTEAD, A. T. *Western Asia in the Days of Sargon of Assyria*, 1908.

OPPENHEIM, A. L., in *A.N.E.T.*, 284-7.

THIELE, E. R. *The Mysterious Numbers of the Hebrew Kings*, 1951, 122-5.

WEIDNER, E. F. 'Silkan(he)ni, König von Musri', *A.f.O.* xiv (1941) 42f.

v SENNACHERIB'S SIEGE OF JERUSALEM

The account of the siege of Jerusalem by Sennacherib (705-681 B.C.), of which his own version dated in 691 B.C. is here translated, has given rise to one of the most debated historical problems of the O.T. It raises the question whether the non-Assyrian accounts refer to one or two campaigns by Sennacherib in the West, of which the first was his third campaign in 701 B.C., in the fourteenth year of Hezekiah, who was the focus of the anti-Assyrian forces in the West, and the second, following his operations against Arabia, between 689 and 686 B.C. It is clear that the detailed Hebrew account agrees with the Assyrian that Sennacherib captured many Judaean towns and villages and besieged Jerusalem, and that Hezekiah paid tribute to the Assyrians (2 Kings xviii.3-16 ; cp. Is. xxxvi.1f.). The Assyrian account of the siege, though worded as a personal narrative, need not imply that the king was himself present at Jerusalem, and his palace reliefs depict him in camp at Lachish (see p. 69), from which he sent an embassy demanding the surrender of the city by Hezekiah (2 Kings xix.8f.). Nor does the Assyrian history claim the capture of Jerusalem. The Hebrew story tells how the advance of an Egyptian army under Tirhakah led to a second embassy and another demand for the surrender of the Judaean capital. Hezekiah, encouraged by the prophet Isaiah, refused to give in. The O.T. account continues with a brief statement of the sudden smiting of the Assyrian army by the angel of Yahweh, which caused the return of Sennacherib to Nineveh, where he was later assassinated (see p. 70).

The majority of scholars consider that the reference to Tirhakah and to the death of Sennacherib, soon after his defeat and return to Nineveh, imply two distinct campaigns against Jerusalem. On this theory, the Assyrians defeated the Syrian, Philistian and Egyptian allies, devastated the town and villages of Judah, and surrounded Jerusalem long enough to force Hezekiah to release Padi and pay tribute, in the year 701 B.C. In another campaign, about fifteen years later, it is thought that Sennacherib suffered a crushing defeat shortly before his death, and to which he makes no reference in the Annals. The O.T., on this view, has telescoped the two campaigns into one. However, the evidence supporting this hypothesis is by no means beyond dispute ; for example, the dates of Tirhakah, who was for at least six years co-regent with Shabataka, are not certainly known. At present it would seem that he would be only nine years of age in 701 B.C., but further evidence might well give a closer date for his birth than c. 710 B.C. Moreover, there is no indication in 2 Kings xix.37 of the time which elapsed between Sennacherib's return and his assassination (verse 36). On any view some years must have elapsed between these two events. Support for the single campaign theory, still maintained by some scholars, has been sought in the silence of the Babylonian Chronicle which readily recorded any major Assyrian reverse ; but the Babylonian narrative of these years is so full of local data that arguments of this kind can never be decisive.

The smiting of the Assyrian army (2 Kings xix.35) is reflected in the account by Herodotus (ii.141), thought to echo an Egyptian version, of 'a multitude of field-mice which by night devoured all the quivers and bowstrings of the enemy, and all the straps by which they held their shields', so that 'next morning they commenced their flight, and great numbers fell, as they had no arms with which to defend themselves'. This has been considered to indicate a plague in the ranks of the army, but the Assyrian account has no hint of this. There is no special reason to suppose that Sennacherib intended to invade Egypt, and that his failure to follow up the victory claimed at Eltekeh might cover some major defeat, or that a drawn battle and the raising of the siege of Jerusalem are in themselves sufficient basis for a legend of the utter rout of Sennacherib handed down by the O.T. and Herodotus. While accepting the coincidences of all accounts at certain general points, it would seem wisest to avoid dogmatic interpretations of details on which the extant sources might appear to disagree.

Merodoch-Baladan (Marduk-apal-iddina II) sought for allies in his struggle against Assyria either during or after his brief rule at Babylon (703-1 B.C.), and his emissaries were sympathetically received by Hezekiah who showed himself outstandingly anti-Assyrian throughout his reign (2 Kings xx.12-19).

Texts

(a) In my third campaign I marched against Hatti. The awful splendour of my lordship overwhelmed Luli, king of Sidon, and he fled far off over the sea and died (an infamous death). The fearsome nature of the weapon of the god Ashur, my lord, overwhelmed Great Sidon, Little Sidon, Bit-Zitti, Zariptu, Mahalliba, Ushu, Akzib (and) Akku, his strong walled cities, places where there were food and drinking facilities for his garrisons, and they bowed in submission at my feet. Tuba'alu (Ethba'al) I sat on the throne to be the king and imposed upon him tribute, due to my lordship, (to be rendered) annually without ceasing.

As for Menahem of Samsimuruna, Tuba'alu of Sidon, Abdili'ti of Arvad, Urumilki of Gebal (Byblos), Mitinti of Ashdod, Buduili of Beth-Ammon, Kammusunadbi of Moab (and) Aiarammu of Edom, all of them kings of Amurru ; they brought valuable gifts,—heavy submission gifts—before me for the fourth time and kissed my feet. But as for Sidqa, king of Ashkelon, who did not bow in submission to my yoke, I deported and sent away to Assyria his ancestral gods, himself, his wife, his sons, his daughters, his brothers and the descendants of his ancestors. I set Sharruludari, son of Rukibtu, their former king, over the people of Ashkelon and imposed on him the rendering of tribute, *katre*-presents for (to acknowledge) my lordship so that he now drags at the (yoke-)ropes !

In the course of my campaign, I surrounded, captured and carried off the spoil of Beth-Dagon, Joppa, Banaiabarqa, Azuru, cities belonging to Sidqa, who did not bow in submission at my feet quickly. The officials, nobles and people of Ekron, who had thrown Padi, their king, into iron fetters as one loyal to the treaty and obligations of (imposed on him by) Assyria, had given him up to Hezekiah, the Jew, as an enemy. On account of the offence they had committed, their heart took fright and they implored (help from) the kings of Egypt, (and) bowmen, chariots of the kings of Ethiopia (Meluhha), an innumerable host, and, indeed, they came to help them. In the plain of Eltekeh, their battle array being drawn up over against me, they prepared their weapons. On (the oracular promise of) the help of Ashur, my lord, I clashed and effected their defeat. Amid the battle, my own hands captured alive the Egyptian charioteers and princes, together with charioteers belonging to the Ethiopian king. I besieged and captured the town of Eltekeh and Timnah and carried off spoil from them. I drew near to Ekron and slew the officials and nobles who had committed the crime and hung their bodies on posts around the city. I counted as prisoners of war the citizens who had done hostile and abusive things. I ordered the release of the rest of them, who were not convicted of any crime or misbehaviour, against whom there was no charge. I caused Padi, their king, to come out of Jerusalem and sat him on the throne as lord over them, fixing upon him (the payment of) tribute to my lordship.

But as for Hezekiah, the Jew, who did not bow in submission to my yoke, forty-six of his strong walled towns and innumerable smaller villages in their neighbourhood I besieged and conquered by stamping down earth-ramps and then by bringing up battering rams, by the assault of foot-soldiers, by breaches, tunnelling and sapper operations. I made to come out from them 200,150 people, young and old, male and female, innumerable horses, mules, donkeys, camels, large and small cattle, and counted them as the spoils of war. He himself I shut up like a caged bird within Jerusalem, his royal city. I put watch-posts strictly around it and turned back to his disaster any who went out of its city gate. His towns which I had despoiled I cut off from his land, giving them to Mitinti, king of Ashdod, Padi, king of Ekron, and Sillibel, king of Gaza, and so reduced his land. Moreover, I fixed upon him an increase in the amount to be given as *katre*-presents for my lordship, in addition to the former tribute, to be given annually. As for Hezekiah, the awful splendour of my lordship overwhelmed him, and the irregular and regular troops which he had brought in to strengthen Jerusalem, his royal city, and had obtained for his protection, together with 30 talents of gold, 300 talents of silver, precious stones, antimony, large blocks of red stone, ivory (inlaid) couches, ivory arm-chairs, elephant hide, elephant tusks, ebony-wood, box-wood, all kinds of valuable treasures, as well as his daughters, concubines, male and female musicians he sent me later to Nineveh, my lordly city. He sent a personal messenger to deliver the tribute and make a slavish obeisance.

Taylor Prism (British Museum No. 91032) ii.34-iii.41.(Plate 4) (*b*) And Luli, king of Sidon, fearing to fight me, fled to Cyprus (Iadnana), which is (an island) amid the sea, and sought refuge. In that same year he died infamously through awe inspired by the weapon of the god Ashur, my lord. I sat Tuba'al on his royal throne and fixed upon him tribute (due) to my overlordship. I laid waste the wide district of Judah (*Iaudi*) and made the overbearing and proud Hezekiah, its king, bow submissively at my feet.

Bull Inscription

(*c*) I took away from Luli his right to rule. Tuba'alu I sat on his throne and imposed tribute to my lordship upon him. I overthrew the wide district of Judah. I imposed my (yoke-)ropes upon Hezekiah, its king.

Nineveh (Nebi Yunus) Slab Inscription

Notes

(*a*) *Great Sidon.* The places listed are all between Tyre and Sidon. *Mahalliba* lies five miles north-east of Tyre and is the Meheleb or Ahlab of Jud. i.31.

katre-presents. The gifts sent or brought by foreigners to the Assyrian king vary, in accordance with the standing of the offerer, between gifts made in the normal exchange of greetings (*tamartu*), presents voluntarily bestowed (*igise*), or required as tokens of respect or good will (*shulmu*), and tribute (*biltu*) imposed as regular dues (*madattu*) or amounts to be paid according to an agreement (*katre*).

Eltekeh and Timnah lie *c.* five miles south-west and south of Gezer respectively, i.e. between Jerusalem and Ashdod.

Hezekiah the Jew (*Hazaqia iaudaia*). Literally 'Hezekiah the Judaean'. The omission of the title 'king' may imply that the description is here used in a deprecatory manner.

strong walled towns would include Lachish (as 2 Kings xviii.13f.).

stamping down earth-ramps up which protected battering-rams were moved to knock bricks off the thinner upper wall. This operation is shown in the reliefs of Sennacherib's siege of Lachish in the British Museum (see p. 69).

watch-posts strictly around it indicates a close blockade rather than a military assault on the city. This may support the view that Sennacherib's primary objective at this time was to oppose the Egyptians advancing on Eltekeh.

to strengthen Jerusalem. There is no reason to believe that the preparations made by Hezekiah were made at the last minute. 2 Chr. xxxii.2-8 and Is. xxii.9ff. show a predetermined and careful plan to reinforce the garrison and water-supplies by the construction of the Siloam Tunnel (pp. 209ff.).

30 talents of gold. . . . The payment imposed on Hezekiah, as recorded in

2 Kings xviii.14ff., while agreeing with the amount of gold stated here, mentions *300* talents of silver, but makes no reference to the other items, unless these are included in 'the treasures of the king's house'.

sent me later to Nineveh may indicate that the tribute was paid after the sudden return of Sennacherib to Assyria following the battle of Eltekeh. There is no certainty, however, that the events recorded in Sennacherib's annals follow a strictly chronological order within any one campaign or year.

(*b*) *I laid waste the wide district of Judah* (*Iaudi*). Cp. Text *c* 'I overthrew'. This is a brief summary of the operations described in full in Text *a* as reprisals against the outlying districts of Judah for Hezekiah's refusal to hand Jerusalem over to the Assyrians.

Bibliography

ALBRIGHT, W. F. 'The Date of Sennacherib's Second Campaign against Hezekiah', *B.A.S.O.R.* No. 130 (1953) 8-11.

HONOR, L. L. *Sennacherib's Invasion of Palestine*, 1926.

LUCKENBILL, D. D. *The Annals of Sennacherib*, 1924.

OPPENHEIM, A. L., in *A.N.E.T.*, 287f.

VI SENNACHERIB BEFORE LACHISH

Although Sennacherib makes no mention in his Annals of his sack of the city of Lachish, he had himself depicted, on the wall relief of his royal palace at Nineveh, sitting on the throne in his camp outside the conquered city of Lachish, surrounded by his officers, while representatives from the stricken town paid homage, and the captives, including women and children, were led past. It was from Lachish that the Assyrian king sent his emissaries to parley with Hezekiah at Jerusalem (2 Kings xviii.17), but by the time of their return he had left for Libnah (2 Kings xix.8). Those who hold the view that Sennacherib campaigned only once in Palestine in 701 B.C. assume that Lachish was among the cities assaulted and captured in that year (see above, pp. 64f. ; 2 Kings xviii.13). Those who maintain the two-campaign theory assume that, if Lachish was captured in that year, it must have been used as an Assyrian head-quarters in the subsequent campaign. On either view the prominence given by the sculptures of Sennacherib to this event underlines his failure to capture Jerusalem, despite the emphasis given to the siege of the capital of Judah in his written records. Above the bas-relief of the king is the following caption.

Text

Sennacherib, king of all, king of Assyria, sitting on his *nimedu*-throne while the spoil from the city of Lachish passed before him.

British Museum Relief No. 124911

Notes

his nimedu-throne. As shown by this relief, it was a portable high throne or chair with arms, high back and a footstool.

the city of Lachish (modern Tell ed-Duweir) was excavated by the Wellcome-Marston Archæological Research Expedition to the Near East between 1932 and 1938. During the ninth and eighth centuries B.C. the city was surrounded by a double wall with recesses and towers set at intervals, similar to those shown on the Assyrian relief. Iron arrow-heads, stone sling-shots and other weapons testify to the siege which led to the wholesale destruction of the city which marked the end of Level III *c.* 700 B.C.

Bibliography

FRANKFORT, H. *The Art and Architecture of the Ancient Orient*, 1954, Pl. 101.
LUCKENBILL, D. D. *The Annals of Sennacherib*, 1924, 156.
PRITCHARD, J. B. *The Ancient Near East in Pictures relating to the Old Testament*, 1955, 371-4.
TUFNELL, O. *Lachish III, The Iron Age*, 1953, 55f.

VII THE DEATH OF SENNACHERIB (681 B.C.)

The Babylonian Chronicle (Text *a*) clearly states that Sennacherib was murdered by his son, but 2 Kings xix.36f. (and Is. xxxvii.37f.) in a brief and direct statement records that 'Sennacherib king of Assyria departed, and went and returned, and dwelt at Nineveh. And it came to pass, as he was worshipping in the house of Nisroch his god, that Adrammelech and Sharezer *his sons* smote him with the sword : and they escaped into the land of Ararat. And Esarhaddon his son reigned in his stead'. The Assyrian texts of his successors, however, make no explicit reference to this event, and there appear to be discrepancies as to his murderer and place of death.

Esarhaddon, the son of the influential Nakiya-Zakutu, West Semitic wife of Sennacherib, was chosen to be crown-prince only after the death of two elder brothers and in face of opposition from his brothers and some district-governors, in the year 687 B.C.

Plate 4   The Taylor Prism of Sennacherib

Plate 5   Babylonian Chronicle Tablet : Nebuchadrezzar's
Capture of Jerusalem, 16 March 597 B.C.

His brothers thereupon incited Sennacherib against him so that he fled to hide in the west, probably Cilicia. It would seem that while he was away, his father was murdered in the month of Tebet (Dec./Jan.) 681/0 B.C., for the prism inscription (Text *b*), itself dated in 673/2 B.C., relates events in their chronological order. Some scholars, however, see in Esarhaddon the head of a pro-Babylonian party which contrived the murder, and thus account for his lack of direct reference to his father's death. But this might be merely a formal avoidance of an unpleasant subject, since in the same text he berates his brothers and, if the murderer, he would hardly have erected a mausoleum as 'the avenger' of his father and been aggrieved when a contemporary failed to send condolences. It is known that the rebels were defeated by Esarhaddon's allies in the land of Hanigalbat, and this may have led to the flight into Armenia of two of them, possibly Arad-Melek and Nergal-shar-usur, whose names are preserved in the forms Adramelus and Nergilus by the late Greek writer Abydenus. The variations in the sources concerning the murderer might be because one of the two brothers mentioned in the O.T. tradition was cited by the Babylonian Chronicle (Text *a*) as the elder, or even as the temporary occupant of the throne. The constant reference to 'brothers' in the Assyrian text might support the O.T. account, but otherwise nothing is known of sons by these names.

The act of Ashurbanipal thirty-two years later need not necessarily be interpreted as a revenge, for ritual murder is not attested elsewhere, nor need it be located at Babylon rather than at Nineveh. Any Babylonian connection with his father's death is linked with the known pro-Babylonian policy of Esarhaddon who, while crown-prince, had been governor of the southern capital. The Rassam cylinder does not specify Babylon, and Sennacherib is not known to have returned to Babylon after he had sacked it in 689 B.C.

'The house of Nisroch' is possibly the Temple of Nusku, or Ninurta, at Nineveh (or Calah). Those who place the murder in Babylon would emend the O.T. text to read 'Marduk'. It would seem that the extant texts provide insufficient evidence for the elucidation of the mysterious circumstances surrounding the death of Sennacherib, and that they may be interpreted as agreeing in general with the O.T. texts.

Texts

(*a*) On the 20th of the month Tebet, his son killed Sennacherib, king of Assyria, during a rebellion. For 23 years Sennacherib had exercised kingship over Assyria. The rebellion continued from the 20th of the month Tebet to the 2nd of the month Adar. On the 18th of the month Adar, Esarhaddon, his son, sat on the throne in Assyria.

Babylonian Chronicle

(*b*) My own father chose me out as chief with due ceremony in a gathering of all my brothers, speaking as follows : 'This is the son who shall succeed me' ; he enquired also of the gods Shamash and Adad by oracle, and they responded with a sure affirmative : 'He is thy replacement' . . . The fact of my succession overbore my brothers, who abandoned that which the gods (had settled) and trusted to their own violence. Plotting evil, they initiated against me slander and false reports which were contradictory to the will of the gods. With unfriendly disloyalty they continually spoke in hatred behind my back. . . . The gods caused me to stay in a hiding-place and spread their good shelter over me and thus preserved me for the kingship. Thereupon my brothers raved and did everything that was not good against both gods and men and plotted evil, even drawing the sword within Nineveh against divine authority. They butted at each other like young kids in order to exercise the kingship. . . .

Nineveh Prism of Esarhaddon, i.10-44

(*c*) As for those common men whose slanderous mouths had spoken derogatory things against my god Ashur and had plotted against me, the prince who reveres him, I tore out their tongues and abased them. As a posthumous offering at this time I smashed the rest of the people alive by the very figures of the protective deities between which they had smashed Sennacherib, my own grandfather. Their cut up flesh I fed to the dogs, swine, jackals, birds, vultures, to the birds of the sky, and to the fishes of the deep pools.

Rassam Cylinder of Ashurbanipal, iv.65-76

Notes

(a) *Esarhaddon, his son.* So 2 Kings xix.37. The introduction of the personal name when citing a new king is the common practice of the Chronicler and does not of itself prove that the son is a different person from the murderer, 'his son', who killed Sennacherib.

(b) *everything that was not good . . . drawing the sword within Nineveh* might include the assassination of Sennacherib (see above).

to exercise the kingship might imply that one or *more* claimed the kingship during the rebellion.

(c) *As a posthumous offering.* This was no common Assyrian practice and appears to be Ashurbanipal's interpretation of the meaning of the death of this group of rebels.

figures of the protective deities, i.e. the colossal *shedu* and *lamassu*, stone winged bulls with human heads, and other figures which guarded the main doorways of Assyrian palaces and temples.

Bibliography

HIRSCHBERG, H. *Studien zur Geschichte Esarhaddons, Königs von Assyrien,* 1932.

OPPENHEIM, A. L., in *A.N.E.T.,* 288.

SMITH, S. *C.A.H.,* III, 1925, 79.

THOMPSON, R. CAMPBELL. *The Prisms of Esarhaddon and Ashurbanipal,* 1931, 7ff.

VIII ESARHADDON'S SYRO-PALESTINIAN CAMPAIGN

After the internal political disturbances on the death of his father Sennacherib (see pp. 70f.) had been settled, Esarhaddon (681-669 B.C.) responded vigorously to the challenge of foreign affairs. Apart from Elamite intrusions, Babylonia was quiet, and his attention was directed initially to the nothern border and to ensuring the payment of tribute by the kings of Cyprus, Syria and Palestine, so that, after raiding the Arabs in 676 B.C., the whole Assyrian force was free to campaign against Egypt. The Ethiopian king of Egypt, Tirhakah, had incited Ba'al of Tyre to revolt and was constantly trying to stir up opposition to Assyria. The Annals of Assyria which record in detail Esarhaddon's successes in Egypt follow the account of his operations against Tyre, Sidon and the Syrian coast with a list of tributaries, including Manasseh of Judah, whose submission at this time is hinted at in 2 Chr. xxxiii.11 ('the captains of the host of the king of Assyria, which took Manasseh . . . and carried him to Babylon'). There is no reference, however, in the Assyrian texts to his temporary deportation to Babylon. Esarhaddon himself is mentioned in 2 Kings xix.37, Is. xxxvii.38 and Ezra iv.2.

Text

I called out the kings of the Hatti-land and the Trans-Euphrates area ; Ba'al, king of Tyre, Manasseh, king of Judah, Qaush-gabri, king of Edom, Musuri, king of Moab, Sil-Bel, king of Gaza, Metinti, king of Ashkelon, Ikausu, king of Ekron, Milki-ashapa, king of Gebal, Matan-ba'al, king of Arvad, Abi-ba'al, king of Samsimuruna, Pudu-il, king of Beth-Ammon, Ahi-milki, king of Ashdod—12 kings of the sea coast. Ekishtura, king of Edi'il (Idalion), Pilagura, king of Kitrusi (Chytrus), Kisu, king of Sillu'a (Soli), Ituandar, king of Pappa (Paphos), Erisu, king of Silli, Damasu, king of Kuri (Curium), Atmesu, king of Tamesi, Damusi, king of Qartihadasti, Unasagusu, king of Ledir (Ledra), Bususu, king of Nuria—10 kings of Iadnana (Cyprus), an island ; —a total of 22 kings of the Hatti-land, the seashore and the island. I sent all of these to drag with pain and difficulty to Nineveh, the city of my dominion, as supplies needed for my palace, big beams, long posts and trimmed planks of cedar and cypress wood, products of the Sirara and Lebanon mountains, where for long they had grown tall and thick ; also from their place of origin in the mountains the forms of winged bulls and colossi made of *ashnan*-stone, female colossi and *abzaztu* thresholds, slabs of limestone, of *ashnan*-stone, of breccia both large and fine grained, of yellow limestone, of pyrites.

Notes

This list of tributaries is repeated by Esarhaddon's successor, Ashurbanipal (669-632 B.C.) in his Annals (I.24f.). It is likely that the continued allegiance of these same western kings was sought by Assyria during the new campaign undertaken by Assyria against Egypt in the first year of Ashurbanipal.

Manasseh, king of Judah (Menasi shar mat Iaudi), is called *Minse* by Ashurbanipal. The subservience and loyalty of these kings was, it seems, tested by the order to transport building materials to Assyria. While some would provide materials and others labour, it is likely that the more remote tributaries would send gold and silver. If this was so, the eighth century Assyrian letter, found at

Nineveh (*British Museum Tablet* K. 1295), which lists tribute received from Palestine, may refer to this occasion. It tells of gold sent by the inhabitants of Beth-Ammon and Moab, silver from Edom, and '10 manas of silver from the inhabitants of Judah'. These sums, like the labourers, were collected by district officers appointed by the Assyrians.

the forms of winged bulls, i.e. the rough-hewn outlines of the colossal stone figures were dragged to the city as unfinished blocks, and are so depicted on the sculptures of Sennacherib.

ashnan, abzuztu. The meanings of these words are unknown.

Bibliography

Borger, R. *Die Inschriften Asarhaddons Königs von Assyrien,* 1956.

Oppenheim, A. L., in *A.N.E.T.,* 291.

Pfeiffer, R. H. *State Letters of Assyria,* 1935, No. 96.

Thompson, R. Campbell. *The Prisms of Esarhaddon and Ashurbanipal,* 1931, 25l.

ix THE BABYLONIAN CHRONICLE

After the death of Ashurbanipal (*c.* 632 B.C.), the Assyrian hold over Babylonia gradually weakened until in 626 B.C. the Babylonians proclaimed their independence under Nabopolassar, the founder of a strong native Chaldæan Dynasty. Although no Annals comparable with those written by the preceding Assyrian kings have survived, the history of this period until the fall of Babylon to Cyrus in 539 B.C. is recorded in the Babylonian Chronicle, a unique, reliable, objective, and probably contemporary, statement of the principal events of each year. The following extracts from the Chronicle, of which the extant texts cover the years 626-622, 610-594, 556, 555-539 B.C., illustrate both its nature and the major events of those years to which reference is made in the O.T.

(a) The Fall of Nineveh (612 B.C.)

The sack of the ancient Assyrian capital was the subject of oracles by the prophets Nahum (i.1ff.) and Zephaniah (ii.13ff.). It was followed by a renewed intervention by Egypt in Asia (see p. 77), and by the increasing domination of 'Assyria' and, later, of Syria, by the Babylonians. Both these nations henceforth exerted considerable influence on Judah. Nineveh fell to a combined attack by the Medes, Babylonians and Scythians :

Text

(In the fourteenth year) the king of Babylonia called out his army and marched to . . ., the king of the Umman-manda and the king of Babylonia met each other in . . . Kyaxares made . . . the king of Babylonia to cross and they marched along the Tigris river bank and pitched camp by Nineveh. From the month of Sivan to the month of Ab they (advanced?) only three. . . . They made a strong attack on the citadel and in the month of Ab, [on the . . . th day the city was taken and] a great defeat inflicted on the people and (their) chiefs. On that same day Sin-shar-ishkun, the Assyrian king, [perished in the flames]. They carried off much spoil from the city and temple-area and turned the city into a ruin-mound and heap of debris . . . of Assyria moved off before [the final attack?] and the forces of the Babylonian king [followed them]. On the twentieth of Elul Kyaxares and his army returned to his land ; the Babylonian king and his army marched as far as Nisibin. Booty and prisoners . . . and of the land of Rusapu were brought before the Babylonian king at Nineveh. In the month of [. . . Ashur-uballit] sat on the throne in Harran as king of Assyria.

The Babylonian Chronicle—British Museum 21901, 38-50

Notes

(*In the fourteenth year*) of Nabopolassar, i.e. 613/2 B.C.

the Umman-manda, or barbarian hordes, have been thought to be either another description of the Median confederation of tribes under Kyaxares, or the Scythian tribes from the northern hills.

Ab is the month of July/Aug. (612 B.C.).

they (*advanced?*) with difficulty, perhaps aided by breaches made in the walls by abnormally high spring floods (so Nah. i.8 ; Xenophon, *Anabasis*, iii.4ff.).

Sin-shar-ishkun, the last king of Assyria at Nineveh (628-612 B.C.), probably died in the flames as related in the later Greek story of Sardanapallus.

a ruin-mound (Arabic *tell*). The remains of the city walls and citadel of ancient Nineveh have been partially excavated, and can be seen by the east bank of the river Tigris opposite Mosul. The ruins are now known as Tell Kuyunjik and Tell Nebi Yunus ('Ruin-mound of the Prophet Jonah'). See Zeph. ii.13.

(*b*) The Egyptian Intervention in Palestine and Syria (610-609 b.c.)

When Ashur-uballit had withdrawn from Nineveh to Harran to establish the Assyrian royal court there, he was supported by Egyptian troops with whose aid he held the city for two years. Harran fell in 609 b.c. to a combined assault by the Scythians (Umman-manda) and the Babylonians. To bring adequate support, Necho II, king of Egypt, had to march through Palestine to capture Carchemish and then cross the Euphrates to Harran. This move brought him into conflict with Judah, whose king Josiah was seeking to regain control of former Israelite territory. Josiah's untimely intervention at Megiddo resulted in his death on the battlefield (2 Chr. xxxv.20-5). This must have occurred in 609 b.c., for the Babylonian Chronicle for the next year makes no further reference to Ashur-uballit or to the Egyptians.

Text

In the sixteenth year, in the month of Iyyar, the Babylonian king called out his army and marched to Assyria. From the [month of Sivan?] to the month of Marcheswan they marched about victoriously in Assyria. In the month of Marcheswan the Umman-manda [who had come to the he]lp of the Babylonian king united their armies and marched to the city of Harran [against] Ashur-uballit who had claimed the Assyrian throne. As for Ashur-uballit and the army of Egypt which had come [to help him], the fear of the enemy fell on them, they abandoned the city and . . . crossed [the river Euphrates]. The Babylonian king reached Harran . . . captured the city, they carried off much spoil from the city and temple. . . .

In the [seventeenth year], the month of Tammuz, Ashur-uballit, king of Assyria, a great Egyptian army . . . crossed the river, and marched against the city of Harran to conquer it . . . they slew the garrison which the Babylonian king had stationed there . . . and he besieged the city of Harran. Until the month of Elul he assaulted the city, but although he did not take it, they withdrew. . . .

Notes

the army of Egypt, possibly the vanguard of the main Egyptian army from Carchemish (modern Jerablus) which had been captured to form a fortified post guarding the crossing of the river Euphrates.

which had come [*to help him*]. So 2 Kings xxiii.29, '*al* meaning 'on behalf of ' rather than 'against' ; cp. 2 Chr. xxxv.20 ; Jer. xlvi.2.

a great Egyptian army may show that a special effort was made in this year (609 B.C.), and that King Necho II was present in person, not merely at Megiddo, but at Carchemish (for O.T. references, see above).

(c) THE BATTLE OF CARCHEMISH (605 B.C.) AND THE SUBMISSION OF JUDAH

During the years 607-606 B.C. the Babylonians, under the aged Nabopolassar, fought defensively in the middle Euphrates area against the Egyptians based on Carchemish, but were finally forced to withdraw. In contrast, the vigorous action of the young crown-prince Nebuchadrezzar in the following year resulted in the overwhelming Babylonian defeat of the Egyptians at Carchemish itself and the swift domination of Syria and parts of Palestine. This resounding victory certainly influenced the prophet Jeremiah who thereafter advocated submission to the now demonstrably more powerful Babylonians. Judah appears to have submitted to Nebuchadrezzar soon after the battle and to have sent hostages to Babylon, among them possibly Daniel (Dan. i.1 ; Berossus in Josephus, *Contra Apionem* 1.19). In the following year Jehoiakim became a vassal.

Text

In the twenty-first year the king of Babylon stayed in his own country while the crown-prince Nebuchadrezzar, his eldest son, took personal command of his troops and marched to Carchemish which lay on the bank of the river Euphrates. He crossed the river (to go) against the Egyptian army which was situated in Carchemish and . . . they fought with each other and the Egyptian army withdrew before him. He defeated them (smashing) them out of existence. As for the remnant of the Egyptian army which had escaped from the defeat so (hastily) that no weapon had touched them, the Babylonian army overtook and defeated them in the district of Hamath, so that not a single man [escaped] to his own country. At that time Nebuchadrezzar conquered the whole of the land of Hatti. For twenty-one years Nabopolassar had been the king of Babylonia. On the eighth of Ab he died ; in the month of Elul Nebuchadrezzar returned to Babylon and on the first day of the month of Elul he sat on the royal throne in Babylon.

In the accession-year Nebuchadrezzar went back again to the Hatti-land and marched victoriously through it until the month of Sebat. In the month of Sebat he took the heavy tribute of the Hatti-land back to Babylon. In the month of Nisan he took the hands of Bel and the son of Bel and celebrated the New Year Festival.

In the first year of Nebuchadrezzar he mustered his army in the month of Sivan and went to the Hatti-land. He marched about victoriously in the Hatti-land until the month of Kislev. All the kings of the Hatti-land came before him and he received their heavy tribute. He marched to the city of Ashkelon and captured it in the month of Kislev.

British Museum Tablet No. 21946, 1-18

Notes

In the twenty-first year. The battle of Carchemish took place probably in May or June, as it occurred before the death of Nabopolassar who died on the eighth of Ab of this year (16 Aug. 605 B.C.).

the Egyptian army which was situated in Carchemish. Excavations of the town and citadel by C. L. WOOLLEY and T. E. LAWRENCE in 1912-14 show that the city was burned about this time. Egyptian objects, and a shield probably borne by a Greek mercenary in the service of Necho II, testify both to the occupation and to the defence of the city.

At that time Nebuchadrezzar conquered the whole of the land of Hatti. The swiftness of this advance is mentioned also by the writer of 2 Kings xxiv.7. 'The land of Hatti' was at this time a Babylonian designation for the territory west of the Euphrates including *all* Syria and Palestine.

he took the heavy tribute back to Babylon, including possibly at this time (spring 604 B.C.) Daniel and Ezekiel among the prisoners.

All the kings of the Hatti-land came before him. Among the kings who submitted were the rulers of Damascus, Tyre and Sidon, and Jehoiakim of Judah, who was to be a faithful vassal for three years (604-601 B.C.) from this time (2 Kings xxiv.1).

Ashkelon. A papyrus letter in Aramaic appealing urgently for help from a Pharaoh against a Babylonian army which had already reached Aphek may have originated in Ashkelon at this critical time (see pp. 251ff.). The fall of Ashkelon may have occasioned the public fast proclaimed in Jer. xxxvi.1-9.

(d) THE CAPTURE OF JERUSALEM (597 B.C.)

Following the submission of Syria and Palestine (called Hatti), Nebuchadrezzar contented himself with an annual march into the area to collect the tribute which he had imposed. Then in 601 B.C. he personally led his army direct to Egypt to battle with Necho II who, however, so severely defeated him that for eighteen months the Babylonians were forced to remain at home recovering and re-equipping their forces. There is no mention of this battle in O.T. or extant Egyptian sources, but it would seem likely that it caused Jehoiakim of Judah to cease paying tribute to Babylon (2 Kings xxiv.1) and, despite the warnings of Jeremiah, to rely upon Egypt who perhaps encouraged him by their intrigues. However, in 599/8 B.C. the Babylonians despoiled the Arab tribes, as described in Jer. xlix.28-33, as a step in preparation for the advance on Judah in the next year. The following Babylonian account can be compared in detail with the O.T. account of the fall of Jerusalem in 597 B.C. as given in 2 Kings xxiv.10-18 ; 2 Chr. xxxvi.9f.

Text

In the seventh year, in the month of Kislev, the Babylonian king mustered his troops, and, having marched to the land of Hatti, besieged the city of Judah, and on the second day of the month of Adar took the city and captured the king. He appointed therein a king of his own choice, received its heavy tribute and sent (them) to Babylon.

British Museum Tablet No. 21946 rev. 11-13. (Plate 5)

Notes

the seventh year of Nebuchadrezzar (598/7 B.C.) as recorded in 2 Kings xxiv. 10f. in the month of Kislev. The Babylonian army was mustered in the month commencing 29 Nov. 598 B.C. or about three months before Jerusalem was captured. While this confirms that Judah was the main objective of this year's expedition, it may also indicate that the call-up resulted from the news of the death of Jehoiakim (see below).

the city of Judah ((al)ia-a-hu-du), i.e. Jerusalem. A similar spelling occurs in the almost contemporary Jehoiachin ration tablets from Babylon (see pp. 84ff.). Cp. 2 Kings xxiv.10f.

the second day of the month of Adar, i.e. 16 March 597 B.C., thus giving a firm date in both O.T. and Babylonian chronology.

captured the king, i.e. Jehoiachin, together with his mother, servants, royal household, and certain soldiers and craftsmen (2 Kings xxiv.12).

a king of his own choice. Nebuchadrezzar appointed the twenty-one year old Mattaniah to succeed his nephew Jehoiachin and changed his name to Zedekiah (2 Kings xxiv.17). The use of a new name marked the subservience of Judah on oath to Babylon.

its heavy tribute would include the treasures from the Temple and royal palace (2 Kings xxiv.13 ; 2 Chr. xxxvi.10).

and sent (them) to Babylon. The Babylonians marched off all the prisoners and booty 'at the return of the year' (2 Chr. xxxvi.10), i.e. about fifteen days after Jerusalem had fallen to the Babylonians, when Adar (the twelfth month— Feb./March) was followed by the spring month Nisan (March/Apr.), the first month of the new year, which was was also called Nebuchadrezzar's eighth regnal year (2 Kings xxiv.12 ; see D. N. FREEDMAN, *B.A.* xix (1956) 56).

This part of the Chronicle shows that Jehoiakim died on 7 Dec. 598 B.C., i.e. three months and ten days before the capture of Jerusalem (2 Chr. xxxvi.9). This falls before the Babylonians reached Judah, whereas 2 Chr. xxxvi.6 seems to imply that Jehoiakim had been taken prisoner by Nebuchadrezzar himself earlier. But cp. 2 Kings xxiv.6. The Chronicle does not give sufficient detail for any check to be made of the statement by Josephus (*Antiq. Jud.* X.6) that Nebuchadrezzar first gained entrance into Jerusalem on a false promise of leniency but later changed his mind and besieged the city, whereupon Jehoiachin surrendered to save the city from destruction.

(e) BABYLON's DOWNFALL (539 B.C.)

The advent of Cyrus (Is. xliv.28, xlv.1 ; cp. 2 Chr. xxxvi.22f.) and the punishment of Babylon were the constant themes of the later prophets of Israel (e.g. Is. xiii, xxi ; Jer. l-li), while the actual fall of the ancient capital is implied in Dan. v.30f. One text, sometimes called the Nabonidus Chronicle, gives a few details of the capture of the city by the Persians in 539 B.C. There are many difficulties raised by both the O.T. and Babylonian records which must await further clarification.

Text

[In the seventeenth year of Nabonidus] . . . Nabu went out from Borsippa for the procession of Bel . . . the king entered the temple of Eturkalamma from. . . . Bel went out and performed the New Year Festival according to the full ritual. In the month of . . . the gods of the city Marad, Ilbaba and the gods of Kish, Ninlil, . . . from Hursag-kalamma entered Babylon. Until the end of the month the gods of Akkad . . . those from every direction, entered Babylon. The gods from Borsippa, Kutha . . . and Sippar did not come in. In the month of Teshrit, while Cyrus was attacking the Babylonian army at Opis by the River Tigris, the people of Babylonia revolted and panicked, but he (Nabonidus) slew (some of) the people. On the 15th day, when Sippar was taken without a battle, Nabonidus fled. On the 16th day, Ugbaru, the district-governor of Gutium, and the troops of Cyrus entered Babylon without battle. Afterwards Nabonidus was captured when he returned to Babylon. Until the end of the month, the shield-bearing Gutians surrounded the temple of Esagila, but none carried arms in Esagila or in its (adjacent) religious buildings, and no prescribed time for a ceremony was missed. On the 3rd of Marcheswan Cyrus entered Babylon and they waved branches before him. Peace settled on the city (and) Cyrus proclaimed peace to Babylon. Gubaru, his district-governor, appointed local governors in Babylon. From the month of Kislev to the month of Adar, the Babylonian gods which Nabonidus had made to come into Babylon . . . returned to their sacred cities. In the month of Marcheswan, in the night of the 11th day, Ugbaru died. In the month of [Marcheswan the . . . th day, the wi]fe of the king died. From the 27th day of Marcheswan until the 3rd day of Nisan (public) mourning [was made] in Babylonia, all the people put ashes on their heads. On the fourth day Cambyses, son of Cyrus, went . . .

Nabonidus Chronicle, iii.5-24

Notes

[*In the seventeenth year of Nabonidus*], i.e. 539 B.C.

Ugbaru, Gubaru was a Babylonian official in southern Babylonia before he was made governor of Gutium in the time of Nebuchadrezzar. He apparently offered his services to Cyrus *c.* 548 B.C. According to Xenophon, this Gobryas made a forced march to take Babylon by surprise while Cyrus advanced on Sippar (Xenophon, *Cyropædia*, IV.6, VII.5, 26-30). Gubaru has sometimes, but wrongly, been identified with 'Darius the Mede' of Dan. v.31, vi.1, 38. The recent discovery of a text of Nabonidus from Harran which refers to the 'King of the Medes' in 546 B.C. reopens the whole question of the historicity of this Median, and makes it possible that 'Darius the Mede' was but another name and title for Cyrus himself. If this is so, Dan. vi.29 would read 'in the reign of Darius, even in the reign of Cyrus the Persian'; cp. 1 Chr. v.26, Tiglath-pileser and Pul being one person, cp. p. 57.

On the 3rd of Marcheswan Cyrus entered Babylon, i.e. on 29 Oct. 539 B.C., or sixteen days after the city had capitulated to Gubaru.

the Babylonian gods . . . returned to their sacred cities. Further details of the decree showing the leniency of Cyrus towards captured peoples are preserved in a cylinder inscription of Cyrus. Since the exiled Jews had no images, this decree would presumably allow the return of the captured Temple vessels to Jerusalem.

Cambyses succeeded his father as king of Babylon (530-522 B.C.).

Bibliography

OPPENHEIM, A. L., in *A.N.E.T.*, 304f. (for *a* above).

SMITH, S. *Babylonian Historical Texts relating to the Capture and Downfall of Babylon,* 1924 (for *b* above).

WISEMAN, D. J. *Chronicles of Chaldæan Kings (626-556 B.C.) in the British Museum,* 1956, 23-31, 67-9 (for *c* above), 32-7, 73 (for *d* above).

D. J. WISEMAN

The Jehoiachin Tablets

MASS deportation as an instrument in the subjugatory policies of Babylonia and Assyria is first mentioned in cuneiform documents from the time of Shalmaneser I (*c.* 1280-1261 B.C.). Sargon II (721-705 B.C.) makes specific mention of the captivity of the ten tribes of Israel in the year 721 B.C. (D. D. LUCKENBILL, *Ancient Records of Assyria and Babylonia*, II, 1927, 26 ; cp. 2 Kings xvii.6). Until comparatively recently, however, no reference in cuneiform sources was to be found to the captivity of Judah. There was indirect evidence, viz. the occurrence in business documents from Nippur of the time of Artaxerxes I and Darius II of many personal names, similar to many well-known O.T. names found in Ezra and Nehemiah, and these were assumed to be those of descendants of the deportees. We have now from the time of Nebuchadrezzar II (604-562 B.C.) texts which throw new light on the treatment of the young King Jehoiachin, who went into captivity in 597 B.C. It was known from Jer. lii.31ff. (cp. 2 Kings xxv.27ff.) that he had been pardoned some thirty-seven years later by Evil-Merodach (561-560 B.C.) and given a daily allowance. The new texts, which belong to a much earlier period (595-570 B.C., the tenth to the thirty-fifth year of Nebuchadrezzar II) refer to the monthly rations of oil allotted to Jehoiachin.

The texts were found along with a large number of other cuneiform tablets at the site of ancient Babylon during excavations carried out there by R. KOLDEWEY from 1899-1917. They were stored in a barrel-vaulted underground building consisting of rows of rooms not far from the famous Ishtar Gate. The room in which they were found was connected with the palace by a stairway. Most probably they were part of the records of an official in charge of rations, perhaps of the *rab-šamni*, the 'oil purveyor'. They deal mainly with deliveries of oil and barley to prisoners and other foreigners residing in Babylon.

The contribution which the brief references in these texts to Jehoiachin (*Yaʾu-kīnu*) and his contemporaries make to our knowledge of conditions during the exile is highly significant. From 2 Kings xxiv.12 ('And Jehoiachin the king of Judah went out to the king of Babylon, he, and his mother, and his servants, and his princes, and his officers : and the king of Babylon took him in the eighth year of his reign') we know that Jehoiachin had submitted to Nebuchadrezzar and, moreover, that his submission seemed to be in the nature of a voluntary act. When he is next mentioned, thirty-seven years have passed. Here we learn that 'Evil-Merodach king of Babylon, in the year that he began to reign, did lift up the head of Jehoiachin king of Judah out of prison ; and he spake kindly to him, and set his throne above the throne of the kings that were with him in Babylon. And he changed his prison garments, and did eat bread before him continually all the days of his life. And for his allowance, there was a continual allowance given him of the king, every day a portion, all the days of his life' (2 Kings xxv.27ff.). From this it is clear that he had hitherto been treated as a prisoner. The term 'prison' may not, of course, imply anything more than house-arrest, which is the impression given by these texts. It is probable that he and the princes and the nobles were housed together in the South Citadel (where the barrel-vaulted building was), and the distribution of oil would seem to indicate that they had their own kitchen.

The reference to the five sons of the king raises a problem. As Text c is dated in the thirteenth year of Nebuchadrezzar, and, as we know from 2 Kings xxiv.8, Jehoiachin was only eighteen years of age when he was carried off in the eighth year of Nebuchadrezzar, this would mean that the sons must have been born during the first five years of captivity. While, however, it is possible that the reference is to brothers of Jehoiachin, sons of Jehoiakim, it seems more probable that Jehoiachin's own sons are meant, since they are referred to as still in the hands of a Jewish attendant (Kenaiah). Shealtiel, therefore, the eldest son of Jehoiachin and the father of Zerubbabel, must have been born about 598 B.C. Thus Zerubbabel could be considerably older than has hitherto been supposed when Haggai was prophesying.

Other Judaeans are mentioned by name in the texts : Urmilki, Gaddiel (cp. Num. xiii.10), Shelemiah (cp. Ezra x.39 ; Neh. xiii.13), and Semachiah (cp. 1 Chr. xxvi.7 ; the name also occurs in the Lachish letters).

Apart from the captives from Judah, the texts contain the

names of many other recipients, including kings and artisans, of rations (mainly oil and barley, but on occasion also dates and spices). Whether all these people were exiles, or whether some were employees of the king, it is impossible to say. They were drawn from Philistia, Phoenicia, Elam, Media, Persia, Egypt, Lydia and Cilicia. We have thus a glimpse of the cosmopolitan character of life in Babylon at the period of the Exile.

Texts

(*a*) To Ya'u-kīnu, king [of the land of Yaudu].

(*b*) ½ (PI) for Ya'u kīnu, king of the land of Ya[hu-du]
2½ *sila* for the fi[ve] sons of the king of the land of Yahudu
4 *sila* for eight men, Judaeans [each] ½ [sila]

(*c*) ½ (PI) for Ya'u [-kīnu]
2½ *sila* for the five sons . . . .
½ (PI) for Yakū-kinu, son of the king of the land of Yakudu
2½ *sila* for the five sons of the king of Yakudu by the hand of Kanama.

(*d*) . . . . Ya]'u- kīnu, king of the land of Yahudu
[. . . . . the five sons of the king] of the land of Yahudu by the hand of Kanama.

Notes

(*a*) The name of the land of Judah is preserved on the reverse of this tablet.

(*b*) The measure *sila* was a little under 1½ pints and *PI* was about 6½ gallons.

Bibliography

ALBRIGHT, W. F. 'King Joiachin in Exile', *B.A.* v (1942) 49-55.

DAICHES, S. *The Jews in Babylonia in the Time of Ezra and Nehemiah*, 1910.

KLAMROTH, E. *Die Jüdischen Exulanten in Babylonien (B.W.A.T.,* 1912).

KOLDEWEY, R. *Das Wieder Erstehende Babylon*, 1925, 90ff.

OPPENHEIM, A. L., in *A.N.E.T.*, 308.

THOMAS, D. WINTON. 'The Age of Jeremiah in the Light of Recent Archæological Discovery', *P.E.Q.*, 1950, 5-8.

WEIDNER, E. F. 'Jojachin, König von Juda, in babylonischen Keilschrifttexten', in *Mélanges Syriens offerts à Monsieur R. Dussaud*, II, 1939, 923-35.

WISEMAN, D. J. *Chronicles of Chaldæan Kings (626-556 B.C.) in the British Museum*, 1956.

W. J. MARTIN

Nebuchadrezzar's Expedition to Syria

THE lines translated below occur in one of two rock inscriptions. On each side of the old narrow road through the valley of Brissa, which Assyrian and Babylonian armies had to take in order to reach and secure the Mediterranean north of Beirut, is an inscription cut into the rock face. Both inscriptions tell of the pious works performed by Nebuchadrezzar II (604-562 B.C.) in Babylon, Borsippa and other cult centres. One inscription includes a record of the liberation of the district and of the people of Lebanon, which reads as follows.

Text

At that time mount Lebanon, the [cedar] mountain, luxuriant forest of Marduk, sweet scented, . . . over which an enemy alien held sway and was taking away its produce. Its population were scattered and had taken refuge in distant places. In the strength of Nabu and Marduk my lords, I drew up [my troops] in array for battle against Lebanon to [take it]. I cleared out its enemy on the heights and in the lowlands and I made glad the hearts of the land. I gathered together its scattered population and brought them back to their place. A thing which no former king had done (that is) I broke up the towering mountains, I ground (?) the limestone, and (thus) I opened up approaches and made a straight way for the cedars. I made the Arakhtu canal carry, as though they were reeds, the hardy, tall, stout cedars, of surpassing quality and impressively black of aspect, solid products of mount Lebanon, to Marduk my king. In Babylon [I . . .] mulberry wood. I made the peoples dwell in safety in mount Lebanon. I saw to it that they had none to terrorise them, that no harm whatsoever (came to them). I have (set) (this) stele (as evidence) of my lasting sovereignty.

Notes

Lebanon. For long Syria was under the power of Assyria. After the fall of Nineveh (612 B.C.) it was coveted and contested by both Egypt and Babylonia. The reason is plain. Whoever filled the power vacuum in Syria would command the local mineral and vegetable wealth, 'gold, silver, copper, precious stones, the produce of the mountains', and also 'the yield of the sea', i.e. the commerce of the Mediterranean.

luxuriant forest of Marduk. An Egyptian building inscription speaks of 'fresh cedar which his majesty (Amen-hotep III, *c.* 1413-1377 B.C.) cut in the country of god's land', a term for eastern lands in general, but here for Lebanon. Marduk's title to the forest is based on its conquest by his servant Nebuchadrezzar II.

cedars of Lebanon are 'the trees of Yahweh' (Ps. civ.16). On one of the Brissa inscriptions Nebuchadrezzar II is shown standing before a cedar. The symbolism of this may be seen from the passage in Ezekiel where 'the Assyrian was a cedar' (xxxi.3ff.).

The *Arakhtu canal* takes off from the Euphrates above Babylon and rejoins it south of the city. Here the name is probably used for the Euphrates itself.

to Marduk, indicating the primary use of the cedar wood, i.e. for the roofing of gates of temples and shrines of the great gods of Babylon. The Hebrews, as also Egyptians, Sumerians and Assyrians, used cedar woods in the building of temples and palaces.

Clearly, Nebuchadrezzar II's case against the enemy alien was not that he carried off the cedars, but that he himself was thereby prevented from carrying them off. Hab. ii.17 and Is. xiv.4ff., 8, 12 are taken by some to refer to Nebuchadrezzar's harsh treatment of the inhabitants of the Lebanon. In cuneiform sources his cruelty is reported only in connection with the population of the Amanus, i.e. the Anti-Lebanon region.

Bibliography

OPPENHEIM, A. L., in *A.N.E.T.*, 307.

RAVN, O. E. *Herodotus' Description of Babylon*, 1942.

SMITH, S. *Babylonian Historical Texts*, 1924.

WISEMAN, D. J. *Chronicles of Chaldæan Kings (626-556 B.C.) in the British Museum*, 1956.

T. FISH

Texts relating to Nabonidus

NABONIDUS, king of Babylon (555-539 B.C.), thought of himself as heir to the mission of two illustrious predecessors, Nebuchadrezzar and Neriglissar, and to their armies. His failure was due to his origins and tactlessness and to political forces at home and abroad.

Nabonidus had ties with far away Harran where his mother became high priestess of the Moon-god. His piety towards his mother and her god partly explains his piety towards both the city and the god of Harran. He protests his devotion to the deities of Akkad, but he offended local susceptibilities by introducing into Babylon deities who did not belong there.

More relevant to his failure was the political situation in his day. Within Babylonia itself the years since the death of Nebuchadrezzar had been years of unrest and violence against the crown. Nebuchadrezzar's son and successor, Evil-Merodach (2 Kings xxv.27), on whose succession Jehoiachin of Judah was set free (561 B.C.), was assassinated after reigning two years. Neriglissar reigned but three years. Nabonidus' immediate predecessor, a mere child, Labashi-Marduk, was murdered within a year of his accession.

Five years after Nabonidus came to the throne, Cyrus overcame Astyages the Mede, whose capital, Ecbatana, he made the capital of his enlarged kingdom (549 B.C.). Nabonidus reacted to this victory by moving his army into Arabia Felix, leaving his son Belshazzar in control of Babylonia and its army. Later he returned to Babylonia and to defeat.

Texts

(a) At the beginning of my lasting kingship they (the great gods) showed me a vision in a dream. Marduk, the great lord, and Sin, the lamp of heaven and earth, were in attendance. Marduk said to me, 'Nabonidus, king of Babylon, on thy cart-horses bring bricks, build Ekhulkhul, and let Sin, the great lord, take up his residence within it.' In fear I spoke to Marduk, lord of the gods, 'This temple which thou tellest (me) to build, Umman-manda encompasses it with his strong forces.' Marduk said to me, 'The Umman-manda of whom thou speakest, he, his land, and the kings who go at his side, will not exist for much longer. At the beginning of the third year, Cyrus, king of Anshan, his youthful servant, will come forth. With his few forces he will rout the numerous forces of the Umman-manda. He will capture Astyages, the king of the Umman-manda, and will take him prisoner to his country.' Such were the words of the lord of the gods, Marduk, and of Sin, lamp of heaven and earth, whose command is unalterable.

(b) May I Nabonidus, king of Babylon . . . may I have my fill of life. As for Belshazzar, my first born, my dear offspring, grant that his days be long (O Shamash).

(c) (O Moon god) preserve me, Nabonidus, king of Babylon, from Sin. To me give the gift of long life, and as regards Belshazzar, my first born son, my dear offspring, put in his heart reverence for thy high divinity.

(d) Seventh year : the king in Tema' ; the crown-prince, his officials, and his army in Akkad. The king came not to Babylon ; the god Nabu came not to Babylon ; the god Bel did not go out ; the festival of the New Year was omitted.

Notes

(a) Nabonidus is not named in the O.T., but his reign was fateful for Jews and others exiled in Babylon.

dream. It may be noted that most of the dreams recorded in the O.T. occur in books contemporary with, or later than, the Captivity, and especially in Ezekiel, Daniel and Zechariah.

Ekhulkhul 'the house of joy', abode of the Moon-god, Sin, of Harran in Aram, and a provincial capital by the Balikh river, under the Assyrians.

Umman-manda have been identified variously with Medes, Scythians, and Bactrians. The name may stand for a confederacy of armed powers under Media.

capture Astyages. The capture of the king of the Medes, Astyages (549 B.C.), is dated 'the 6th year' of Nabonidus in the Nabonidus Chronicle.

(b-d) In the book of Daniel (v.1f., 11, etc.) Belshazzar is king of Babylon. Contemporary inscriptions name Nabonidus, not Belshazzar, 'king of Babylon'.

There is no evidence, but it may be presumed, that Nabonidus elected Belshazzar to act as vice-regent in his absence (553-545 B.C.). This means that Belshazzar had political power, backed by force, in the capital for more years than had his father Nabonidus. The circumstance that oaths were taken in the joint names of Nabonidus and of Belshazzar underlines the latter's authority in the land. *Tema'* is perhaps Taima in the Nejd (R.V. Tema in Jer. xxv.23, etc.).

Bibliography

DOUGHERTY, R. P. *Nabonidus and Belshazzar*, 1929.

OPPENHEIM, A. L., in *A.N.E.T.*, 306.

SMITH, S. *Isaiah Chapters xl-lv* (Schweich Lectures 1940), 1944.

T. FISH

The Cyrus Cylinder

(Plate 6)

THE opening lines of the inscription are incomplete but their general tenor is clear.

Babylonia had been, before Cyrus, inefficiently administered by reason of the appointment of 'weaklings' to high office. There had been hostility to local cults, including those of the city of Ur, and even to that of Marduk. Authority had put an end to daily offerings. The entire population were being destroyed under a 'yoke without respite', perhaps corvée work.

Text

(lines 9 ff.) The lord of the gods became furiously angry at their complaints and [forsook] their borders. . . . The gods who dwelt amongst them left their dwellings, in anger at having brought (them) into Babylon. Marduk . . . turned (his face) to all their habitations which were in ruins and (to) the population of Sumer and Akkad, who were like men dead, and he had compassion. He scoured all the lands for a friend, seeking for the upright prince whom it would have to take his hand. He called Cyrus, king of Anshan. He nominated him to be ruler over all. He made the land of Guti, all the warrior band of Manda, submit to him. The blackheaded people whom he (i.e. Marduk) put in his (Cyrus') power, to them he (Cyrus) tried to behave with justice and righteousness. Marduk the great lord, compassionate to his people, looked with gladness on (his) good deeds and his upright intentions. He gave orders that he go against his city Babylon. He made him take the road to Babylon and he went at his side like a friend and comrade. His vast army, whose number like the waters of a river cannot be determined, with their armour held close, moved forward beside him. He got him into his city Babylon without fighting or battle. He averted hardship to Babylon. He put an end to the power of Nabonidus the king who did not show him reverence. The entire population of Babylon, the whole of Sumer and Akkad, princes and governors, bowed to him (Cyrus) and kissed his feet. They were glad that he was king. Their faces lighted up. The master by whose aid the mortally sick had been made alive, all had been preserved from ruin and . . . [For this] they praised him and honoured his name. I am Cyrus, king of the world, great king, mighty king, king of Babylon, king of the land of Sumer and Akkad, king of the four quarters, son of Cambyses, great king, king of Anshan, grandson of Cyrus, great king, king of Anshan, descendant of Teispes, great king, king of Anshan, progeny of an unending royal line, whose rule Bel and Nabu cherish, whose kingship they desire for their hearts' pleasure. When I, well-disposed, entered Babylon, I set up the seat of dominion in the royal palace amidst jubilation and rejoicing. Marduk the great god caused the big-hearted inhabitants of Babylon to . . . me. I sought daily to worship him. My numerous troops moved about undisturbed in the midst of Babylon. I did not allow any to terrorise the land of [Sumer] and Akkad. I kept in view the needs of Babylon and all its sanctuaries to promote their wellbeing. The citizens of Babylon . . . I lifted their unbecoming yoke. Their dilapidated dwellings I restored. I put an end to their misfortunes. At my deeds Marduk, the great lord, rejoiced, and to me, Cyrus, the king who worshipped him, and to Cambyses, my son, the offspring of (my) loins, and to all my troops he graciously gave his blessing, and in good spirits before him we [glorified] exceedingly his high [divinity]. All the kings who sat in throne rooms, throughout the four quarters, from the Upper to the Lower Sea, those who dwelt in . . ., all the kings of the West Country who dwelt in tents, brought me their heavy tribute and kissed my feet in Babylon. From . . . to the cities of Ashur and Susa, Agade, Eshnunna, the cities of Zamban, Meturnu, Der, as far as the region of the land of Gutium, the holy cities beyond the Tigris whose sanctuaries had been in ruins over a long period, the gods whose abode is in the midst of them, I returned to their places and housed them in lasting abodes. I gathered together all their inhabitants and restored (to them) their dwellings. The gods of Sumer and Akkad whom Nabonidus had, to the anger of the lord of the gods, brought into Babylon, I at the bidding of Marduk, the great lord, made to dwell in peace in their habitations, delightful abodes. May all the gods whom I have placed within their sanctuaries address a daily prayer in my favour before Bel and Nabu, that my days be long, and may they say to Marduk my lord, ' May Cyrus the king who reveres thee, and Cambyses his son. . . .'

Notes

to take his hand, i.e. in the procession rite at the New Year Festival. Isaiah (xlv.1) has 'Thus saith the Lord to his anointed, to Cyrus, whose right hand I have holden'.

He called Cyrus, king of Anshan. In this text it is Marduk who calls him, but in a text found at Ur it is Sin, the Moon-god, who gives him victory. In the O.T. Yahweh elects him (Is. xliv.28, xlv.1ff.). His own god was Ahura-Mazda, creator of heaven and earth, and of man. Anshan's precise locality is uncertain. It was both city and district in the north-east of Elam.

he went at his side. Cp. 'I will go before thee' (Is. xlv.2).

without fighting or battle. According to the Nabonidus Chronicle, 'Ugbaru, the governor of Gutium, and the army of Cyrus entered Babylon without a battle'. (Nabonidus had already fled, and was, perhaps, later killed.) It is surmised that the Babylonian Ugbaru is the Gobyras of Xenophon, a traitor and leader of the Babylonian malcontents. For the fate of Babylon, cp. Is. lvi-lxvi.

From . . . to the cities of Ashur. Perhaps here the text named western lands as far as the Mediterranean and including Judah.

I gathered together all their inhabitants and restored (to them) their dwellings. No Babylonian text records Cyrus' liberation of the Jews in particular. On this point O.T. evidence is clear ; cp. Ezra i.1-11. In Isaiah (xliv.24f., 28, xlv.13) Cyrus is commissioned to rebuild Jerusalem and the temple. Micah (v) foretells restoration under Cyrus.

In the Persian Empire created by Cyrus there were four capital cities. Three were in Persia, viz., Ecbatana, Susa and Parsagadae. The other capital was Babylon. Cyrus styles himself 'King of Babylon, king of the lands', and in Babylon he received the submission and tribute of governors and kings of all the lands, including the deserts, between the Mediterranean and the Persian Gulf.

Bibliography

CAMERON, G. G. *History of Early Iran*, 1936.

GHIRSHMAN, R. *Iran* (Pelican Books), 1954.

LANE, W. H. *Babylonian Problems*, 1923.

OPPENHEIM, A. L., in *A.N.E.T.*, 315.

T. FISH

Plate 6　The Cyrus Cylinder

The Murashu Tablets

In 1893 an American Expedition working at Nippur, about sixty-five miles south-east of Babylon, found seven hundred and thirty cuneiform clay tablets written between 455 B.C. and 403 B.C., during the time of the Persian (Achaemenid) kings of Babylon, Artaxerxes I, Darius II, and Artaxerxes II.

The tablets belonged to a business house in Nippur run by the Murashu family. This house is often described as a banking house. The description may pass if it is remembered that the bank did not exchange money and that the 'capital' was almost exclusively *immobilia*. The clients were mainly land-owners and farm-workers resident in central and southern Babylonia.

Texts

a) A specified amount of barley belonging to Iddin-ellil, son of Belshunu, on orders from Rimut son of Murashu (stands) against Nabu-iddin, son of Ninurta-etir. In the month of Ayyar in the 38th year, the barley (to the amount stated above), as measured by Iddin-ellil at Nippur, he will hand over at the gate of the silo. (Names of four witnesses and of the scribe). Nippur, the month of Nisan, 19th day, 38th year of Artaxerxes, king of the lands. Thumb nail mark of Nabu-iddin.

b) Quantities of silver, meal, a cask of sweet beer, a sheep, rent for the year 41 of the fiefs of X and of Y and his partners, which are at the disposal of Ellil-shum-iddin, son of Murashu. The silver, the cask of sweet beer, a sheep, the meal, which are the rent for the year 41, X and Y have received from the hands of Ellil-shum-iddin, son of Murashu ; they have been paid. (Names of seven witnesses. Seal imprint of X and Y. The scribe was the son of Ellil-shum-iddin). Nippur, month of Tashrit, 22nd day, 41st year of Artaxerxes.

Notes

The books of Ezra, Nehemiah and Chronicles are contemporary with the Murashu tablets. The two sources contain many personal names. Of the names on the Babylonian texts, a small proportion are names found in the contemporary Hebrew books. From this it emerges only that during the fifth century B.C. there were Jews in central and southern Babylonia. Contrary to what is often stated, Murashu and his sons were not Jews : the business house in their name was not a Jewish business house. Jews did business with Murashu and Sons, but so did Babylonians, Persians, Aramaeans and Egyptians.

The two texts translated above have been chosen because they illustrate the non-Jewishness of the business. On both tablets it is stated that the transaction was witnessed on days when, according to Jewish law, no servile work should be done, i.e. during the feasts of Passover and of Tabernacles. Other contracts involve usury in circumstances where usury is contrary to Jewish law.

Bibliography

CARDASCIA, G. *Les Archives de Murashu*, 1951.

MEEK, T. J., in *A.N.E.T.*, 221f.

T. FISH

The Babylonian Theodicy

THE Babylonian Theodicy is a debate which attempts to reconcile the concept of divine justice prevailing in the world with actual experience. It asks why the righteous suffer, and so it falls into the same category as the book of Job. In form it is an acrostic poem, which consisted, when complete, of twenty-seven stanzas of eleven lines each. A sufferer, who cites his own calamities, and a friend, who tries to uphold orthodox views, take alternate stanzas. The text itself, like the Song of Songs, contains no indications of the change of speaker, but this want has been supplied in the translation. The eleven lines of each stanza begin with the same sign, and the twenty-seven cuneiform signs read together form a sentence :

' I, Saggil-kinam-ubbib, the incantation priest, am benediction-priest of the god and the king'.

This knowledge of the author's name, though almost unique in cuneiform literature, adds very little to the understanding of the poem, since nothing is known about him. On general grounds of style and language the date of composition can be fixed as probably between 1400 and 1000 B.C. The text has been assembled from thirteen fragments recovered from later Babylonian and Assyrian libraries, but only two-thirds of the whole are preserved. The text is difficult, but help is forthcoming from a cuneiform commentary which explains many of the words.

There is no direct connection between the Theodicy and the book of Job. The similarities arise from a common intellectual background in which both writers expect to find justice in the world, and are perplexed when the righteous suffer. Neither Hebrews nor Babylonians had any concept of recompense in a future life, so that any rewards or punishments had to be meted out in this life. The monotheism of the Hebrew writer allowed the problem to be stated in simple terms. Yahweh controls the universe, and the suffering of his servant Job cannot but be at his command, or at least with his approval. The agencies bringing the suffering receive no attention. The only question in the discussion is, Why does Yahweh so will ? The Babylonians had a more complex universe filled with major and minor deities, as well as with evil demons. The situation was correspondingly more complex. On the one hand the personal deities should protect their devotees as their part of a well understood agreement. On the other hand the great gods responsible for ordering the universe should not have made men prone to wickedness and oppression. Evil demons do not seem to worry the writer. Apparently he considered them controlled by the greater forces in the universe.

The answers given to the questions are significantly different. In the book of Job the basic tenets are so strongly held that a logical impasse results. The answer then is that man has no right to question the Almighty about the workings of his inscrutably just will. The Theodicy does not really formulate an answer to the dilemma that experience hardly bears out the view that divine justice ultimately prevails. The friend indeed makes a certain concession when he admits that the righteous may not enjoy a full measure of bounty (line 240). This problem is then dropped, and both agree that miscarriages of justice frequently occur. The friend explains that the gods made men so inclined, but in so doing the basic assumptions have been broken down. If the gods are concerned to uphold justice in the world, how can they have made men prone to injustice ? The writer does not seem to have realised the implications of his conclusion. At least he makes no attempt to answer the problem which he has unconsciously raised.

Text

SUFFERER
 (*In the damaged opening lines he addresses his friend*)
5 Where is the wise man of your calibre ?
 Where is the scholar who can compete with you ?

 Where is the counsellor to whom I can relate my grief ?
 I am finished. Anguish has come upon me.

 I was a youngest child ; fate . . . my father ;
10 My mother who bore me departed to the Land of No Return ;
 My father and mother left me without a guardian.

FRIEND

Respected friend, what you say is gloomy ;
You let your mind dwell on evil, my dear fellow.

You make your fine discretion like an imbecile's ;
15 You have reduced your beaming face to scowls.

People in fact give up and go the way of death ;
It is an old saying that they cross the river Hubur.

When you consider mankind as a whole,

    . . . it is not . . . that has made the impoverished first-
       born ri[ch.]
20 Whose favourite is the fattened rich man ?

He who waits on his god has a protecting angel ;
The humble man who fears his goddess accumulates wealth.

*   *   *   *   *   *   *

SUFFERER

45 I bow to you, my co[mrade], I grasp your wi[sdom.]
. . . . the utterance of [your words.]
. . . . come, let me [say something to you.]

The onager, the wild ass, who filled itself with . . .
Did it pay attention to the giver of assured divine oracles ?

50 The savage lion who devoured the choicest flesh,
Did it bring its flour offering [to] appease the goddess's anger ?

. . . the *nouveau riche* who has multiplied his wealth,
Did he weigh out [pre]cious gold for the goddess Mami ?

[Have I he]ld back offerings ? I have prayed to my god,
55 [I have] pronounced the blessing over the goddess's regular
       sacrifices . . . .

FRIEND

O [pa]lm, tree of [we]alth, my precious brother,
Endowed with all wisdom, jewel of g[old]

You are as stable as the earth, but the plan of the gods is
       remote.

Look at the superb wild ass on the [plain ;]
60 The arrow will follow the gorer who trampled the fields.

Come, consider the lion that you mentioned, the enemy of
  cattle ;
For the crime which the lion committed the pit awaits him.

The bloated *nouveau riche* who heaps up goods
Will be burnt at the stake by the king before his time.

65 Do you wish to go the way these have gone ?
Rather seek the lasting reward of the gods !

SUFFERER

Your mind is a north wind, a pleasant breeze for the peoples ;
Your fine advice is pure and choice.

Just one word would I put before you.

70 Those who neglect the god go the way of prosperity,
While those who pray to the goddess are impoverished and
  dispossessed.

In my youth I sought the will of my god ;
With prostration and prayer I followed my goddess.

But I was bearing a profitless corvée as a yoke.
75 My god decreed, instead of wealth, destitution.

A cripple is the man over me ; a lunatic is the man in front
  of me.
The rogue has been promoted, but I have been brought low.

*   *   *   *   *   *   *

FRIEND

235 As for the rogue whose favour you seek,
His . . . . soon vanishes.

The godless cheat who has wealth,
A death-dealing weapon pursues him.

Unless you seek the will of the god, what luck have you ?
240 He that bears his god's yoke never lacks food, though it be
  sparse.

Seek the kindly wind of the gods ;
What you have lost over a year you will make up in a
  moment.

SUFFERER

I have looked around society, but the evidence is contrary.
The gods do not impede the way of a devil.

245 A father drags a boat along the canal
While his first-born lies in bed.

The first-born son pursues his way like a lion ;
The second son is happy to be a mule driver.

The heir stalks along the road like a bully ;
250 The younger son will give food to the destitute.

How have I profited that I have bowed down to my god ?

I have to bow beneath the base fellow that meets me ;
The dregs of humanity, like the rich and opulent, treat me
with contempt.

FRIEND

O wise one, O savant who masters knowledge,
255 In your anguish you blaspheme the god.

The divine mind, like the centre of the heavens, is remote ;
Knowledge of it is difficult ; the masses do not know it.

Among all the creatures that Aruru formed
The prime offspring is altogether. . . .

260 In the case of a cow the first calf is lowly,
The later offspring is twice as big.

A first child is born a weakling,
But the second is called a heroic warrior.

Though a man may observe what the will of the god is, the
masses do not know it.

SUFFERER

265 Pay attention, my friend, understand my ideas,
Heed the choice expression of my words.

People extol the word of a strong man who is trained in
murder,
But bring down the powerless who has done no wrong.

They confirm the wicked whose crime is. . . .
270 Yet suppress the honest man who heeds the will of his god.

They fill the sto[re house] of the oppressor with gold,
But empty the larder of the beggar of its provisions.

They support the powerful, whose . . . is gui[lt,]
But destroy and drive away the weak in his poverty.

275 And as for me, the penurious, a *nouveau riche* is persecuting me.

FRIEND

Narru, king of the gods, who created mankind,
And majestic Zulummar, who dug out their clay,

And mistress Mami, the queen who fashioned them,

Gave perverse speech to the human race.
280 With lies, and not truth, they endowed them for ever.

Solemnly they speak in favour of a rich man ;
'He is a king,' they say, 'riches go at his side.'

But they harm the poor as though he were a thief ;
They lavish slander upon him and plot his murder,

285 Making him suffer every evil like a criminal, because he has
no protection.
Terrifyingly they bring him to his end, and extinguish him
like a flame.

SUFFERER

You are kind, my friend ; behold my grief.
Help me ; look on my distress ; know it.
I, though humble, wise, and a suppliant,
290 Have not seen help and succour for a moment.
I have trodden the square of my city unobtrusively ;
My voice was not raised, my speech was kept low.
I did not raise my head, but looked at the ground,
I did not worship even as a slave in the company of my
assoc[iates.]
295 May the god who has thrown me off give help !
May the goddess who has [abandoned me] show mercy !
For the shepherd Shamash gu[ides] the peoples like a god.

Notes

Lines 5ff. Unlike the book of Job, the speakers in this dialogue maintain a marked politeness to the end. Some scholars have suspected sarcasm, but needlessly. The friend never attributes the dire straits of his interlocutor to some horrible sin, which confirms the existence of mutual respect. Generally the tone of the Theodicy is less tense than that of the book of Job.

Lines 9ff. Here the writer adumbrates the main topics of his dialogue (i) Why are the powerful allowed to oppress the weak ? (ii) Why has the first-born advantages over the younger sons ?

Line 17. The *Hubur* is the Babylonian Styx, the river which had to be crossed on the way to the underworld.

Lines 21f. *god, goddess*. Ordinary Babylonians had no access to the great gods like Marduk or Nabū, and for their personal needs adopted small private gods who, if properly supplied with offerings, interceded with the great gods on behalf of their clients. These are the gods and goddesses referred to without name in the Theodicy.

Lines 45-66. The orthodox view that personal gods can assure prosperity is countered by examples of the impious who enjoy the fruits of their crimes, yet disregard deities altogether. The reply is that their success is short-lived, and ends in disaster ; cp. Ps. xxxvii.10. It is certainly striking that two of the examples are from the animal kingdom.

Line 53. *Mami* is the mother goddess ; cp. line 278.

Line. 62. The cuneiform commentary explains *pit* by 'underworld' (cp. Ps. xxx.3, etc.).

Line 244. *devil*, as in colloquial English, is used here metaphorically for a human tormentor.

Lines 245-64. Here the sufferer, a youngest child himself, complains of the advantages which the first-born enjoyed in Babylonian (as in Hebrew) society. The answer, that nature redresses this lack of balance by making the later offspring more robust, need not be substantiated by statistics. Readers will know sufficient examples supporting this statement to understand that it is an empirical observation. It must be remembered that in the ancient world mothers commonly experienced childbirth before they were fully grown.

Lines 265-86. The oppression to which the writer refers is clearly miscarriage of justice.

Line 276f. *Narru* is a name of Enlil according to the cuneiform commentary, one of the chief gods of the Sumerian pantheon who eventually became merged with Marduk. *Zulummar* is a name of Ea, one of the great gods of the Babylonian pantheon.

Bibliography

LANDSBERGER, B. 'Die babylonische Theodizee', *Z.A.* 43 (1936) 32-76.

PFEIFFER, R. H., in *A.N.E.T.*, 438-40.

W. G. LAMBERT

Babylonian Moral Teachings

THE various documents which portray the Babylonian view on life, spread as they are over more than a millennium, do not, of course, present a uniform picture. Hedonism, pessimism, pacifism are all represented. Yet there is an approach to life which can be considered orthodox. It demands the performance of the proper duties to the gods and to men, and it promises in return a goodly measure of health and prosperity. Instructions in this way of life circulated in several different forms. A compilation of admonitions was connected with the name of the Sumerian flood hero Ziusudra. The Sumerian work is preserved, though not yet published. A small fragment of a Babylonian translation is preserved on a fragment of a tablet written about 1100 B.C. in Assyria. It is not a coincidence that Noah received some admittedly very different instructions on disembarking from the ark, according to Gen. ix.1-7. A better-known Babylonian work of the same category is the Counsels of Wisdom, which is treated below. Moral teachings are also contained in some hymns, especially in those to gods of justice. In Sumerian a hymn to Nanshe includes a very eloquent ethical section, and a famous hymn to Shamash is the classic of Babylonian preceptive hymns. Selections from this are also given below. The Psalter likewise has examples of didactic liturgy (Pss. xv, xxiv. 3-6).

It appears that several of the matters of conduct which receive attention in Babylonian writings were also matters of concern to Hebrew writers, for example, guarding one's speech (Prov. x.19), leaving a neighbour's wife alone (Exod. xx.17), corruption in law courts (Exod. xxiii.6ff.), two standards of weights and measures (Amos viii.5), and injustice towards poor borrowers (Exod. xxii.25ff.). The idea too of promising material rewards for the observance of the injunctions is common to both literatures. There is, however, this difference, that the Babylonians had no god whose holiness was such that his worshippers must conform to his standards. Not even Shamash is extolled for his own virtues, though he was certainly conceived as having them.

In the O.T., however, the concept of the holiness of Yahweh results in a deeper moral tone, and more penetrating exhortations. The similarities, when studied in the whole context of the two cultures, are undoubtedly not coincidental, but result from a common heritage on which both are built.

1 COUNSELS OF WISDOM

These are a collection of short sections of moral precepts, distinguished from each other by content and metre. Originally the work extended for about one hundred and sixty lines, of which less than half remains. Both beginning and end are missing, a loss which obscures any literary framework into which the sections may have been fitted. Only the most slender evidence for dating exists. To the writer the feel of the work is that of the Cassite period (1500-1000 B.C.), though an Old Babylonian date (1800-1500 B.C.) cannot be positively excluded. The copies were all written between 700 and 400 B.C.

Text

31 Do not frequent a law court,
   Do not loiter where there is a dispute,
   For in the dispute they will have you as a testifier,
   Then you will be made their witness,
35 And they will bring you to a lawsuit not your own to affirm.
   When confronted with a dispute, go your way ; pay no attention to it.
   Should it be a dispute of your own, extinguish the flame !
   Disputes are a covered pit,
   A strong wall that scares away its foes.
40 Though a man forget it, it remembers him and lays the accusation.
   Do not return evil to the man who disputes with you ;
   Requite with kindness your evil-doer,
   [Pay] back justice to your enemy,
   Be devoted to your adversary.
45 If your ill-wisher is . . . ., nurture him.
   Do not set your [mind] on evil [doing.]

57 Do not insu[lt] the downtrodden and . . . .
   Do not vent your anger on them as an autocrat.
   With this a man's god is angry,

60 It is not pleasing to Shamash, who will requite him with e[vi]l.
   Give food to eat, beer to drink ;
   Grant what is asked, provide for and honour.
   In this a man's god takes pleasure ;
   It is pleasing to Shamash, who will requite him with favour.
65 Do charitable deeds, render service all your days.

72 Do not marry a prostitute, whose husbands are legion,
   A temple harlot, who is dedicated to a god,
   A courtesan, whose favours are many.
75 In your trouble she will not support you,
   In your dispute she will be a mocker ;
   There is no reverence or submissiveness with her.
   Even if she dominate your house, get her out,
   For she has directed her attention elsewhere.
80 (*Variant:* She will disrupt the house she enters, and her
       partner will not assert himself.)

127 Do not utter li[bel, s]peak what is of good report.
    Do not say evil things, speak well of people.
    One who utters libel and speaks evil,
130 Men will waylay him with the retribution of Shamash.
    Beware of careless talk, guard your lips ;
    Do not utter solemn oaths while alone,
    For what you say in a moment will follow you afterwards.
    But exert yourself to restrain your speech.
135 Every day worship your god.
    Sacrifice and benediction are the proper accompaniment of
        incense.
    Present your free-will offering to your god,
    For this is proper toward the gods.
    Prayer, supplication, and prostration
140 Offer him daily, and you will get your reward.
    Then you will have full communion with your god.
    In your wisdom study the tablet.
    Reverence begets favour,
    Sacrifice prolongs life,
145 And prayer atones for guilt.
    He who fears the gods is not slighted by . . . . . .
    He who fears the Anunnaki extends [his days.]

Notes

Lines 41-5. This is not 'loving one's enemies', nor even 'heaping coals of fire upon his head' (Prov. xxv.22). The previous lines warn men against becoming embroiled in a lawsuit. These lines offer practical advice on achieving this end. Similar advice is offered to rulers in The Cuthean Legend of Naram-Sin—'Respond to their wickedness with kindness, to kindness with gifts and exchanges, but do not go forth before them' (lines 170ff., translation of O.R. GURNEY, *Anatolian Studies*, v (1955) 109). This whole text is written around the moral that pacifism is the best policy for a ruler.

Lines 60, 64. These lines include aphorisms which probably had a very wide oral circulation, as they also appear in the Shamash Hymn (lines 100, 106, 119 below), and in the Aramaic version of the Words of Ahikar (*A.N.E.T.*, 428, vi.92f.).

Lines 72-80. Both street- and cult-prostitutes were exceedingly common in ancient Babylonia, and their activity seems generally to have been accepted as a respectable profession. As worded, this section merely condemns them as unsuitable as wives. Simple observation might well suggest that a woman of this kind will have a strong, self-willed character, but it is still possible that a moral revulsion at this institution may have been rationalised in this thought.

The story of Judah and Tamar (Gen. xxxviii) shows an attitude to prostitution which is very similar to that of the Babylonians and Assyrians; as a class such women were tolerated, though it was a serious offence for a married woman to engage in this practice; serious, because it was an offence against her husband. No restrictions were put on men, however, in this respect, whether married or not. Elsewhere in the O.T. prostitution is fully condemned. A particularly striking warning against it is contained in Prov. vii. In the other similar condemnations found in Prov. i-ix it may be noted that in ix.13 the phrase 'knoweth nothing' is probably more correctly translated 'is not still' (*J.T.S.*, N.S. iv (1953) 23 f.): the thought is thus similar to that of line 77. From Amos onwards the prophets denounce cult prostitution (Amos ii.7; Hos. iv.11-18; Jer. ii.20). It became indeed a symbol for any debased form of religion.

Lines 127-34. Two other sections of the Counsels of Wisdom not included here also deal with restraint in speech, and it is a common topic in the book of Proverbs (e.g. x.19), and is found also in Egyptian Wisdom literature (e.g. *A.N.E.*, 420, iv.1). The basis of the section under discussion seems to be a magic conception of speech as something which cannot be withdrawn once it has been uttered, but remains operative, even if it returns onto the head of the speaker. The account of the blessing of Jacob and Esau (Gen. xxvii), when Isaac was unable to take back the blessing which Jacob had gained by trickery, shows that this same idea of the solemn utterance was known among the Hebrews (cp. Is. lv.11).

Line 147. *the Anunnaki* are the underworld gods.

Bibliography

LANGDON, S. H. 'A Tablet of Babylonian Wisdom', *P.S.B.A.*, xxxviii (1916) 105-16, 131-7.

—— *Babylonian Wisdom*, 1923, 88-92 (also printed in *Babyloniaca* vii (1923) 216-20.).

PFEIFFER, R. H., in *A.N.E.T.*, 426f.

II THE SHAMASH HYMN

This hymn to the sun-god, the Mesopotamian god of justice, is one of the finest cuneiform hymns. It extends for two hundred lines, and the greater part of it is well preserved. Although Shamash was never one of the first-ranking gods, his worship was always common, and he was perhaps the most popularly revered god in all periods. In this hymn he is praised as the giver of light, and for the care which he bestows on every creature. His all-seeing eyes miss nothing in the universe, and thus moral conduct is his concern.

The copies, with one exception, are Assyrian, and from the seventh century B.C. The one exception is Babylonian, and is probably a little later. The text was probably composed not earlier than 1000 B.C., though some of the material incorporated may be Old Babylonian (1800-1500 B.C.).

Text

88 A man who cove[ts] his neighbour's wife
Will . . . . before his appointed day.

90 A fiery demon and . . . . is prepared for him,
Your weapon will strike at him, and there [will be no]ne to save.

[His] father will not stand in his defence,
And at the judge's command his brothers will not plead.

He will be caught in a copper trap that he did not foresee.

95 You destroy the horns of a scheming villain,
. . . .
You give the unscrupulous judge experience of fetters.

Him who accepts a bribe and yet lets justice miscarry you
   make bear his punishment.

He who receives no bribe but takes the part of the weak,
100 It is pleasing to Shamash, and he will prolong his life.

A circumspect judge who pronounces just verdicts
Controls the palace and lives among the princes.

What is he benefited who invests money in unscrupulous
   trading missions ?
He is disappointed in the matter of profit and loses his
   capital.

105 He who invests money in distant trading missions and pays
   one shekel per . . .,
It is pleasing to Shamash, and he will prolong his life.

The merchant who [practises tr]ickery as he holds the
   balances,
Who uses two sets of weights thus lowering the . . .,
He is disappointed in the matter of profit and loses his capital.

110 The honest merchant who holds the balances [and gives] good
   weight,
Everything is presented to him in good measure . . . .

The merchant who practises tr[ickery] as he holds the corn
   measure,
Who weighs out loans [of corn] by the minimum standard,
   but requires a large quantity in repayment,

The curse of the people will overtake him before his time ;
115 If he demanded repayment before the agreed date, there
   will be guilt upon him.

His son will not assume control of his property,
Nor will his brothers take over his estate.

The honest merchant who weighs out loans of corn by the
   [maxi]mum standard, thus multiplying kindness,
It is pleasing to Shamash, and he will prolong his life,

120 He will enlarge his family, gain wealth,
And like the water of a never failing spring [his] descendants
   will never fail.

Notes

Lines 98f.   The crime is not the acceptance of a *bribe*—this was little different from a lawyer's fee—but failure to secure justice for the plaintiff or defendant, as the case may have been, after he had paid his money.   The opposite is the virtuous attorney who helps the poor without charge.

Lines 103-06.   These are references to foreign trade, the economics of which are not fully understood.

Bibliography

GRAY, C. D.   *Shamash Religious Texts*, 1901, 9-23 (also printed in *A.J.S.L.* xvii (1901) 129-45).

STEPHENS, F. J., in *A.N.E.T.*, 387ff.

VON SODEN, W.   *Sumerische und akkadische Hymnen und Gebete*, 1953, 240-7.

W. G. LAMBERT

Prayer to any God

THIS prayer, bearing the title 'Prayer to any god', is written in Sumerian, a language superseded by Akkadian, except for liturgical purposes, soon after 2000 B.C. Still in use, through religious conservatism, in the seventh century B.C., the prayer, like many other Sumerian texts, was given an interlinear Akkadian translation (cp. the reading of the O.T. in Hebrew with an accompanying Aramaic rendering (Targum) in N.T. times). Like some O.T. psalms, it was probably originally composed for the exclusive use of the king. Its severe liturgical form, characteristically Sumerian, distinguishes it from the vast majority of Akkadian private prayers, and it lacks their variety of thought and language. In common with numerous psalms in the Psalter, it consists of a number of paragraphs of unequal length. Some of these are in a form based upon the responsive litanies or processional psalms of Sumerian public liturgies. Thus lines 1-10, 39-50, 59-63 each comprise a series of short invocations of monotonous similarity, in the second or third person, to which uniform liturgical formulas are appended. Elsewhere also occur groups of lines (13-16, 17-20, 26-9, 30-4, 35-8, 51-3, 56-8, 64f.) with parallel beginnings or endings. In a few O.T. psalms a litany style, probably with musical, perhaps congregational, responses, is found, for example, in Pss. cv.9ff., cxxxv.19f., and especially in Pss. cxviii and cxxxvi, whose recurring formula 'His mercy endureth for ever' is also often cited outside the Psalter (e.g. in Jer. xxxiii.11) ; cp. also the refrains in Ezek. xxxii. 20-31 and Is. ix.8-x.4 (and v.25). For small groups of lines with identical openings, see Pss. xxix, ciii, cxv, cxviii, cxxxv, cl, and Is. v.8-24. For the interchange of second and third persons in invocations, cp. Pss. lxviii, lxix, lxxxix, etc. These stylistic correspondences may, but need not, imply Babylonian influence.

Like most Babylonian, and many O.T., penitential psalms, the prayer contains confessions of sin, a description of the suppliant's misfortunes, pleas for pardon, and a promise to adore the deity. The chief penitential psalms in the O.T. are Pss. vi, xxv, xxxii, xxxviii, li, cii, cxxx and cxliii. Resemblances in thought and language to Babylonian prayers sometimes occur in them, as elsewhere in the Psalter, and may be due to indirect Babylonian influence from an early, or even a later, time.   While, however, traces of Canaanite influence have been plausibly conjectured, there is no clear instance of borrowing from Babylonian, and the style, phraseology and ideas are, on the whole, very different and much more varied and artistic.

Babylonian prayers show none of the noblest features of O.T. psalms, such as monotheism, love of the deity, and trust in divine love, nor is there any consciousness of an obstacle to God's forgiveness in the sinner's moral character and outlook.   There are, however, close connections with lower and more primitive Israelite ideas, some of which survived into the official post-exilic cult.   In Babylonia, as in Israel, certain traditional moral and ceremonial customs were regarded as divinely ordained and equally obligatory, any breach, even unwitting, normally incurring divine displeasure and consequent punishment.   Misfortunes, including sickness, were in general interpreted as direct retributive divine acts to be obviated or cured only by remorse, confession, plea for pardon, and prescribed expiatory ceremonies. This Sumerian prayer was probably part of a lengthy ritual which included prayers to several named deities with sacrificial offerings and a variety of symbolic purificatory acts.

The Akkadian translation does not always strictly render the Sumerian, and the closing formulas are frequently summarised in both versions by one word, or by a 'ditto' sign, or are even omitted altogether.   Missing parts of the text cannot be certainly restored.

SUMMARY OF THE PRAYER.   Lines 1-10, appeal for forgiveness ; lines 11-29, confession of sin and appeal for forgiveness ; lines 30-8, description of the penitent's sufferings (continued in line 55) ;   lines 39-50, renewed appeal for forgiveness ;   lines 51-3, plea of universal human ignorance ;   lines 54-63, renewed reference to the penitent's sufferings with appeal for forgiveness and promise to adore the deity ; lines 64f., concluding appeal, repeating the formula of lines 1-10.

Text

(Of) my lord—may the anger of his heart to its place return ;
(Of) the god who is unknown—to its place (return) ;
The mother-goddess who is unknown—to its place (return) ;
The god, known or unknown—to its place (return) ;
5 The mother-goddess, known or unknown—to its place (return) ;
The heart of my god—to its place (return) ;
The heart of my mother-goddess—to its place (return) ;
The god and my mother-goddess—to its place (return) ;
The god w[ho is angry] with [me—to its place (return)] ;
10 The mother-goddess [who is angry with me—to its place (return)].
The transgression [I have committed]—I know not ;
The sin [I have sinned]—I know not.
A good name—[may the god pronounce] for me (?) ;
A good name—[may my mother-goddess pronounce] for me (?) ;
15 A good name—[may the god na]me ;
A good name—[may my mother-goddess name].
Food [of my god (?)—unwittingly I have ea]ten ;
Water of a cesspool (?)—[unwittingly I have] drunk ;
What was forbidden by my god—unw[ittingly] I have eaten ;
20 What was forbidden by my mother-goddess—unwittingly I have trodden.
My lord—my transgressions are many, my sins are great ;
My god—my transgressions are many, my sins (are great) ;
My mother-goddess—my transgressions are many, my sins (are great) ;
God, known or unknown—my transgressions are many, my sins (are great) ;
25 Mother-goddess, known or unknown—my transgressions are many, my sins (are great).
The transgression I have committed—I know not ;
The sin I have sinned—I know not ;
The forbidden thing I have eaten—I (know) not ;
The forbidden thing (ground) I have trodden—I (know) not.
30 The lord in the anger of his heart has looked at me ;
The god in the rage of his heart has turned on me ;
The mother-goddess is angry with me and has made me ill ;
The god, known or unknown, has afflicted me ;
The mother-goddess, known or unknown, has caused me anguish.

35 I keep seeking help, but no one takes my hand ;
I have wept, but to my side they have not come ;
I utter laments, but no one hears me ;
I am in anguish, I am overwhelmed, I do not see (light).
The god who is merciful—(to him) I turn, my prayer I speak ;
40 My mother-goddess—her foot I kiss, before her (?) I crawl ;
The god, known or unknown— . . . [I spe]ak (?) ;
The mother-goddess, known [or unknown]— . . . [I spe]ak (?),
My lord, tu[rn to me] . . . ;
Mother-goddess, lo[ok upon me] . . . ;
45 God, known [or unknown, turn to me] . . . ;
Mother-goddess, known [or unknown, look upon me]. . . .
How long, [my (?)] God—[until the anger of thy heart rests] ?
How long, my mother-goddess—[until the anger of thy heart
rests] ?
How long, god known or unknown—until the anger of [thy]
heart [rests] ?
50 How long, mother-goddess, known or unknown—until thy hostile
heart returns to its place ?
Mankind is dumb and knows nothing ;
Mankind—name whom one may—what know they ?
Whether one does wrong or does right one knows not.
My lord, thou wilt not strike down thy servant ;
55 Into the waters of a morass he has been cast ; take thou his hand.
The sin I have sinned—turn thou to good ;
The transgression I have committed—may the wind carry away !
My iniquities (which are) many—like a garment strip off.
My god—the transgressions seven times seven, my transgressions,
forgive.
60 My mother-goddess—the transgressions seven times seven, (my
transgressions, forgive.)
God, known or unknown—the transgressions seven times seven,
(my transgressions, forgive.)
Mother-goddess, known or unknown—the transgressions seven
times seven, (my transgressions, forgive.)
My transgressions forgive, and I will celebrate thy praises.
May thy heart, like the heart of one's mother who bore—to its
place return ;
65 (Of one's) mother who bore and of (of one's) father who begot—
to its place return.

Notes

Lines 1-10. *my lord.* The invocations are addressed to the unidentified deity or deities, whose anger is believed by the suppliant to have occasioned his misfortune. The word 'my', which is occasionally added, probably does not refer to the suppliant's personal protecting god or goddess ; cp. note on line 6. 'Lord' (Bel) is a title of many Babylonian gods, though later reserved especially for Marduk (O.T. Merodach, Jer. l.2) of Babylon (cp. Is. xlvi.1 ; Jer. li.44). Its Hebrew equivalent, Baal, used of the chief Canaanite god, was for a time applied to Yahweh (cp. Hos. ii.16, and the name Bealiah in 1 Chr. xii.5), but later Adonai, with the same meaning, superseded it, and was also later regularly substituted in reading for 'Yahweh' ; hence the common rendering of 'Yahweh' by 'the LORD' in the R.V. *anger of his heart.* In the O.T. also misfortunes are attributed to God's wrath at sin (cp. Pss. vi.1, lxxix.5f.), and there, too, the heart is considered one of the seats of the emotions (joy, sorrow, fear, etc.), and is said to 'grow hot' with anger (Ps. xxxix.3). *to its place* (*return*), like boiling liquid that subsides as it cools. The O.T metaphor is of fire that is kindled (Deut. xi.17, xxxii.22), poured out (Jer. vii.20), and consumes (Ps. xc.7), but may be pacified (Prov. xvi.14) and turn away (Num. xxv.4). *unknown.* Babylonian gods were so numerous in early times that even the priests did not know the names of all. Sumerian prayers often invoke long lists of divine names, but later most of the gods were forgotten, or were regarded as relatively unimportant servants of the few great gods to whom alone prayer was addressed by name. This is the only extant Babylonian prayer reserved for an unnamed (because unknown or, at least, unidentified) god or goddess, but many prayers include, among their invocations to named gods, one to the 'unknown' god or goddess (cp. Acts xvii.23). *the mother-goddess.* Literally 'the mother, the *ishtar*'. Normally, the title 'mother' is omitted when this noun is used. The attributes of all Babylonian gods are, in general, identical, and this helped to foster strong monotheistic tendencies, although true monotheism was not achieved. Each god had a female counterpart or consort, but these consorts were little more than names and were, from early times, frequently identified with Ishtar, the great mother-goddess, whose name was also used as a common noun, meaning 'goddess'. She is the 'queen of heaven' of Jer. vii.18, xliv.17, 25. Her Phœnician counterpart was Ashtoreth (1 Kings xi.5), and a multiplicity of such goddesses was worshipped in Canaan (cp. Jud. ii.13 ; 1 Sam. vii.4, xxxi.10). A female consort of Yahweh was worshipped in the fifth century B.C. by the Jews of Elephantine in Egypt. *my god, my mother-goddess.* This is possibly, but not certainly, a reference, as in some Babylonian prayers, to the personal protecting deities who interceded for the suppliant before the great gods. They seem to have been akin to the household gods of the Babylonians and Hebrews (O.T. teraphim, Gen. xxxi.19; Jud. xviii.7), and could, like other gods, be alienated by sin and placated by repentance. Somewhat similar were the protecting geniuses sent by the great gods to 'stand beside', or 'go in front of', a man ; cp. O.T. angels (Gen. xxiv.7, xlviii.16 ; Pss. xxxiv.7, xci.11 ; Is. lxiii.9).

Lines 11-20. *I know not.* The suppliant admits unwitting sins (lines 21-25,

57-62), but denies conscious guilt (lines 11-12, 17-20, 26-9), and protests universal human ignorance of divine laws (lines 52-4). He does not deny that unwitting offences deserve punishment. Similarly in the O.T., involuntary sins are regularly punished (1 Sam. xiv.27, 43f. ; 2 Sam. vi.6f.) The priestly legislation deals largely with atonement for unintentional sins (Lev. iv.27f., v.15), including natural physical defilement (Lev. xii.1-8 ; cp. xxii.4). O.T. psalmists often make a general, never specific, acknowledgement of sin (e.g. Pss. xli.4, li.3), but sometimes they protest their innocence (e.g. Pss. xxvi, xliv.17f.), and the problem of innocent suffering is recognised in the book of Job and elsewhere. *A good name*, i.e. virtually, a happy destiny ; cp. the O.T. phrases 'regard for good' (Jer. xxiv.5), and 'remember for good' (Neh. xiii.31). But the metaphor may be juridical, of rehabilitation and declaration of immunity from penalty ; 'name' in the O.T. sometimes means reputation (Gen. xii.2 ; Ruth iv.14 ; cp. Phil. iv.3). A parallel O.T. idea is inscribing a man's name in the book of life (cp. Ps. lxix.28). *Food*, i.e. consecrated food, forbidden to the laity ; cp. Lev. xxii.14 ; Mark ii.26. The O.T. sometimes cites ritual and moral offences together as if indistinguishable and equally heinous (Is. lviii.9-14 ; Ezek. xviii.6f.). Although the Babylonians and Israelites both recognised the grave importance of morality, no specific ethical offences are ever mentioned in the psalms of either people. *Water*. Stagnant or polluted water was, like other unhealthy substances, considered by the Babylonians to cause ritual uncleanness ; cp. the O.T. lists of prohibited foods in Lev. xi ; Deut. xiv. *trodden*, e.g. in or around a temple, unapproachable by the laity, or approachable only after special precautions. In Israel, no gentile was allowed within the Temple court (Neh. xiii.7f. ; Acts xxi.28). Only priests might enter the Temple (Heb. ix.6), only the high-priest the inner sanctuary (Lev. xvi ; Heb. ix.7). The scene of a theophany was also holy (Gen. xxviii. 16f. ; Exod. iii.5).

Lines 21-30. *my transgressions are many, . . . great.* Cp. Ps. xxv.11 ; Jer. xiv.7. *looked at me.* The gods were believed to scrutinise, from the sky, and, in appropriate cases, to punish men's actions (cp. Job xxxiv.21, xl.11f. ; Ps. xi.4 ; Prov. xv.3). But in both Babylonian and O.T. prayers God usually 'looks' in mercy ; cp. line 44 below.

Lines 31-40. *made me ill.* Descriptions of sickness and misery are usual in Babylonian and O.T. penitential psalms ; cp. Job xvi.7ff., xix.6ff. ; Pss. xxii.6ff., 12-18, xxxviii.2-12, lxxxviii.3-9, 15-18, cii.3-11. *afflicted* is a common phrase in the Psalter, e.g. Pss. lxxxviii.7, cxix.75. *seeking help, but no one takes my hand*, like a man in a bog (line 55) ; cp. Job xix.16 ; Pss.xviii.41, cxlii. 4; Is. xli.13, xlii.6. *wept, utter laments.* Cp. Pss. vi.6ff., lxix.3, 10, cii.5. In Babylonia and Israel grief was displayed rather than restrained. *no one hears me.* Cp. Job xix.7. *do not see (light)*, in the sense of deliverance, healing and happiness. The phrases 'see light' and 'see the sun' are thus used in Babylonian prayers ; cp. Job xxxiii.28, 30 ; Ps. cxviii.27 ; Is. ix.2, lix.9. Physical blindness can scarcely be intended ; cp. also Ps. cxlvi.8 ; Is. xxix.18, xxxv.5, xlii.7. *merciful*, a flattering epithet, perhaps genuinely meant ; cp. Pss. li.1, lxxxvi.15, ciii.8. *her foot I kiss.* The language is metaphorical ; cp., in the literal sense, 1 Kings xix.18 ; Ps. ii.12 ; Hos. xiii.2. *I crawl* (cp. Is. ii.8f.), a gesture to excite pity ; cp. Josh. vii.6 ; Ps. xliv.25. A commoner O.T. phrase is 'humble oneself', metaphorically, before God (e.g. 2 Kings xxii.19).

Lines 41-50. *turn to me.* Cp. Ps. lxix.16. *look upon me,* in mercy (contrast line 30) ; cp. Ps. lxxxiv.9. *How long?* is a common ejaculation in Akkadian and O.T. psalms ; cp. Pss. xiii.1f., lxxix.5, xc.13.

Lines 51-60. *Mankind is dumb,* i.e. unable to justify itself before God ; cp. Job iv.17ff., ix.2f., 12, 14ff, xxv.4ff. ; further Ps. xxxix.9 ; Is. liii.7 *knows nothing.* The O.T. sometimes emphasises man's involuntary ignorance (Job viii.9, xi.7f., xiii.23 ; Pss. xix.12, cxliii.8; Prov. xx.24), but usually regards knowledge as attainable and ignorance as blameworthy (Ps. xxxii.8f., liii.1, 4 ; Prov. i.7, 22). *name whom one may.* Literally 'whatever names are named'. *Thou wilt not strike down* is apparently an expression of trust in divine mercy, a feature characteristic of O.T. psalms (e.g. Ps. xvi.8, 10) ; but perhaps 'thou canst not strike down' is a better translation. *thy servant.* Cp. Pss. xxvii.9, lxix.17, lxxxvi.2, cxliii.12. *a morass.* Cp. Ps. xl.2, lxix.1, 2, 14f. *turn thou to good,* i.e. change punishment into blessing ; cp. Ps. cxviii.25. There is no idea here of overruling evil for good, as in Gen. l.20. *may the wind carry away* is a common Akkadian and O.T. metaphor ; cp. Ps. i.4, xxxv.5, lxviii.2 ; Hos. xiii.3. *like a garment strip off.* Cp. the symbolic changing of the high-priest's garments in Zech. iii.4, clothing with righteousness (Job xxix.14 ; Ps. cxxxii.9), salvation (2 Chr. vi.41 ; Is. lxi.10), cursing (Ps. cix.18f.), and shame (Ps. xxxv.26), and the metaphor of sin as a stain on a garment (Is. i.18 ; Rev. vii.14). *seven times seven,* i.e. an indefinitely large number. Seven and its multiples are often thus used in Babylonian and O.T. literature ; cp. Gen. iv.24 ; Ps. lxxix.12 ; Matt. xviii.22. The suppliant magnifies his self-accusations to mollify the outraged deity as one would an earthly king. *forgive.* Literally 'unloose', like a fetter ; cp. Ps. cxvi.16 ; Acts viii.23 ; Rom. viii.21.

Lines 61-65. *celebrate* (literally 'praise') *thy praises,* a vow, consequent upon deliverance ; cp. Gen. xxviii.20ff. ; Ps. li.18f. Such a vow often closes an Akkadian or O.T. prayer, e.g. Pss. vii.17, xiii.6, lxi.8. *mother.* Cp. Is. xlix.15. *father.* Cp. Ps. ciii.13 ; Mal. iii.17.

Bibliography

DRIVER, G. R., in *The Psalmists,* ed. D. C. SIMPSON, 1926, 109-75.

HOOKE, S. H. *Babylonian and Assyrian Religion,* 1953.

JASTROW, M. *Die Religion Babyloniens und Assyriens,* revised ed., I, 1905 ; II, 1912. See especially II, 101-06.

—— *Aspects of Religious Belief and Practice in Babylonia and Assyria,* 1911.

OESTERLEY, W. O. E., *The Psalms,* 1939.

STEPHENS, F. J., in *A.N.E.T.,* 391f.

WIDENGREN, G. *The Accadian and Hebrew Psalms of Lamentation as Religious Documents,* 1937.

C. J. MULLO WEIR

Texts from Ras Shamra

(Plate 7)

THESE texts from Ras Shamra, the ancient Ugarit, on the north Syrian coast, from which we have selected extracts from legends and myths in alphabetic cuneiform, come from an archæological context *c.*1400 B.C., and, according to certain colophons to tablets of the Baal-text, were redacted in their extant form at that time. Their finished form, however, indicates a considerable period of literary elaboration, possibly four centuries. Thus customs and institutions to which the texts refer are not necessarily current in precisely the form in which they are described, but are related to the heroic past. In principle, however, and often in detail, there are striking correspondences with Hebrew life and culture. Hebrew literary conventions have Canaanite proto-types, and there is a close dialectic affinity between Hebrew and Ugaritic.

I THE LEGEND OF KING KERET

This is probably the torso of a larger text, and is extant in three tablets, the first well preserved and the others more fragmentary, amounting in all, including probable restorations, to some five hundred half-couplets. As a royal saga this text, like that of Aqht, is of great value for the study of kingship and social conventions in pre-Israelite Canaan.

Text

I   A ROYAL WOOING

> Keret came down from the roof,
> He prepared food for the city,
> Wheat for Beth Hubur.
> He parched bread of the fifth,
> 5 Food of the sixth month.[1]
> The crowd mustered [2] and came forth,
> The élite of the fighting men [3] mustered,

Plate 7   Tablet from Ras Shamra : The Legend of King Keret

Then forth came the crowd together ;
His host was abundant in freemen,
10 Three hundred times ten thousand,[4]
Marching in thousands like a rainstorm,
Even in tens of thousands as winter rain.[5]
After[6] two two marched,
After three all of them.
15 The solitary man shut up his house,
The widow hired a substitute,
The sick man rose from his bed,
The blind man gave his benediction.[7]
The bridegroom produced the bride-price,
20 Burning to claim his wife,
Yea, to acquire[8] his beloved.
As locusts which occupy the fields,
As hoppers the desert marches,[9]
They went a day, a second (day) ;
25 After that, at sunset on the third (day)
They reached the shrine of Atherat of Deposits,[10]
Even (the shrine of) the Goddess of Oracles[11] ;
There Keret of Th'[12] made a vow.
'As surely as Atherat of Deposits is present,
30 Even the Goddess of Oracles,
If I take Hurriya into my house,
If I bring the damsel[13] into my court,
Two-(thirds) of her will I give in silver,
Yea, a third in gold.'[14]
35 They went a day, a second (day),
A third, a fourth day.[15]
After sunset on the fourth day
He reached Udum[16] the Great,
Even Udum Abundant in Water.
40 They abode at the city,
They watched at the town.
To and fro in the fields plied the women
          cutting wood,[17]
Congregating in the open places.
To and fro at the well plied the women
          drawing water,
45 Filling (the jars) at the spring.[18]

They tarried a day, a second (day)
A third, a fourth day,
A fifth, a sixth day,
Then at sunrise on the seventh day

50 Did King Pabil pay attention
To the sound of the bellowing of his bull,
To the sound of the braying of his ass,
To the lowing of his ploughing-ox,
To the barking of his tawny [19] hound . . .
(*King Pabil sends messengers to Keret with terms*)

55 'Take silver and electrum, [20]
Gold in token of her value,
And a henchman perpetual, three horses,
A chariot [21] which stands in the stable of (thy)
        humble servant, [22]
Take, O Keret, peace-offerings in peace.

60 Harm not Udum the Great,
Even Udum Abundant in Water.
Udum is the gift of El,
The present of the Father of Men. [23]
Depart, O King, from my house,

65 Withdraw, O Keret, from my court.'
Then answered Keret of Th' :
'For what purpose are silver and electrum to me,
(Gold) in token of her value,
And a perpetual henchman, three horses,

70 A chariot which stands in the stable of a
        humble servant ?
Nay, but what I have not in my house do thou give.
Give me the damsel Hurriya,
The fairest of the offspring of thy first-born,
Whose grace is as the grace of Anat, [24]

75 Whose beauty is as the beauty of Athtarat,
Whose eyeballs are as the sheen of lapis-lazuli,
Whose eyelids are as bowls of cornelian,
For in my dream El granted, [25]
In my vision the Father of Men,

80 Offspring should be born to Keret,
Even a lad to the Servant of El.' [26]

II 'A DIVINITY THAT DOTH HEDGE A KING'

'How say they Keret is the son of El,
The offspring [27] of the Kindly One and the Holy ?
Or do gods die,
85 The offspring of the Kindly One not live ?' [28]

III CANAANITE EXORCISM

Then declared El, the Kindly, the Merciful.
'Sit, my sons, on your seats,
Even on your princely thrones.
I myself will resort to magic,
90 And will stay the power of the disease,
Driving out the sickness.'
With dung his hand he fills,
With goodly dung . . . he moulds.[29]

IV A CANAANITE ABSALOM

Yasib [30] too sits in the palace,
95 And his inwards instruct him.[31]
'Go to thy father, Yasib,
Go to thy father and say,
Repeat to Keret of Th' :
"Hear, and may thine ear be alert !
100 By slow degrees thou art growing old,
And in the tomb [32] thou wilt abide.
Thou hast let thy hands fall into error,[33]
Thou dost not judge the case of the widow,
Nor decide the suit of the oppressed.[34]
105 Sickness is as thy bedfellow,
Disease as thy concubine.
Descend from thy rule that I may be king,
From thy government that I may be enthroned".'

Notes

[1] By this ritual the new crop was made available for common use. For fire as a means of desacralisation, cp. Lev. ii.14. *Bread of the fifth, food of the sixth month* refers presumably to barley and wheat which are harvested in that order.

[2] This word *ngb* was taken by the first commentators as meaning the Negeb in the South of Palestine. This and other geographic references have since been abandoned by most scholars.

[3] Literally 'the fighting men of the fighting men'. Hebrew also forms the superlative in this way. The military aspect of the expedition is a fiction, preserving the conception of winning the bride by force. The modern Arabic peasantry in Palestine still speak of 'snatching a bride'.

[4] This is obvious hyperbole. Another possible translation is 'henchmen, hundreds of myriads'. The word for 'three' and 'henchmen' is *thlth*, which corresponds to Hebrew *shlsh*. This word means 'a captain of chariotry' in Exod. xiv.7, xv.4 and elsewhere.

[5] The word is a shorter form of the Hebrew *yrh*, 'the early rains' of the O.T.

[6] On internal evidence and from the Arabic cognate it is plain that the word *'athr* is a preposition here and does not signify 'Asher', as was first thought.

[7] Our meaning is established by Arabic cognates. The blind man, incapable of active service, can at least speak an auspicious word, which had the effect, it was thought, of influencing Providence by auto-suggestion ; cp. 'Go up to Ramoth-gilead, and prosper !' spoken to Ahab by prophets at the gate of Samaria (1 Kings xxii.12).

[8] This is a disputed passage. On our interpretation the verb has an exact parallel in Hos. iii.2 and in 1 Sam. xxiii.7.

[9] The reference is not so much to the number of the locusts, a frequent figure in the O.T., as to the progress of a swarm.

[10] *Atherat* is the mother-goddess, Asherah of the O.T. In the text *'athrt tsrm* is generally taken as 'Atherat of the Tyrians', and phonetically this is possible, though we prefer to take *tsrm* as a common noun cognate with an Arabic word *tsurra* 'a bundle'.

[11] *'elt tsdynm* is generally taken as 'the Goddess of the Sidonians'. We take *tsdynm* as a common noun cognate with the Arabic word *tsaday* 're-echo'.

[12] From administrative texts from Ras Shamra a clan Th' is known to have been very influential. The word has been taken here as 'noble', in which case it would be cognate with a well-known Hebrew word *shō'a*.

[13] The word *ghlmt* is the same as that mistranslated 'virgin' in the Immanuel oracle in Is. vii.14. In the light of the Ugaritic word the root may be determined by its Arabic cognate as meaning 'one lustful', i.e. 'sexually mature'.

[14] Probably relative to the bride-price.

[15] Conventional rather than actual numbers are a hallmark of saga. So Laban pursues Jacob seven days (Gen. xxxi.23), the Nile runs blood for seven days (Exod. vii.25), and the Ark is among the Philistines seven months (1 Sam. vii.1), etc.

[16] Not the Edom of the O.T., as was first thought, but a city.

[17] The occupation may be an allusion to the age of the girls, as among modern

Arab peasantry, where a girl approaching puberty is actually termed 'a hewer of wood and a drawer of water'.

[18] Did the King expect to see his bride-to-be here, as Rebecca and Zipporah were found at the well ? It must be remembered that the saga is cast in the heroic past, the age of grand simplicity.

[19] Possibly 'hungry', or 'whining', after Arabic cognates. The reference is to the privations suffered through the 'siege' of Keret.

[20] Literally 'pale yellow metal', as distinct from 'ruddy gold' (khrs), the word used in the following couplet.

[21] This suggests a date for the text c.1800 B.C., when the horse and light war-chariot were introduced into Western Asia. When the Keret text was composed horses and chariots were still apparently rareties.

[22] A deferential form of address as in Hebrew; cp. Ps. lxxxvi.16, where 'the son of thy handmaid' is found in parallelism with 'thy servant'.

[23] The stock epithet of El, the senior god of the Canaanite pantheon. The kin-title probably denotes the authority of El in the moral sphere.

[24] The most active goddess in the Ras Shamra mythology, the sister of Baal and his champion when he is in eclipse. Her cult is indicated in Palestine in the place-names Beth-anath in Naphtali (Josh. xix.38), Beth-anoth in Judah (Josh. xv.59), and possibly Anathoth, the home of Jeremiah in Benjamin (Jer. i.1, xi.21, etc.).

[25] As among the early Hebrews dreams were regarded as the medium of revelation.

[26] On internal evidence *Servant of El* is specifically a title of the king. In Hebrew psalms also the king is termed 'the Servant of God', e.g. Pss. cxxxii.10, cxliv.10, lxxxix.3, 20, 39. The 'Servant' denotes the 'worshipper', i.e. the king as representing the people as a religious community on high cultic occasions before their god. After the abolition of the Hebrew monarchy the people could still be thought of in terms of their royal representative of former times, e.g. Is. xlii.1-4, xlix.1-6, lii.13-liii.12.

[27] *shpch*. Cp. Hebrew *mishpāchāh* 'family'.

[28] Elsewhere in the text the king is termed 'the son of El', who is, however, also 'the Father of man', or perhaps better, 'the Father of the community'. The king, however, represents the community before the god, especially in the cult, where he is 'the Servant of god' *par excellence* (cp. note 26). In the present passage, with its somewhat extravagant language, we have a projection of cultic ideology, the king being the embodiment of his people before their god and the representative of the god to the people. For the Hebrews the king, who symbolised the kingship of God, i.e. Order against Chaos, was regarded as the son of God by adoption, e.g. Pss. ii, cx, this being a social, rather than a physical, relationship. Even among the Hebrews, however, this could give rise to the conception that the king was 'god', e.g. Ps. xlv.6, 'Thy throne, O God, is for ever and ever'.

[29] The verb indicates that the missing word signified an image. The transference of sickness to an external body was a common conception in Babylonian medicine. This principle lies at the base of the Hebrew practice of transferring the sins of the people to the scapegoat (Lev. xvi).

30 From a verb cognate with an Arabic root meaning 'to succeed'.
31 The same verb as in the Hebrew phrase 'my reins instruct me' (Ps. xvi.7).
32 Literally 'cave', a cognate of the Hebrew word for 'cave'.
33 'That the righteous put not forth their hands unto iniquity' (Ps. cxxv.3).
The last word in Hebrew is the same as *error* in the Ras Shamra passage.
34 From the Aqht text also we learn that

> 'Deciding the case of the widow,
> Judging the suit of the orphan'

was specifically the office of the king ; cp. Deut. x.18 ; Is. i.17 ; Ps. lxviii.5.

II THE LEGEND OF AQHAT, SON OF DAN'EL [1]

This text is extant on three tablets, of which the last is badly
damaged. It is almost certain that at least one tablet followed.
The extant text, including three fragments concerning the
Rephaim, which probably belong to it, and with probable
reconstructions of fragmentary text, amounts to some three
hundred half-couplets. In this text saga has already passed into
myth.

Text

I THE IDEAL SON

Then on the seventh day Baal proffered his
    intercession
For the impotence of Dan'el the Dispenser of
    Fertility,[2]

. . . .

'Then bless him, O Bull El, my father,[3]
5 Grant him thy benediction, O Creator of Created
    Things,[4]
And may there be a son for him in the house,
Even a scion in the midst of his palace,
One who may set up the pillar of his ancestral god [5]
In the sanctuary, the refuge [6] of his clan,
10 Who may pour out his drink-offering [7] to the ground,
Even to the dust wine after him,
Who may heap up the platters [8] of his company,
Who may drive away any who would molest his
    night-guest,[9]
Who may take his hand when he is drunk,

15 Support him when he is full of wine,[10]
   Who may eat his slice in the temple of Baal,
   Consume his portion in the temple of El,[11]
   Who may plaster his roof when it is muddy,[12]
   Who may wash his garment when it is dirty.' [13]

II   A MAIDEN'S DUTIES

20 'Hear, O Maiden [14] who bearest water on thy
     shoulder,
   Who sweepest the dew from the barley,[15]
   Who knowest the course of the stars . . .' [16]

III   A MORTAL'S REPULSE OF A GODDESS

   'Fabricate not, O Virgin ; [17]
   To a hero [18] thy words are trash.
25 As for mortal man, what does he get as his latter
     end ?
   What does mortal man get as his inheritance ?
   Glaze [19] will be poured out on my head,
   Even plaster [20] upon my pate,
   And the death of all men will I die,
30 Yea, I will surely die.'

IV   A GREAT DROUGHT

   Thereupon Dan'el, the Dispenser of Fertility,
     imprecates [21]
   The clouds with heat in the season of rain,
   The clouds which rain in the season of summer
     fruit,[22]
   The dew which falls on the grapes.
35 'For seven years may Baal be restrained,
   For eight He who Mounteth the Clouds,[23]
   Without dew, without showers,
   Without upsurging of the lower deep,[24]
   Without the drum-roll, the voice of Baal.' [25]

Notes

[1] Not Daniel, but *Danel*, as in Ezek. xiv.14, 20 (Hebrew text), and in the denunciation of the king of Tyre, (Ezek. xxviii. 3) suggesting that the prophet was familiar with Phœnician literature.

[2] This word, the subject of certain doubt, is a participle. It may be from a root, found also in Hebrew, meaning 'healing'. In Gen. xx.17 it refers to the restoration of fertility to the harem of Abimelech of Gerar, and in 2 Kings ii.21 to the restoration of the fertilising properties of the spring of Jericho ; hence our translation. The influence of the king over nature is a well-known conception in the ancient East, and is the basis of the conception of the Golden Age in Nature in the Messianic hope (cp. Ps. lxxii.5, 16).

[3] *El* being the father of the divine family in Canaanite religion, it is likely that his title, the Bull, signified his procreative power.

[4] The word *Creator* means the same as 'builder'. The same verb is used of God's creation of Eve in Gen. ii.22.

[5] The verb *set up* is the root of *matsēbāh*, used in the O.T. of standing stones of sacral significance, and also of images. The classic example of such a pillar signifying also in Hebrew tradition the presence of the God of the family, is Jacob's pillar at Bethel (Gen. xxviii).

[6] Literally 'hiding place'. With a slight phonetic variation of the initial consonant the word is used also in Hebrew in this sense, e.g. in Ps. xxvii.5.

[7] This word, generally taken to mean 'smoke', i.e. of sacrifice or incense, is cognate with the Arabic verb meaning 'to drip'. In this and the following line the reference is to funerary offerings, for which drains were provided in Late Bronze Age (fourteenth century B.C.) tombs excavated at Ras Shamra, and also, remarkably enough, in tombs in Israelite Samaria. In the Hadad inscription from Zenjirli in North Syria, which is to be dated in the first half of the eighth century B.C., we read (lines 17f.)—'May the soul of Panammu eat with thee, and may the soul of Panammu drink with thee !' (see G. A. COOKE, *A Text-Book of North-Semitic Inscriptions*, 1903, 162).

[8] The word is found in Hebrew meaning large flat tablets, e.g. the tablets on which Moses received the law. We visualise the large wooden tray of Bedouin hospitality. The ideal son must be a generous host.

[9] The host, as among the Bedouin, is the protector of his guests, as Lot in Sodom (Gen. xix.1-11), and the Levite's host at Gibeah (Jud. xix.16).

[10] Cp. Is. li.18 (of Jerusalem) : 'There is none to guide her among all the sons whom she hath brought forth ; neither is there any that taketh her by the hand of all the sons that she hath brought up'. The son must see that his parent's decency is safeguarded in secular or sacred conviviality. For wine-bibbing at sacred festivals, cp. Amos ii.8 ; Hos. vii.5 ; Deut. xiv.26, xxxii.38.

[11] The reference here is to communion-meals whereby the solidarity of the group, which was essentially a religious body, was realised, one member with another, and all with their god. This was done by all partaking of a common sacrifice, technically known in Hebrew as *shelāmîm*, mistranslated as 'peace-offerings'. (The true nature of this sacrifice was emphasised by W. R. SMITH, *Religion of the Semites*, third ed., 1927, 237.) The solidarity of the community

is visualised here in the cult of Baal, the power of Providence in nature, and of El, whose domain was more specifically the social sphere.

[12] The flat roofs of eastern houses are still rolled with little stone rollers after rain.

[13] So that no one, particularly a woman, by whom evil influences, for the primitive mind, had more ready access, should 'put a ju-ju on it'. The garment, having direct contact with a man's body, was thought of as representing the man himself. In a Greek graffito from a Phœnician tomb of the third century B.C. at Beit Jibrin in South Palestine a lover states that he has secured the garment of his lass (J. R. PETERS and H. THIERSCH, *Painted Tombs of Marissa*, 1905). By cutting off the skirt of Saul's mantle David was probably regarded as having permanent power over Saul (1 Sam. xxiv.1ff.).

[14] The word *pght* is found in administrative texts from Ras Shamra as a common noun. It may be the same as Puah, the name of one of the Hebrew midwives in Egypt (Exod. i.15).

[15] This may refer to gathering green weeds as fodder for the animals. In any case it indicates the early rising of the maiden.

[16] This probably does not refer to astrology, but simply to her industry both early and late, as the good woman in Prov. xxxi.15, 18 'riseth also while it is yet night . . . her lamp goeth not out by night'.

[17] The stock epithet of the goddess Anat in these texts.

[18] This word *ghzr* 'young man, warrior' has a little-known Hebrew cognate 'ōzēr, found in 1 Chr. xii.1, denoting a military class, and probably in Ps. lxxxix.20 denoting 'a youth'.

[19] Figurative for 'white hair'. H. L. GINSBERG detected the word (in Hittite *zap-zagu*), and he proposes to read it in Prov. xxvi.23, i.e. *kesapsāgīm metsuppeh 'al chāres* 'like glaze overlaid on a potsherd' for *keseph sīgīm metsuppeh 'al chāres*, literally 'silver of dross overlaid on a potsherd' (*B.A.S.O.R.* No. 97 (1945) 22 ; No. 98 (1945) 20f.)

[20] Literally 'potash' after an Arabic cognate. This denotes white hair or baldness. This negative view of the destiny of the individual is characteristic of Hebrew thought in the pre-exilic period. It finds expression later too, e.g. in Ecclesiastes and among the Sadducees, though in Pharisaism and in kindred sects, from whom much apocalyptic matter in the Apocrypha emanated, there was a more 'lively' hope.

[21] For this aspect of the royal office, cp. note 2. The verb is cognate with the Arabic verb 'to pray', which, as far as we can ascertain, is not used in the sense in which we take the Ugaritic word. Hence some scholars interpret the present passage as a prayer for moisture in time of drought, and not as a curse. The words, however, follow a mourning rite, hence we take the passage as a curse. In favour of the former interpretation the text in the immediate sequel describes Dan'el as engaged in rites to revive nature after drought. That is not to say, however, that a long interval did not intervene. The epic moves swiftly in time and space.

[22] *Rain* is rare in Palestine in summer, though the heavy dew may fall as heavily as rain and is heralded by clouds. Rain is expected any time after August (Elul) ; cp. the folk-saying, 'As for Elul, its verge is soaked by rain'.

23 i.e. Baal, whose proper name is known from these texts as Hadad, the most active deity in the Canaanite fertility cult, and manifest in winter storms and rain. His stock epithet is 'He who Mounteth the Clouds', *rkb'rpt*. This imagery is transferred to Yahweh in Deut. xxxiii.26 and Ps. civ.3, and in Ps. lxviii.4, where Yahweh is entitled *rōkēbh ba'arābhōth*, mistranslated 'him that rideth through the deserts'.

24 The third of the three sources of moisture in these regions, the rain, the dew, and the springs ; cp. Deut. xxxiii.13, 'for the precious things of heaven, for the dew, and for the deep that coucheth beneath', and 2 Sam. i.21, where the unsatisfactory text has been emended on the basis of the Ras Shamra passage, which is strongly suggested, to read *hārē haggilbōa' 'al tal we'al mātār 'aleykem weshera' tehōmōth* 'Ye mountains of Gilboa, let there be neither dew nor rain upon you, nor upsurging of the deeps' (H. L. GINSBERG 'A Ugaritic Parallel to 2 Sam. i.21', *J.B.L.* lvii (1938) 209-13).

25 i.e. thunder, said in the O.T. to be the voice of God. Often the plural 'voices' (unqualified) is used in this sense, e.g. Exod. ix.23, etc.

III THE BAAL MYTHS

The vicissitudes of Baal are described on seven fragmentary tablets, amounting, with probable reconstructions of damaged text, to about fourteen hundred half-couplets. Another tablet, also damaged, describes the temporary eclipse of Baal, here named Hadad, 'the Thunderer'. We regard the first four tablets as a separate myth describing the conflict of Baal and the tyrannical waters, and the other three as an account of the conflict of Baal and Death. In the former myth Baal is the power of Providence in Nature, and the myth of how he won his king-ship we regard as appropriate to the Autumnal New Year Festival, when the same theme of the kingship of God was celebrated among the Hebrews.[1] This Canaanite myth greatly influenced Hebrew thought and did much to broaden the Hebrew conception of the power and influence of Yahweh. In the second myth Baal is the principle of fertility in vegetation in conflict with the power of sterility. This myth we believe to have been related to seasonal ritual throughout the year of the Syrian peasant. Here the influence on Hebrew literature was confined to language and imagery.

Text

I BAAL IS KING !

(*The arrogant Sea has cowed the divine assembly* [2] *into submission, but Baal stands forth as their champion,* [3] *and is supported by the divine craftsman, 'the Skilful and Percipient One'*)

Then up speaks the Skilful and Percipient One.
'Have I not told thee, O Prince Baal,
Have I not declared, O Thou who Mountest the
     Clouds [4] ?
Behold, thine enemies, O Baal,
5 Behold, thine enemies thou shalt smite,
Behold, thou shalt subdue thine adversaries. [5]
Thou shalt take thine eternal kingdom,
Thy sovereignty everlasting.' [6]

. . . .

(*The divine craftsman fashions two maces for Baal, named according to their purpose 'Driver' and 'Expeller'* [7])

Then soars and swoops the mace in the hand of Baal,
10 Even as an eagle in his fingers.
It smites the head of Prince Sea,
Between the eyes [8] of Judge [9] River
Sea collapses and falls to the ground,
His strength is impaired ;
15 His dexterity fails.
Baal drags him away and disperses him,[10]
He annihilates Judge River.

. . . .

'Let Baal reign.' [11]

II THE PRIMORDIAL ENEMIES OF BAAL [12]

20 'What enemy rises up against Baal,
What adversary[13] against Him who Mounteth
     the Clouds ?
Have I not slain Sea, beloved of El [14] ?
Have I not annihilated River, the great god ?
Have I not muzzled the Dragon,[15] holding her in a
     muzzle ?

25 I have slain the Crooked Serpent,[16]
  The Foul-fanged with Seven Heads.[17]
  I have slain the Beloved of the earth-deities,
  Even Death, who passes on his way with prodigious
      haste,
  I have slain the Bitch of the gods, Fire,
30 I have annihilated the daughter of El, Flame,
  Smiting and dispossessing the Flood,
  Who would drive Baal from the crags of Saphon.' [18]

III   MOURNING FOR BAAL

  'Dead is Baal the Mighty,
  Perished is the Prince, Lord of the Earth.'
35 Then the Kindly El, the Merciful,[19]
  Comes down from his throne ; he leaps to the
      footstool ;
  And from the footstool he leaps to the ground.
  He lets down his turban in grief ;
  On his head is the dust in which he wallows [20] ;
40 He tears asunder the knot of his girdle ;
  He makes the mountain re-echo with his
      lamentation,
  And his clamour to resound in the forest.
  Cheeks and chin he rends,
  His upper arm he scores,[21]
45 His chest as a garden-plot,
  Even as a valley-bottom his back he lacerates.
  . . . .
  Anat too goes and ranges
  Every mountain to the heart of the earth,
50 Every hill to the midst of the fields.[22]
  She comes to the pleasant land of pasture,
  The fair field of the fat grazings ;
  She comes upon Baal fallen to the ground.

IV   A HARVEST RITE

  She [23] seizes Death, the Son of El ;
55 With a blade she cleaves him ;
  With a shovel she winnows him ;
  With fire she parches him ;

With a millstone she grinds him ;
In the field she sows him ;
60 His remains the birds eat,
The wild creatures consume his portions ;
Remains from remains are scattered.[24]

V THE REVIVAL OF BAAL

In a dream of El, the Kindly, the Merciful,
In a vision of the Creator of Created Things,
65 The heavens rain oil,
The wadis run with honey.[25]
El, the Kindly, the Merciful rejoices,
His feet on the footstool he sets,
He relaxes reserve [26] and laughs.
70 He raises his voice and cries :
'I shall sit and take my ease,
And the soul shall repose in my breast,
For Baal the Mighty is alive,
For the Prince, Lord of the earth, exists.'

Notes

[1] The most direct evidence for the cult of Yahweh as King at the great autumn festival is Zech. xiv.16f., where the worship of Yahweh as King is associated with the Feast of Tabernacles.

[2] So in Ps. lxxxii Yahweh is the only effective god in the divine assembly.

[3] So Marduk in the Babylonian myth of the conflict of Cosmos and Chaos, which was proper to the Spring New Year Festival.

[4] Cp. II, note 23.

[5] Cp. Ps. xcii.9 : 'For, lo, thine enemies, O Lord,
For, lo, thine enemies shall perish ;
All the workers of iniquity shall be scattered'.

[6] Kingship won in conflict with the powers of disorder is the theme of the present piece and of Hebrew psalms and passages in the prophets which probably re-echo the language of the cult. The closest parallel in the O.T. is Ps. cxlvi.10 : 'The Lord shall reign for ever,
Thy God, O Zion, unto all generations'.

[7] Cp. the two pillars at the porch of the Temple, Jachin ('He shall establish') and Boaz ('In it is strength'), 1 Kings vii.21 ; 2 Chr. iii.17.

[8] A word-play on the double meaning of ʿn in Ugaritic and also in Hebrew, viz. 'spring', 'eye'.

[9] As in the case of the Hebrew 'Judge', shōphēt, in Ugaritic thpt, denoted more than a judicial functionary.

[10] Cp. Ezek. xxix.3ff., xxxii.2-6, where Pharaoh, called 'the Dragon' (*tannīm*, see below note 15), is dismembered and scattered over the land.

[11] Probably a cultic cry ; cp. 'The Lord reigneth' in Ps. xciii, where, incidentally, the enemies of God, as in the Ras Shamra myth, are the waters. In the Psalms, particularly those celebrating the kingship of Yahweh, in the Prophets, and in Apocalyptic writings, the enemies of God are repeatedly spoken of as threatening waters or monsters of the deep.

[12] Here Anat, the sister of Baal, speaks. In another context Baal is said to have killed the Crooked Serpent (see below note 16). The myth as extant does not describe these exploits, and the uncertainty as to who killed the monsters seems to indicate an older myth now vaguely remembered.

[13] The feminine singular is used as a collective, as occasionally in Hebrew.

[14] Probably a euphemism.

[15] *tnn*, the *tannīm* of Ezek. xxix.3, xxxii.2, and *tannīnīm* of Gen. i.21 ; Ps. lxxiv.13, cxlviii.7, and Job vii.12, where, as in the Ras Shamra myth, it is associated with the sea as an enemy of God.

[16] Later in the same myth it is said of Baal :

> 'Though thou didst slay Lotan the Primæval Serpent,
> Didst make an end of the Crooked Serpent,
> The Foul-fanged with Seven Heads'.

Cp. Is. xxvii.1, 'In that day the Lord . . . shall punish

> Leviathan the Primæval Serpent (*liwyāthān nāchāsh bārīach*)
> Even Leviathan the Crooked Serpent (*liwyāthān nāchāsh ʿaqallāthōn*)
> And he shall slay the dragon (*tannīm*) that is in the Sea'.

Here the adjectives qualifying Leviathan are the same as in the Ras Shamra passage. Job xxvi.13 also refers to the Primæval (R.V. 'swift') Serpent (*nāchāsh bārīach*).

[17] Ps. lxxiv.13 refers to the breaking of the heads of the dragon (*tannīn*), which seems to reappear in Rev. xii.3, in the 'great red dragon, having seven heads'.

[18] This mountain on the northern horizon of Ras Shamra, modern Jebel el-Aqra and Mount Kasios of the Greeks, was the seat of Baal, who was thus Baal Saphon. Classical and archæological evidence suggests that Baal Zephon mentioned in the Exodus from Egypt (Exod. xiv.2) was a shrine of the Canaanite Baal. The fact that in Ps. xlviii.2 Jerusalem as the seat of Yahweh, 'the great King', is described as 'the sides' (better 'extremities') 'of the north', seems to indicate the vestiges of a Baal-liturgy, the prototype of the cult of Yahweh as King at the Autumn New Year Festival.

[19] These are the stock epithets of El in the Ras Shamra texts, denoting his authority in the moral sphere. They recall God's epithets of 'Gracious and Merciful' (*channūn werachūm*) of Joel ii.13 ; Jonah iv.2 ; Pss. cxi.4, cxii.4, cxlv.8, etc.

[20] The same verb is used for a mourning rite, usually wallowing in ashes (Jer. vi.26 ; Ezek. xxvii.30) ; in Mic. i.10, as here, wallowing in dust is mentioned.

[21] Literally 'marks with three scores', i.e. with the nails of the three fingers.

[22] The search for the dead deity by a goddess is a common motive in the fertility cult throughout the Near East ; cp. the search of Isis for Osiris, of

Ishtar for Tammuz, of Demeter for Kore. The mourning for Baal as a vegetation deity in eclipse suggests the weeping for Tammuz, also a vegetation deity, by the women of Jerusalem in the sixth month (Ezek. viii.14), and, more directly, the public mourning for Hadad-Rimmom (the Canaanite Baal) in the Valley of Megiddo (Zech. xii.11). Was the ritual counterpart to the mourning of the Virgin Anat on the mountains not that annually practised in Israel also by the virgins on the mountains of Gilead, this being later somewhat artificially invested with historical significance through association with Jephthah's daughter (Jud. xi.37-40) ?

[23] Viz. Anat, the most active goddess in the Ras Shamra mythology.

[24] Underlying this passage is a rite of desacralisation, see above, I, 1, note 1 ; cp. Lev. ii.14, the offering of the first sheaf, 'green ears of corn dried by the fire, even corn beaten out of full ears'.

[25] Cp. 'flowing streams of honey and butter' (Job xx.17), 'then will I . . . cause their rivers to run like oil' (Ezek. xxxii.14), 'the mountains shall drop sweet wine, and all the hills shall melt' (Amos ix.13), and 'the mountains shall drop down sweet wine, and the hills shall flow with milk' (Joel iii.18).

[26] Or, more literally, 'opens the passage of his jaws'. Cp. the anthropomorphisms of the O.T., e.g. 'the nostril of God grew hot', i.e. 'was angry', etc.

Bibliography

DE LANGHE, R. *Les Textes de Ras Shamra-Ugarit et leurs Rapports avec le Milieu Biblique de l'Ancien Testament*, 2 vols., 1945.

DRIVER, G. R. *Canaanite Myths and Legends*, 1956.

DUSSAUD, R. *Les Découvertes de Ras Shamra (Ugarit) et l'Ancien Testament*, 1941.

GASTER, T. H. *Thespis*, 1950.

GINSBERG, H. L., in *A.N.E.T.*, 129-55.

GORDON, C. H. *Ugaritic Literature*, 1949.

GRAY, J. 'Ugarit : a Canaanite Metropolis of the Bronze Age', *E.T.* lxvi (1955) 326-30.

—— 'The Ras Shamra Texts : a Critical Assessment', *H.J.* liii (1955) 113-26.

SCHAEFFER, C. F. A. 'The Cuneiform Texts of Ras Shamra' (Schweich Lectures 1936), 1939.

J. GRAY

Egyptian Documents

The 'Israel Stele' of Merenptah
The Hymn to Aten
A Penitential Psalm
The Instruction for King Meri-ka-re
A Dispute over Suicide
The Tale of the Two Brothers
The Teaching of Amenemope
Love Songs

The 'Israel Stele' of Merenptah

(Plate 8)

WHEN Merenptah (*c.* 1223-1211 B.C.) succeeded to the throne of his father Ramesses II, he was well advanced in years. Apparently unrest in Egypt's Asiatic possessions followed his accession, for the concluding lines of the inscription here translated suggest that he quelled revolts in Palestine and Syria. This alleged punitive attack seems to have taken place during Merenptah's third regnal year. There is no reference to the incident in the O.T., and some scholars would doubt the historicity of his claims to an Asiatic conquest. The Egyptian myth of the invincible, divine Pharaoh often led to grandiloquent claims of victory over enemies that cannot be reconciled with historical evidence. There are, however, scattered pieces of information which lend support to belief in such a Palestinian campaign. At any rate, we may rest assured that it had little enduring effect, for Egypt's hold on her dwindling Asiatic empire was becoming increasingly tenuous.

In his fifth year Merenptah was faced with a threat of far greater magnitude, when he was forced to secure his western borders against an invasion by the Libyans, reinforced by hordes of Sea Peoples. These latter were the result of mass migrations of Indo-European folk from Europe who crossed the Mediterranean in search of new homes. Among the groups which comprised the attacking force were Achaeans, Tyrsenians, Lycians, Sardinians and Sicilians. Merenptah succeeded in inflicting a resounding defeat on his enemies and averted the danger for a time. His victory over the Sea Peoples, however, afforded but a temporary respite, for forty years later Ramesses III was to be confronted with an even greater array of such invaders, among whom were the Philistines, who, upon their defeat, settled on the Palestinian coastal plain.

To commemorate his redoubtable achievement, Merenptah appropriated a black granite stele, originally set up nearly a century and a half earlier by Amenhotep III, and on the reverse side inscribed a series of hymns of victory. This he set up in his

mortuary temple at Thebes, while at the same time a duplicate
was carved on the great temple at Karnak. This latter now
survives only in fragments. The present translation renders
somewhat less than half of the original hieroglyphic text.

Text

The sun, dispelling the cloud that was over Egypt,
    Letting To-meri see the rays of the sun disc ;
Removing the copper mountain from the neck of the patricians,
    Giving breath to the plebeians who were shut in ;
5 Slaking the desire of Memphis over their foes,
    Making Tjanen rejoice over his adversaries ;
Opening the doors of Memphis which had been blocked up,
    And letting its temples receive their food(-offerings). . . .

The sole one, restoring the courage of hundreds of thousands,
10   For breath enters their nostrils at the sight of him ;
Breaking into the land of Temeh in his lifetime ;
    Putting eternal terror into the hearts of the Meshwesh ;
Making the Libyans, who had trampled Egypt, retreat
    With great dread in their hearts because of To-meri ;
15 Their advanced troops abandoned their rear,
    Their feet did not stand firm, but ran away ;
Their archers cast away their bows,
    The hearts of their running men were faint from travelling ;
They loosened their water-skins, which were thrown to the
    ground,
20   Their packs were untied and cast away.

The wretched enemy prince of Libya
    Fled alone in the depth of night ;
No feather was on his head, his feet were unshod,
    His wives were seized in his presence ;
25 The grain(?) for his food was taken away,
    He had no water in the water-skin to sustain him.
His brothers' faces were fierce enough to slay him,
    One fought the other amongst his leaders.
Their tents were burned and reduced to ashes ;
30   All his belongings became food for the soldiers.

When he reached his (own) country, in grief,
> Every survivor in his land was discontented at
> > receiving him. . . .

Great rejoicing has risen in Egypt,
> Jubilation has issued from the towns of To-meri ;
35 They recount the victories
> Which Merenptah wrought in Tehenu :
'How beloved he is, the victorious ruler !
How exalted is the king among the gods !
How fortunate he is, the master of command !
40   Ah, how pleasant it is to sit when one is engaged in chatter !'

One may walk freely on the road,
> Without any fear in the hearts of men.
Fortresses are left to themselves ;
> Wells are open, accessible to messengers ;
45 The ramparts of the encircling wall are secure in the sunlight
> Until their watchmen awake.
The Medjay are stretched out in sleep,
> The Tjukten hunt in the fields as they wish. . . .

The princes lie prostrate, saying, 'Salaam' !
50   Not one lifts his head among the Nine Bows.
Destruction for Tehenu ! Hatti is pacified ;
> Canaan is plundered with every evil ;
Ashkelon is taken ; Gezer is captured ;
> Yanoam is made non-existent ;
55 Israel lies desolate ; its seed is no more ;
> Hurru has become a widow for To-meri ;
All the lands in their entirety are at peace,
> Everyone who was a nomad has been curbed by King
> > Merenptah.

Notes

Lines 1-3. The introductory strophe extols Merenptah as the saviour of
Egypt, referring to him as *the sun*. *To-meri* is but another name for Egypt.
The metaphor of a *copper mountain* is used to describe the insupportable burden
of the foreign invaders which, as it were, constricted the necks of the Egyptians
so they could not breathe.

Line 6. *Tjanen* was an ancient god of Memphis, early equated with the god Ptah.

The second strophe describes the victorious Pharaoh defeating the Libyans single-handed (*the sole one*, line 9), since the Egyptian concept of kingship reflected in art as well as in literature portrayed the ruler as invincible, wreaking destruction on the enemy by his own divine power. The Egyptian maintained that it was not the army, but the Pharaoh alone who inflicted defeat on all his foes who fled pell-mell before him.

Lines 11f. *Temeh* is a term for Libya, and the *Meshwesh* were one of the Libyan tribes. So great was the confusion into which the Libyan forces were thrown that the advanced troops fled in disorder, leaving the forces in their rear without protection (line 15). The third strophe vividly depicts the fate of the Libyan ruler as he fled barefoot and empty-handed, without even the distinctive feathered head-dress of the Libyan warriors (line 23).

The following two strophes relate the joy of Egypt at the victory and the security which now prevailed throughout the land.

Line 36. *Tehenu* is yet another name for Libya.

Line 40. The verb rendered *chatter* means properly 'to speak a foreign tongue, to talk gibberish'.

Line 44. The word translated *accessible* is in all probability a Canaanite loanword, cognate with Hebrew *pr'* 'to let loose'. The *wells*, so essential to desert travel, were freely available to the envoys who travelled between Egypt and Western Asia.

Lines 47f. refer to two groups, the *Medjay* and the *Tjukten*. The former were originally a Nubian tribe employed as mercenaries by the Egyptians in the New Kingdom, but in the course of time the term came to mean simply 'police, desert troops'. The Tjukten were a type of soldier in the western desert, and the name is preserved in the O.T. as Sukkiim (2 Chr. xii.3).

The final strophe is of greatest interest to O.T. students, for here occurs the only reference to the name *Israel* in any Egyptian inscription.

Lines 49-54. The word rendered by the Arabic *salaam* is another Canaanite loanword, cognate with Hebrew *shālōm* 'peace, well-being', commonly employed as a greeting. The *Nine Bows* is an Egyptian expression for all subjugated peoples. After Libya (Tehenu), mention is made of *Hatti*, the Hittite kingdom, comprising eastern Asia Minor and northern Syria. Next comes *Canaan*, written in the original with the definite article, as elsewhere in Egyptian texts. For Egyptians the name referred to the Palestinian coastal plain and southern Syria. Then follow two Biblical cities, *Ashkelon* (cp. Jud. i.18 ; Zeph. ii.4 ; Zech. ix.5) and *Gezer* (cp. Josh. x.33), and a further town *Yanoam* not mentioned in the O.T., but identified with modern Tell en-Na'meh and located north of the Sea of Galilee.

Lines 55f. *Hurru* was the land of the Hurrians, the Horites of the O.T., and the term was used in Egyptian texts to refer to Palestine and Syria as far north as the Amorite territory. Since *Israel* is here made parallel with Hurru, we may surmise that the former was not an insignificant tribe, but an important and strong people by this time.   However, the fact that the hieroglyphic determinative for people rather than land is used with the name suggests that Israel was not yet permanently settled.   This would fit the O.T. context, for Joshua's campaigns were most probably conducted during the third quarter of the thirteenth century.   The extravagant claims of conquest, however, may be attributed to the exaggeration appropriate to such royal inscriptions.

Line 56, in addition to an apt metaphor, describing Hurru as husbandless, and so lacking a defender against her enemies, contains a clever paronomasia between *kh'rw* 'Hurru' and *kh'rt* 'widow'.

Bibliography

WILSON, J. A., in *A.N.E.T.*, 376ff.

R. J. WILLIAMS

The Hymn to Aten

AT the time when Egypt was at the height of her career as a world power during the New Kingdom, the land was shaken by a revolutionary religious doctrine which threatened to sweep away the theological dogmas of centuries. The key figure in this iconoclastic movement was the Pharaoh Amenhotep IV who came to the throne *c.* 1370 B.C. to reign as co-regent with his father Amenhotep III (*c.* 1397-1360 B.C.). This youth, frail of body, with the temperament of a dreamer and the fanatical zeal of a reformer, inspired the somewhat extravagant description of him as 'the first individual in human history' (J. H. BREASTED). So romantic a figure has he appeared to historians, that many have credited him with originating the worship of the god Aten and establishing the first monotheistic faith.

There is, however, a continually increasing body of evidence which points to the fact that the cult of Aten had developed before the time of Amenhotep IV, indeed probably as early as the reign of Thutmose IV (*c.* 1411-1397 B.C.). It is likely that the worship of Aten developed from the ancient cult of the Heliopolitan sun-god Re. In the course of time the syncretistic character of Egyptian religious thinking had led to the fusion of the god Re with many other deities such as Atum, Horus, and Amun, with the consequent assimilation of their characteristics and functions. The new cult paid homage to the physical orb of the sun (for which the Egyptian word was *aten*), stripped of its mythological accretions. Hence, except in the earliest period, no images or other representations of Aten were employed other than the figure of the sun disc with its rays extending towards the earth, each ending with a hand beneficently proffering the hieroglyphic symbol for life.

The life-giving powers of the sun were emphasised, as was natural in a land which basks continually in sunshine, and where veneration of the sun was basic to religion. As in the earlier Fifth Dynasty temples to Re, worship was conducted under the open sky in the spacious temple courts. This was in marked contrast to the cults of other deities whose worshippers made

their way through the massive halls of their temples in ever increasing darkness, until at last they reached the sacred shrine
or holy of holies, shrouded in total darkness.

Such was the faith that Amenhotep IV espoused. But only
with his accession as co-regent did the new worship constitute a
threat to other cults, when a vicious attack was directed against
the temples and priesthood of Amon-Re, the state god, whose
main sanctuaries were at Thebes, the capital city. The reasons
for this were not merely religious but undoubtedly also political,
for as a result of its excessive wealth and power, the priesthood
of Amon-Re had become a serious threat to the authority and
stability of the throne. This persecution of Amon-Re meant
not only the suppression of the priesthood and worship in his
temples, but also the effacement of the hated name of Amun
wherever it appeared, since the Egyptian regarded the name itself
as possessing the very essence of the one bearing it. Destruction
of the name, then, equally with the defacement of the sculptured
representations of the deity, constituted an effective method of
wiping out the god's existence. Hence the name Amun was
even chiselled out of his father's royal titulary, and his own name
of Amenhotep changed to Akhenaten in acknowledgment of the
new deity.

By his sixth year Akhenaten had found the capital city of
Thebes unbearable, surrounded as he was by the monumental
evidence of the supremacy of Amon-Re. So it was that he
abandoned it to establish a new capital at Tell el-Amarna in
Middle Egypt. Here, on virgin soil, unpolluted by the temple of
any other deity, a new city was built, the remains of which bear
testimony to the hasty manner of its construction. To it he gave
the name Akhetaten, the 'Horizon of Aten'. In this place,
undisturbed by any traces of the Amun cult, he devoted himself
to the contemplation and service of Aten.

We have described the intolerance of the Aten cult as having
been directed mainly against the worship of Amon-Re. There
were sporadic and unsympathetic attempts to curb the worship
of other deities too, but none of these matched the fury of the
onslaught against the state god. Such a zeal for the exclusive
worship of Aten has led many to claim for Akhenaten the title
of the world's first monotheist. However, the evidence is by no
means decisive on this point. Not only was the campaign against

deities other than Amon-Re conducted in a half-hearted manner, but in the prose introduction to the Aten Hymn itself, Aten is equated with the deities Re-Harakhti and Shu, and later in the hymn also with Re. We shall see below that the hymn's claim for the exclusiveness of Aten is only apparent. We would do well to reserve the term monotheism for Hebrew religion and employ for the religion of Akhenaten a less restrictive term such as monolatry, the worship of one god to the exclusion of others, even though their existence be not denied.

Central to the new faith was the idea of 'living on *ma'at*'. This important term *ma'at*, variously translated 'righteousness', 'justice', or 'truth', meant basically the divinely ordained cosmic order. By the Middle Kingdom it had acquired the overtones of social justice. But Akhenaten's use of it emphasised the aspect of truth, by which he meant the subjective truth of the senses rather than the traditional objective, universal truth. This is consonant with the further observation that the Atenist faith was an intellectual rather than an ethical one, a fact which is apparent in the Aten Hymn. This sensual truth manifested itself in a type of realism in art which, in the earlier phases of the movement, was exaggerated to a degree approaching caricature. The Egyptian love of nature reached an even fuller expression in the new naturalistic paintings which clearly betray the influence of Creto-Mycenaean fresco painting.

Noble though this doctrine may have been in many ways, it failed to win the approval or support of any but Akhenaten's circle of courtiers and adherents. To the people, as from time immemorial in Egypt, the Pharaoh was himself a god, and Akhenaten did not seek to alter this. Only he and his family were privileged to offer worship directly to Aten ; the people directed their prayers to the king, and through him the blessings of Aten were vouchsafed to them. It was inevitable that a doctrine of so contemplative and intellectual a nature would be incomprehensible to the common folk who either ignored it or adopted a hostile attitude towards it. This fact, combined with the lack of a spirit of compromise, so essential to the syncretistically-minded Egyptian, spelled disaster for Atenism. Under Akhenaten's co-regent and successor Smenkhkare, perhaps even before the former's death, a movement for reconciliation with the Amon-Re cult began. Before many years had passed, Atenism was forgotten, and the heretic King Akhenaten was anathematised by later generations.

Akhenaten's speculative dreaming had cost Egypt her empire, so hardly won by the daring exploits of Thutmose III and his successors. The idealistic king's preoccupation with his new faith led to the neglect of his Asiatic domains where the machinations of the wily and powerful Hittite ruler Suppiluliumas, aided by the invasions of the Habiru (from whom the later Hebrews probably derived their name), led to the collapse of Egyptian domination in Western Asia. It was not until the time of Ramesses II (c. 1290-1223 B.C.) that Egypt once again assumed her rôle as an imperial world power.

The great Hymn to Aten is a major document of the new faith as well as a fine example of the Egyptian poetic genius. Only a single copy exists, carved in hieroglyphs on a wall in the tomb of Eye at Tell el-Amarna. As a result of acts of vandalism, a portion of the latter part of the hymn has been lost, and we are dependent on a faulty copy made three-quarters of a century ago. A prose introduction, added when the hymn was inscribed in the tomb, has been omitted from the translation.

Text

Thou dost appear beautiful on the horizon of heaven,
   O living Aten, thou who wast the first to live.
When thou hast risen on the eastern horizon,
   Thou hast filled every land with thy beauty.
5 Thou art fair, great, dazzling, high above every land ;
   Thy rays encompass the lands to the very limit of all thou
      hast made.
Being Re, thou dost reach to their limit
   And curb them [for] thy beloved son ;
Though thou art distant, thy rays are upon the earth ;
10   Thou art in their faces, yet thy movements are unknown (?).

When thou dost set on the western horizon,
   The earth is in darkness, resembling death.
Men sleep in the bed-chamber with their heads covered,
   Nor does one eye behold the other.

15 Were all their goods stolen which are beneath their heads,
      They would not be aware of it.
   Every lion has come forth from his den,
      All the snakes bite.
   Darkness prevails, and the earth is in silence,
20   Since he who made them is resting in his horizon.

   At daybreak, when thou dost rise on the horizon,
      Dost shine as Aten by day,
   Thou dost dispel the darkness
      And shed thy rays.
25 The Two Lands are in festive mood,
      Awake, and standing on (their) feet,
   For thou hast raised them up ;
      They cleanse their bodies and take (their) garments ;
   Their arms are (lifted) in adoration at thine appearing ;
30   The whole land performs its labour.

   All beasts are satisfied with their pasture ;
      Trees and plants are verdant.
   The birds which fly from their nests, their wings are (spread) in
         adoration to thy soul ;
      All flocks skip with (their) feet ;
35 All that fly up and alight
      Live when thou hast risen [for] them.
   Ships sail upstream and downstream alike,
      For every route is open at thine appearing.
   The fish in the river leap before thee,
40   For thy rays are in the midst of the sea.

   Thou creator of issue in woman, who makest semen into
         mankind,
      And dost sustain the son in his mother's womb,
   Who dost soothe him with that which stills his tears,
      Thou nurse in the very womb, giving breath to sustain all
         thou dost make !
45 When he issues from the womb to breathe on the day of his birth,
      Thou dost open his mouth completely and supply his needs.
   When the chick in the egg cheeps inside the shell,
      Thou givest it breath within it to sustain it.

Thou hast set it its appointed time in the egg to break it,
50   That it may emerge from the egg to cheep at its appointed
       time ;
       That it may walk with its feet when it emerges from it.

How manifold is that which thou hast made, hidden from view !
   Thou sole god, there is no other like thee !
Thou didst create the earth according to thy will, being alone :
55   Mankind, cattle, all flocks,
Everything on earth which walks with (its) feet,
   And what are on high, flying with their wings.

The foreign lands of Hurru and Nubia, the land of Egypt—
   Thou dost set each man in his place and supply his needs ;
60   Each one has his food, and his lifetime is reckoned.
Their tongues are diverse in speech and their natures likewise ;
   Their skins are varied, for thou dost vary the foreigners.
Thou dost make the Nile in the underworld,
   And bringest it forth as thou desirest to sustain the people,
65 As thou dost make them for thyself,
   Lord of them all, who dost weary thyself with them,
Lord of every land, who dost rise for them,
   Thou Aten of the day, great in majesty.

As for all distant foreign lands, thou makest their life,
70   For thou hast set a Nile in the sky,
That it may descend for them,
   That it may make waves on the mountains like the sea,
   To water their fields amongst their towns.
How excellent are thy plans, thou lord of eternity !
75   The Nile in the sky is for the foreign peoples,
For the flocks of every foreign land that walk with (their) feet,
   While the (true) Nile comes forth from the underworld for
      Egypt.

Thy rays suckle every field ;
   When thou dost rise, they live and thrive for thee.
80 Thou makest the seasons to nourish all that thou hast made :
   The winter to cool them ; the heat that they(?) may taste thee.
Thou didst make the distant sky to rise in it,
   To see all that thou hast made.

Being alone, and risen in thy form as the living Aten,
85   Whether appearing, shining, distant, or near,
Thou makest millions of forms from thyself alone :
    Cities, towns, fields, road, and river.

Every eye perceives thee level with them,
    When thou art the Aten of the day above the earth (?)
90 When thou didst go away because all men existed,
    Thou didst create their faces that thou mightest not see [thy]self
        [alone],
        . . . one . . . which thou didst make.
Thou art in my heart ;
    There is no other that knows thee,
95 Save thy son Akhenaten,
    For thou hast made him skilled in thy plans and thy might.
The earth came into being by thy hand,
    Just as thou didst make them (i.e. mankind).

When thou hast risen, they live ;
100   When thou dost set, they die.
For thou art lifetime thyself ; one lives through thee ;
    Eyes are upon (thy) beauty until thou dost set.
All labour is put aside when thou dost set in the west ;
    When [thou] risest [thou] makest . . . flourish for the king.
105 As for all who hasten on foot,
    Ever since thou didst fashion the earth,
Thou dost raise them up for thy son who came forth from
        thyself,
    The King of Upper and Lower Egypt, Akhenaten.

Notes

The first strophe extols the splendour of *Aten* as he rises in the heavens. *Re*, the sun-god of Heliopolis, is identified with Aten in line 7, in which there is an example of paronomasia between the words r^c ('Re') and r^c ('limit'). Line 8 means that Aten subdues all lands for Akhenaten. The latter part of line 10 is damaged, and the meaning is thus obscure.

The next two strophes describe the terrors of darkness, when Aten is absent from the sky, as contrasted with the joys of day, when he has returned to pour his beneficent rays on the earth. The striking parallelism between this hymn and Ps. civ in the O.T. has frequently been pointed out. That direct influence of an Egyptian work on Hebrew literature is not unknown is clear from the

demonstrable dependence of Prov. xxii.17 to xxiv.22 on passages in the
Egyptian Teaching of Amenemope. Yet we may wonder how a Hebrew poet,
more than half a millennium later.could have become acquainted with the
central document of a religion which later ages execrated and sought to
obliterate from their memory. Despite the complete eclipse of Atenism after
the death of Akhenaten, however, its influence remained in art and literature,
and many of the ideas contained in the Aten Hymn, itself dependent on earlier
models as we shall see, found expression in later religious works. From sources
such as these the Psalmist may well have obtained his inspiration. With lines
11 to 20 may be compared Ps. civ.20f., and lines 21 to 30 with verses 22f.
The Two Lands (line 25) are Upper and Lower Egypt.

The fourth strophe speaks of Aten's life-giving powers in the world of
nature. This interest in nature, evidenced in lines 31 to 40 and 47 to 51, is
not, however, peculiar to the Atenist faith. It was anticipated in the great
Hymn to Amun contained in a papyrus written in the time of Amenhotep II
(*c.* 1436-1411 B.C.), but utilising sources from a still earlier period. In this
composition similar divine benefactions are attributed to the god Amon-Re,

> 'Who made pasture [for] all beasts,
>   And fruit trees for mankind ;
> Who made that on which the fish in the river may live,
>   And the birds that take wing in the sky ;
> Who gives breath to what is in the egg,
>   And sustains the son of the slug ;
> Who makes that on which gnats may live,
>   And worms and flies likewise'.

As we shall see, this is only one of several features in which the Aten Hymn
reflects the thought of the earlier Amun Hymn.

To turn again to the parallelism with Ps. civ, compare lines 31 to 36 with
verses 11-14 and lines 37 to 40 with verses 25f. The word *ka*, rendered 'soul'
in line 33, designates the protective spirit which formed a part of the personality of every individual, whether human or divine, accompanying him through
life and preceding mortals to the other world. It may often correspond to
'vital force', 'appetite', 'desire', or similar concepts.

The fifth and sixth strophes laud Aten as creator of the universe. Lines
52 to 54 recall the words of Ps. civ.24. Line 53 is commonly cited as evidence
for the monotheistic character of the Atenist faith. But it is clear from the
earlier polytheistic Hymn to Amun already quoted that this is a familiar
literary cliché, for we find the latter addressing Amun in even more extravagant terms :

> 'Thou art the sole one, who madest [every]thing,
>   The only sole one, who madest what exists'.

And again :

> 'The only sole one, who has no peer'.

In the seventh strophe Aten is hailed as a universal god, creating and
sustaining all peoples. Once more, this concern of the deity for all mankind,
regardless of race or colour, is not original with the religion of Akhenaten,

for it is also found in the Hymn to Amun, where this deity is identified with the primæval creator god

'Atum, who made the common folk,
Who varied their natures and made their life,
Who diversified their hues, one from the other'.

The Aten Hymn merely continues the New Kingdom tendency to universalism in religion, which was a corollary to Egypt's imperialism in the political sphere.

Hurru (line 58), the land of the Hurrians, familiar from the O.T. as the Horites, refers to the territory of Palestine and Syria at least as far north as Byblus. Hurru and Nubia respectively were the most northerly and southerly lands known to the Egyptians. With lines 59f., cp. Ps. civ.27. Since the Egyptians knew nothing of the sources of the Nile, they regarded it as bubbling up from the subterranean waters they called Nun (line 63). In lines 66 to 68 Aten is described as the evening, morning, and midday sun respectively.

The eighth strophe tells of Aten's concern for foreign lands. Rain was a rare phenomenon in Egypt, and the author thinks of it as the result of a heavenly Nile dropping its waters from on high to the foreign lands beneath, somewhat like the Hebrew concept of waters above the sky which poured through windows or sluices (Gen. vii.11, viii.2 ; Is. xxiv.18, etc.). With lines 70 to 73 again compare Ps. civ.6, 10, 13.

Aten is viewed as the creator of the seasons in the next strophe. The text is damaged and uncertain at the end of line 80. But it is the first part of the tenth strophe which has suffered most from the wanton mutilation of the inscription, and the meaning of the lines escapes us. The statement that Aten was known to Akhenaten alone (lines 93-96) is confirmation of the fact that only he, with his family, could worship Aten directly. In the translation the name Akhenaten has been substituted for the longer titulary of the king. In the final strophe, line 101 recalls Deut. xxx.20. Line 104 has again suffered damage.

Bibliography

GLANVILLE, S. R. K. 'Amenophis III and his Successors in the XVIIIth Dynasty', in *Great Ones of Ancient Egypt*, 1929, 103-39.
PEET, T. E. 'Akhenaten, Ty, Nefertete and Mutnezemt', in *Kings and Queens of Ancient Egypt*, 1925, 81-116.
WILSON, J. A., in *A.N.E.T.*, 369ff.
—— *The Burden of Egypt*, 1951, ch. ix.

R. J. WILLIAMS

A Penitential Psalm

By the time of the Nineteenth Dynasty (*c.* 1304-1181 B.C.), Egypt had fallen on evil days. Her position as a world power was constantly being assailed. The confident optimism of earlier days had given place to apprehension. The rugged individualism, so characteristic of the Old Kingdom and later, was replaced by an authoritarian state in which the individual was submerged. The concept of Fate grew apace and was utilised by the state religion to give cogency to the necessity for abject subservience to the state-imposed order, for this was man's chief end ! It was inevitable that men should seek refuge in 'otherworldliness', looking expectantly toward the joys to be found in the life to come as compensation for their hard life on earth, and that personal piety should become a characteristic of the age. For the first time in Egyptian literature, this sense of frustration and inadequacy expressed itself in confessions of guilt and appeals for divine mercy. A number of stelæ were inscribed with texts calling upon various deities for forgiveness, much in the style of the penitential psalms familiar to us from Mesopotamian and Hebrew literature (e.g. Ps. li).

Whether we are justified in calling such compositions penitential psalms, however, may well be questioned, for they are far removed from their counterparts in Israel or Babylonia. What makes them so basically different in tenor is probably the fact that the Egyptian never achieved a true concept of sin in the O.T. sense. For him evil was not rebellion against the divine command, but merely an aberration from *ma'at*, the cosmic order—it was evidence of ignorance on his part, as expressed in another such text :

> 'An ignorant and foolish man,
> I knew neither good nor evil'.

Hence it is not surprising to find the Egyptian totally devoid of a sense of true contrition.

The stele selected for translation here, now in the Berlin State Museum (No. 20377), was set up during the reign of the Nineteenth Dynasty ruler Ramesses II (*c.* 1290-1223 B.C.) by a crafts-

man of the Theban necropolis, Nebre by name. Like his son
Nakhtamun, Nebre was an outline draughtsman, an artist whose
function was to draw in red on the tomb walls the outline sketches
of the reliefs which the sculptors would then carve. The hieroglyphic text consists of a series of short strophes in poetic form,
interspersed with prose comments. The latter have been omitted
from the translation. The stele was erected as a token of gratitude
for the recovery of Nebre's son from a serious illness. This
calamity was interpreted as the result of an offence, the details
of which are not given, committed in connection with a cow
belonging to the temple herds of the state god Amon-Re.

Text

Giving praises to Amun :
I compose hymns to him in his name,
  I render him praises to the height of heaven
    And to the breadth of earth ;
5   I recount his might to him who sails downstream
    And to him who sails upstream.

Beware of him !
Proclaim him to son and daughter,
  To great and small ;
10 Tell of him to generations of generations
    Which have not yet come into being.

Tell of him to the fish in the deep,
  To the birds in the sky ;
Proclaim him as the one who knows him not
15   And to the one who knows him.
Beware of him !

Thou art Amun, the Lord of the silent man,
  One who comes at the cry of a poor man.
Were I to call upon thee when I am ill,
20 Thou comest, that thou mightest rescue me,
  That thou mightest give breath [to] him who is weak
  And rescue the one who is shut in.

Thou art Amon-Re, Lord of Thebes,
  Rescuer of him who is in the underworld ;
25 Because thou art [merciful (?)],
  When one calls upon thee,
Thou art the one who comes from afar. . . .

Hymns were composed to him in his name,
  Because of the greatness of his might ;
30 Supplications were made to him in his presence,
  Before the whole land,
On behalf of the outline draughtsman Nakhtamun,
    justified,
  While he was lying ill in a state of death,
Being [under] the power of Amun
35   Because of his cow. . . .

The servant was bent on doing wrong,
  Yet the Lord is bent on being merciful.
The Lord of Thebes does not spend a whole day
    angry ;
  As for his anger, in the completion of a moment
    nothing is left.
40 The wind is turned back to us in mercy ;
  Amun has returned with his breezes.
As thy soul endures, thou wilt be merciful,
  We shall not repeat what has been averted. . . .

I will make this stele in thy name,
45   And establish these hymns for thee in writing
    upon it,
Since thou didst rescue the outline draughtsman
    Nakhtamun for me.
Thus I spoke to thee, and thou didst hear me ;
  See ! I am doing what I said.
Thou art the Lord of him who calls upon thee,
50   Contented with justice, the Lord of Thebes.

Notes

Line 1. The god *Amun*, who was fused with the old Heliopolitan sun-god Re in the form *Amon-Re* (line 23), was the deity of the capital city Thebes and the dynastic god of the New Kingdom. As a god who punished the offender, one must beware of him (lines 7, 16).

Lines 7-16. Note how the verbs of the two strophes in these lines are balanced in reverse : 'beware . . . proclaim . . . tell of'.

Line 17. The *silent man* is a concept which becomes increasingly prevalent during the later New Kingdom. Taciturnity was regarded as a virtue and contrasted with the fiery nature of the passionate man in many texts such as the Wisdom of Ani and the Teaching of Amenemope. In such contexts the term 'silent' bore much the same connotation as 'self-controlled, disciplined'. In the view of the state, such discipline should express itself in resignation, in submission to the larger will of the state. Egypt had now come to resemble Mesopotamia which, from time immemorial, because of its constant insecurity, had exalted obedience as the prime virtue. It is for this reason that the penitential psalm, so common in Mesopotamia, only now makes its appearance in Egyptian literature.

Lines 36-9. The belief that man is inherently evil, the god inherently merciful, can be paralleled in many similar Mesopotamian and Hebrew texts (cp. Pss. lxxviii.38f., cxxx.3f.). The sentiment expressed in lines 38f. is echoed in Pss. xxx.5, ciii.9.

Lines 40f. are supplemented by the sentence in one of the prose comments in this same text : 'I found the Lord of the gods coming as the north wind, with pleasant breezes before him'. The north wind was the cooling wind which brought refreshment and healing to Egypt.

Line 42. The word *ka*, conventionally translated 'soul', refers to the incorporeal, protective spirit that was believed to accompany each person throughout his life, forming part of his personality and corresponding in part to the 'vital force'.

Line 50. The word *ma'at*, here rendered by *justice*, expresses a concept basic to Egyptian thinking which might equally well be translated by 'righteousness' or 'truth'.

Bibliography

BLACKMAN, A. M., in *The Psalmists*, ed. D. C. SIMPSON, 1926, 177-97.

GUNN, B. 'The Religion of the Poor in Ancient Egypt,' *J.E.A.* iii (1916) 81-94.

PEET, T. E. *A Comparative Study of the Literatures of Egypt, Palestine, and Mesopotamia* (Schweich Lectures, 1929), 1931, 88ff.

WILSON, J. A., in *A.N.E.T.*, 380f.

R. J. WILLIAMS

The Instruction
for King Meri-ka-re

THE extract which follows is taken from a work composed by an Egyptian king for the benefit of his son Meri-ka-re, who succeeded him on the throne. The name of the father occurred in a damaged part of the text and is lost, but it has been argued with great plausibility that he was Khety II, who bore the throne-name of Wah-ka-re. This king and his son lived in the period of confusion and anarchy known as the First Intermediate Period, which followed the downfall of the Old Kingdom (c. 2280 B.C.) and which preceded the rise of the Middle Kingdom (c. 2000 B.C.). The Old Kingdom was a feudal state, and when it collapsed the powerful barons of Memphis, Herakleopolis and Thebes strove for supremacy. Eventually the dynasty of Thebes won the day and under the second and third Menthuhoteps (c. 2065-2015 B.C.) Egypt was at last brought under one rule. King Khety II and his son Meri-ka-re belonged to the Herakleopolitan dynasty (Manetho's 9th and 10th Dynasties). They reigned c. 2150-2080 B.C., by which time Memphis had come under Herakleopolitan domination and the struggle was now between Herakleopolis in the North and Thebes in the South. Under Khety III, Meri-ka-re's successor, the power finally passed to the kings of Thebes (Manetho's 11th Dynasty). The Instruction for King Meri-ka-re was thus composed in times of violence and intrigue, and it is in this setting that it must be interpreted and understood.

Three copies of the Instruction, all written on papyrus, have survived. The longest and most complete, but which unfortunately has the first twenty lines badly broken, is on the verso of a papyrus in the Hermitage Museum in Leningrad. Another papyrus containing the text belongs to a Moscow museum, while the third, of which only a part has been published, was last heard of in the private possession of a scholar living in Switzerland.

All three papyri can be assigned on palæographical grounds to a date in the middle of the Eighteenth Dynasty, i.e. c. 1450 B.C. The language in which they are written, however, belongs to an earlier period and is, in fact, the language which was spoken and written round about the rise of the Middle Kingdom. There is thus no reason to doubt the authenticity of the Instruction and its royal authorship. Certainly there is no question of its being composed in a later age and attributed to an earlier author in order to give it prestige and dignity, as is sometimes the case with ancient oriental works.

The three extant copies were written some seven hundred years after the Instruction was composed. It must have enjoyed considerable popularity and have been held in high esteem to have survived so long. Inevitably the text has suffered in transmission : this and the fact that it is written in Eighteenth Dynasty orthography, which often confuses words of identical or similar pronunciation, make it an extremely difficult work to translate. Only a good Middle Kingdom manuscript would clarify many of the obscurities in the text as we now know it.

The Old Kingdom was a period of stability and prosperity. It is therefore natural that the teaching of its sages should have been directed towards the advancement of a man's position in life and the increasing of his material well-being in this world. The downfall of the old order and the resultant strife and uncertainty prevalent throughout the First Intermediate Period caused people to think more deeply and to ponder on moral issues as never before. The Instruction for King Meri-ka-re reflects the moods of the times. Parts of it are practical advice on such subjects as the protection of frontiers and the suppression of revolts, but in the main it is concerned with right conduct and just dealings with one's fellow men. The excerpt presented below is a good sample of the advice offered to Meri-ka-re by his father. It illustrates the high moral plane that the Egyptians had already attained by the time Abraham entered Egypt, and it shows also some of the religious and ethical concepts with which the early Semitic migrants into Egypt would come into contact. It is, of course, impossible to say to what extent these early visitors were influenced by Egyptian beliefs, but they may well have played some part in shaping the moral codes of the later inhabitants of Palestine.

The first paragraph of the excerpt here given begins with an exhortation to act justly and kindly in this earthly life. The king should show kindness and consideration to the distressed, the defenceless, and those who are inferior in station. He should be just and sparing in meting out punishment. At this point a note of hardness creeps in, doubtless prompted by bitter personal experience : show no mercy to rebels and traitors. Next the king is warned not to kill an able man, who might be of service to him, or someone whom he has known since his school-days. The point of the last two sentences, which speak of the behaviour of the soul, is obscure.

The first few sentences advising Meri-ka-re to act justly and to protect the oppressed find their parallel in the utterances of the great eighth-century prophets of Israel. Thus Isaiah says : 'Learn to do well ; seek judgement, relieve the oppressed, judge the fatherless, plead for the widow' (i.17). Jeremiah also says : 'Execute ye judgement and righteousness, and deliver the spoiled out of the hand of the oppressor : and do no wrong, do no violence, to the stranger, the fatherless, nor the widow, neither shed innocent blood in this place' (xxii.3). In Ps. lxxxii.3f. we read :—'Judge the poor and fatherless : do justice to the afflicted and destitute. Rescue the poor and needy : deliver them out of the hand of the wicked'. Nearly fifteen hundred years separate the author of the Instruction for Meri-ka-re and these O.T. teachers, but both are motivated by the same humane feelings.

The second paragraph is concerned with the life after death and is one of the most remarkable utterances that have survived from ancient Egypt. From the earliest times the Egyptians had an unshakable belief in the continued existence of the individual after life on this earth had come to an end, and the words of Meri-ka-re's father represent this belief in its purest and loftiest form.

The Egyptians held that not merely a man's soul, but also his personality and whatever other attributes go to make up the individual, lived on after death. In order that they should do so it was necessary that the physical body should be preserved in its entirety. If the body perished, the soul and the other attributes were rendered homeless. Hence enormous care was devoted to the preservation of the body by mummification and to the preparation of a tomb which was intended to be inviolable. The Fourth Dynasty pyramids and the royal tombs hewn in the cliffs of Thebes by the rulers of the Eighteenth Dynasty are examples of the lengths to which Egyptian kings would go to preserve the body. Daily offerings of food and drink were provided by mortuary priests for the benefit of the deceased, and his tomb was equipped with a bed, chairs, linen, games and other furniture so that he could continue his life as on earth.

Side by side with this concept was another. After death the soul would dwell in heaven with the gods and would lead a happy and care-free existence for the rest of time.

In the Old Kingdom the soul's passage to this Elysium was assured by spells. The oldest which have survived are engraved on the walls of the chambers inside pyramids of the Sixth Dynasty kings and are known as the Pyramid Texts. They form an extensive body of texts and are of the greatest value for the study of the early religious beliefs of the Egyptians.

In the troubled times of the First Intermediate Period, when the Instruction for Meri-ka-re was composed, old ideas were challenged. It was no longer felt that entrance to the future paradise was automatic and could be ensured by spells alone. Surely only the righteous could expect to gain admittance. There must be a judgment of the soul, at which man's deeds on earth would be cited in evidence for or against him. If he had proved unworthy of life with the gods he would be rejected.

It is typical of the ancient Egyptians that they never rejected an old concept but grafted the new on to it, however contra-dictory and illogical the result might be. Belief in the efficacy of spells persisted, and out of the Pyramid Texts grew the so-called Coffin Texts of the Middle Kingdom. These texts were written inside the large wooden box-shaped coffins favoured in that period. In the Eighteenth Dynasty a further development took place, and the Coffin Texts were expanded and modified into the 'Book of the Dead', written on papyri and often furnished with illustrations. The Book of the Dead survived till Roman times after undergoing several recensions, and it gave rise to various other works of a similar character. The manuscripts of the Book of the Dead were placed in the tomb with the deceased.

In one of the vignettes of the Book of the Dead we get further information about the judgment of the soul as it was visualised some six or seven centuries after Meri-ka-re. Osiris presides over a conclave of forty-two judges. The heart of the deceased is weighed in a balance against the symbol of truth. A monster, half crocodile and half hippopotamus, waits to devour the soul which has been found wanting. The god Thoth notes the result on a scroll. It is clear that by this time the purity of the earlier belief had become tarnished. Funerary stelæ of the period show, however, that poor people, who could not afford the expensive manuscripts of the Book of the Dead and the elaborate ritual of spells, still believed that personal righteousness and just dealings would secure them a place with the gods in the next world. Thus the teaching of the great thinkers and moralists of the First Intermediate Period was not in vain.

The Hebrew attitude to the hereafter contrasts strangely with that of the Egyptians. Life after death is seldom mentioned in the O.T., whereas almost every Egyptian text of any length, whatever its nature, contains some reference to it. The Egyptian looked forward to a full and happy life in the next world, whereas the Hebrews expected nothing but a colourless and gloomy existence in Sheol. This is expressed most forcefully by the writer of Ecclesiastes :—'but the dead know not any thing, neither have they any more a reward ; for the memory of them is forgotten. As well their love, as their hatred and their envy, is now perished ; neither have they any more a portion for ever in any thing that is done under the sun' (ix.5f.). And again :—'for there is no work, nor device, nor knowledge, nor wisdom, in the grave, whither thou goest' (ix.10). The Egyptians looked forward to an existence in the company of the gods, but the Hebrews regarded death as the severance of all connection with God. Thus in Ps. vi.5 we find :—'For in death there is no remembrance of thee : in Sheol who shall give thee thanks ?' and is Ps. lxxxviii.4f. :—'I am counted with them that go down into the pit ; I am as a man that hath no help. Cast off among the dead, like the slain that lie in the grave, whom thou rememberest no more ; and they are cut off from thy hand'. Hezekiah, after his recovery from sickness, says :—'For the grave cannot praise thee, death cannot celebrate thee : they that go down into the pit cannot hope for thy truth. The living, the living, he shall praise thee, as do I this day' (Is. xxxviii.18f.).

It is indeed strange that the beliefs of their cultured and powerful neighbours had so little influence on the Hebrews. It may well be that by O.T. times the nobler concepts of the earlier periods had become so encrusted with magic, and the cult of the dead and the concern for the preservation of the mortal remains were so much to the fore, that the Hebrews found nothing to attract them in the Egyptian attitude to death.

In ancient Egypt there were no religious teachers comparable in function with the prophets of the Hebrews. From time to time, however, great thinkers arose and their utterances were carefully committed to writing. Their precepts and their teaching were treasured throughout the centuries and their names were remembered for generations after their death. Like the Hebrew prophets they had a profound influence upon the religious, moral and ethical beliefs of their countrymen. The author of the Instruction for King Meri-ka-re was one such.

Text

DO JUSTICE SO LONG AS THOU ABIDEST ON EARTH. Calm the weeper and oppress not the widow. Do not oust a man from the property of his father. Do not harm officials in respect of their posts.[1] Beware of punishing wrongfully. Do not kill : it shall not profit thee. Punish with caution [2] by beatings—so shall this country [3] be peaceful—except (for) the rebel when his plans have been discovered, for God knows the treacherous of heart, and God requiteth his sins in blood. It is the mild man who . . . . . . a lifetime. Do not slay a man whose good qualities thou knowest, one with whom thou didst chant the writings [4] and read in the inventory. . . . . God, bold of thy step in difficult places. The soul cometh to the place it knoweth : it cannot stray from the paths of yesterday and no magic can oppose it. It cometh to those that give it water.

THE JUDGES [5] WHO JUDGE THE DEFICIENT, thou knowest that they are not lenient on that day of judging the miserable, in the hour of performing (their) duty. It is hard when the accuser is possessed of knowledge.[6] Put not thy trust in length of years [7] : they regard a lifetime as an hour. A man surviveth after death and his deeds are placed beside him in heaps. Eternal is the existence yonder. He who makes light of it is a fool. As for him who reaches it without doing wrong, he shall exist yonder like a god, striding forth like the Lords of Eternity.

Notes

In the Leningrad Papyrus (the only one in which this portion of the text is fully preserved), the first sentence of each of the two paragraphs is written in red. Capitals are used here to reproduce these headings.

[1] *posts*. The Egyptian word is of uncertain meaning and the translation is a guess.

[2] *caution*. The meaning of the Egyptian word is uncertain.

[3] *this country* is a common expression for Egypt, exactly as 'this country' is used by Englishmen in speaking of England.

[4] *with whom thou didst chant the writings*. This expression seems to mean 'with whom you were at school'.

[5] The *Judges* are a tribunal of gods who judge the dead and decide their fate on the basis of their behaviour whilst on earth.

[6] *It is hard when the accuser is possessed of knowledge*, i.e. when the accuser is armed with facts detrimental to the dead person appearing before the divine judges it goes ill with him.

[7] *Put not thy trust in length of years*. However long it may be since a sin was committed, the accuser and the judges will remember.

Bibliography

BREASTED, J. H.   *The Dawn of Conscience*, 1953.

BUDGE, E. A. WALLIS.   *The Mummy*, second ed., 1925.

ERMAN, A.   *The Literature of the Ancient Egyptians*, 1927, 75-84.

GARDINER, A. H.   'New Literary Works from Ancient Egypt,' *J.E.A.* i (1914) 20-36.

SCHARFF, A.   *Der historische Abschnitt der Lehre für König Merikare* (*Sitzungsberichte der Bayerischen Akademie der Wissenschaften, Philosophisch-historische Abteilung*, 1936, Heft 8).

WILSON, J. A., in *A.N.E.T.*, 414-18.

T. W. THACKER

A Dispute over Suicide

THE name of the author of 'A Dispute over Suicide' has not survived. The text is written in hieratic on a papyrus in the Berlin Museum : no other copies are known. The handwriting dates the papyrus to the Middle Kingdom (*c.* 2000-1740 B.C.). It seems probable that the work was composed a few hundred years previously in the First Intermediate Period (*c.* 2280-2000 B.C.), like the Instruction for King Meri-ka-re, when the troubled times caused men to reassess religious and ethical beliefs.

The beginning of the papyrus is missing, but probably not much has been lost. As it has come down to us, the papyrus contains one hundred and fifty-five vertical lines of text, each of about eight words. Thus it would compare in length with one of the shortest books of the O.T.

The 'Dispute' is in the form of a dialogue between an unnamed man, who is weary of life, and his soul. The man speaks in the first person and tries to convince his soul of the desirability of suicide and death. The course of the argument is difficult to follow and the text is very obscure in places, especially the first half where there are parables and metaphors, the point of which often escapes the modern reader. It seems not improbable that the man consistently argues in favour of suicide while his soul attempts throughout to dissuade him, but such is the difficulty of the text that sometimes the attitude of the soul is not clear and scholars hold varying views on the tenor of some of its speeches.

It is impossible to say whether there was an introductory prologue which gave the circumstances of the dispute and which may have mentioned the author's name. In its present mutilated form the papyrus begins with a speech in which the man rebukes his soul for not agreeing to suicide. This is followed by a curt rejoinder on the part of the soul, after which the man makes another speech of some length. The soul's reply begins the excerpt given here : only the first part of it is translated. Up till now the dialogue has been in prose, but at this point the man breaks into verse and his speech contains some thirty-three stanzas, not all of which are translated. The papyrus ends with a brief reply by the soul. In the translation capitals denote words written in red ink.

'A Dispute over Suicide' is remarkable for the extreme views it puts forward. The Egyptians were a happy, light-hearted people, fond of the pleasures of this world ; yet they were not afraid of death. Indeed, they regarded it as an extension of this earthly life, where they would continue to enjoy themselves—if anything to a greater degree than on earth. In the 'Dispute', however, we find the man disillusioned and weary of life, while his soul takes an equally gloomy view of death. The author is clearly challenging the accepted attitudes and beliefs of his day.

The O.T. scholar who reads 'A Dispute over Suicide' is at once reminded of the book of Job. In both works the principal character is a man of gentle and retiring disposition, imbued with a spirit of pessimism. Job, however, is weighed down by his own misfortunes, while his Egyptian counterpart is mainly dismayed by prevailing social conditions.

The use of dialogue to treat a philosophical and religious problem is followed by the author of the book of Job in his presentation of the problem of suffering more than fifteen hundred years later. In the book of Job the technique is much more highly developed than in 'A Dispute over Suicide', where we see the beginnings of this literary genre. There are more characters in the drama and greater use of verse is made. Altogether the book of Job is a much finer and more finished work of art.

The book of Job is unique of its kind in Hebrew literature, but other compositions in the form of dialogue, such as the 'Story of the Eloquent Peasant', were produced in ancient Egypt. Nevertheless it would be unwise to assume that the author of the book of Job has taken over an Egyptian medium and perfected it. Only a small portion of Hebrew literature has survived, and we cannot be sure that the book of Job has not been modelled on lost Hebrew antecedents.

We cannot therefore claim any direct connection between 'A Dispute over Suicide' and the book of Job, but comparison of the two works affords interesting parallels.

Text

My soul opened its mouth to me that it might answer what I had said. If thou recallest burial, it is a sad matter. It is the bringing of tears, making a man sad. It is dragging a man from his house and casting him on the hillside. Thou shalt never go up that thou mayest see the sun. Those who built in granite [1] and who hewed chambers in fine pyramid(s) with good work, when the builders became gods their offering stelæ [2] were destroyed like (those of) the weary ones that died on the dyke, through lack of a survivor, the water having taken its toll, and the sun likewise to whom the fishes of the river banks talk. Listen to me. Behold it is good for men to listen. Follow pleasure and forget care. . . .

I opened my mouth to my soul that I might answer what it had said.

> Behold my name stinks
>> Behold more than the stench of fish
>> On a summer's day when the sky is hot. . . .
> Behold my name stinks
>> Behold more than a woman,
>> About whom a lie has been told to a man.
> Behold my name stinks
>> Behold more than a sturdy lad
>> About whom it is said 'He belongs to his rival'. [3]

> To whom shall I speak today?
>> Brothers are evil,
>> The companions of yesterday do not love.
> To whom shall I speak today?
>> Hearts are rapacious,
>> Every man seizes the goods of his neighbour . . .
> To whom shall I speak today?
>> Men are contented with evil,
>> Goodness is neglected everywhere.
> To whom shall I speak today?
>> One who should make a man enraged by his evil
>> behaviour
>> Makes everyone laugh, though his iniquity is
>> grievous. . . .

To whom shall I speak today?
  The wrongdoer is an intimate,
  The brother with whom one should act is become
      an enemy.
To whom shall I speak today?
  Yesterday is not remembered,
  No one now helps him that hath done (good).
To whom shall I speak today?
  Faces are averted,
  Every man has (his) face downcast towards his
      brethren.
To whom shall I speak today?
  Hearts are rapacious,
  No man has a heart upon which one can rely.
To whom shall I speak today?
  There are no righteous men.
  The land is left over to workers of iniquity. . . .
To whom shall I speak today?
  I am laden with misery
  Through lack of an intimate.
To whom shall I speak today?
  The sin that roams the land,
  It has no end.
Death is in my sight today
  (Like) the recovery of a sick man,
  Like going abroad after detention.
Death is in my sight today
  Like the smell of myrrh,
  Like sitting under an awning on a windy day.
Death is in my sight today
  Like the scent of lotus flowers,
  Like sitting on the bank of drunkenness.
Death is in my sight today
  Like a well trodden way,
  As when a man returns home from an expedition.
Death is in my sight today
  Like the clearing of the sky,
  Like a man attracted thereby to what he knows not.
Death is in my sight today
  Like the longing of a man to see home,

When he has spent many years held in captivity.
Surely he who is yonder [4] shall
    Be a living god,
    Punishing the sin of him who commits it.
Surely he who is yonder shall
    Stand in the barque of the sun,
    Causing the choicest things to be given therefrom
      to the temples.
Surely he who is yonder shall
    Be a man of knowledge,
    Who cannot be prevented from petitioning Re
      when he speaks.

What my soul said to me. Put care aside, my comrade and brother. Make an offering on the brazier and cling to life, according as I (?) have said.[5] Desire me here and reject the West, but desire to reach the West when thy body goes into the earth, that I may alight after thou hast grown weary.[6] Then let us make an abode together.

IT IS FINISHED FROM ITS BEGINNING TO ITS END, AS IT WAS FOUND IN WRITING.

Notes

[1] *Those who built in granite* refers to the kings and nobles of the Old Kingdom who built the great pyramids and who erected fine tombs for themselves in order that their mortal remains should be preserved for ever. Preservation of the physical body was essential for life after death. The sense of the passage is that these kings and nobles are now no better off than poor men who died in the open, without shelter and without relatives to perform the mortuary rites for them. Soon after the great ones *became gods* (i.e. died), their pyramids and tombs were plundered and their offering stelæ were destroyed, thus reducing them to the level of the paupers.

[2] *offering stelæ* were necessary for the mortuary cult. It was believed that the deceased needed food and drink after death. Stelæ were erected on the outside of the tomb, at which such offerings were made. The wealthy endowed mortuary priests to make the offerings daily while the less fortunate relied on relatives and friends.

[3] *his rival*, i.e. the lad's father's rival for his mother's affections. The imputation levelled against the lad is that he is a bastard.

[4] *he who is yonder* is a euphemism for 'the dead'.

[5] *as I (?) have said.* The original has 'as you have said'. The pronoun of the second person is emended to that of the first person.

[6] *grown weary* is a euphemism for 'died'; cp. earlier in the text *like (those of) the weary ones that died on the dyke.*

Bibliography

ERMAN, E.   *The Literature of the Ancient Egyptians*, 1927, 86-92.

FAULKNER, R.   'The Man Who Was Tired of Life', *J.E.A.* xlii (1956) 21-40.

PEET, T. E.   *A Comparative Study of the Literatures of Egypt, Palestine, and Mesopotamia* (Schweich Lectures 1929), 1931, 114-17.

WILSON, J. A., in *A.N.E.T.*, 405ff.

T. W. THACKER

The Tale of the Two Brothers

ONE episode in the Egyptian story 'The Tale of the Two Brothers' has often been compared with the story of Joseph and Potiphar's wife (Gen. xxxix), but it would require much greater similarity of detail between the Egyptian and the Hebrew stories to justify the oft-made suggestion that the Egyptian story is the origin of the incident described in Genesis. Further, parallels to the story can be quoted from the literature of other peoples (cp. the Greek story of the love of Phaedra, the wife of Theseus, for Hippolytus, her husband's son).

'The Tale of the Two Brothers' exists in only one manuscript, Papyrus 10183 in the British Museum, usually known, from the name of its former owner, as the D'Orbiney papyrus. The manuscript is complete, well preserved, and is one of the most beautifully written papyri in hieratic which have survived from antiquity. The colophon at the end of the papyrus makes it clear that the papyrus was written as a literary exercise by the pupil-scribe Ennana, and this fact probably explains the presence of a number of corrupt passages in the text. In some short jottings at the end of the papyrus appears the name of the Crown Prince Sethoy-Meneptah, and from this it may be inferred that the manuscript was written c. 1210 B.C.

The complete tale is a strange mixture of various elements, including folklore and mythology. The two brothers bear the names of gods, and, although at the beginning of the story the scene is laid in an ordinary Egyptian village, the action passes quickly into the realm of faerie where wonderful trees bloom, oxen speak, the Fates prophesy, and marvellous things happen. The purpose of the tale is primarily entertainment.

When the story opens, the reader is told how two brothers, Anupu and Bata, are living together in a village, both going out daily to cultivate their fields. Of the two brothers, Anupu only is married. The extract translated below describes the wife's attempt to seduce her brother-in-law and the flight of the falsely accused Bata. Anupu is prevented by the Sun-god from killing his brother. Bata is able to convince his brother of his innocence, whereupon Anupu returns home and kills his wife. From this point onward the story becomes increasingly an account of those supernatural wonders which are so marked a feature of folklore.

Text

After many days after this they were in the field, and they were in need of seed. Whereupon he (Anupu) sent his younger brother, saying, 'Go, fetch seed for us from the village.' His brother found his elder brother's wife sitting having her hair dressed.[1] Then he said to her, 'Get up, give me seed that I may away, because it is for me my brother is waiting. Do not delay.'

But she said to him, 'Go away. Open the bin and take for yourself what you require. Do not interrupt me in the middle of my hairdressing.'

Then the youth entered his cattle byre and brought out a large vessel, it being his intention to carry away a great quantity of seed. He loaded himself with barley and wheat, and went out bearing them.

Then she said to him, 'How much is that which is upon your shoulder?'

He said to her, 'Three measures of wheat and two measures of barley,[2] five in all upon my shoulder.' So he said to her.

Then she [conversed with] him, saying, 'Indeed, there is great strength in you, for I see your feats of strength daily.' She desired to know him [3] as a male is known.

Whereupon she stood holding on to him,[4] and saying to him, 'Come, let us pass an hour sleeping together. If this pleases you, then I will make beautiful clothes for you.'

Then the youth became like a panther of Southern Egypt for anger because of the evil speech which she uttered to him. She was very much afraid. Then he reasoned with her,[5] saying, 'See, you are like a mother to me. Moreover your husband is like a father to me. He who is my elder is he who has brought me up. What is this great crime which you have said to me? Do not mention it again. I will not tell it to anyone. I will not disclose it to anyone.' He lifted up his burden and took himself off to the field. Then he reached his elder brother, and they continued to work at their task.

Now afterwards at evening his elder brother returned to his

house, while his younger brother rounded up his cattle, and loaded himself with all manner of field produce, and drove his cattle before him to bed them down in their byre which was in the village.

As for his brother's wife, she was afraid because of the utterance which she had spoken.   Whereupon she fetched fat and *pdr*.[6]   She pretended to be like one who has been beaten, with the intent of saying to her husband, 'It was your brother who beat me.'

When her husband came home at evening as was his daily custom, he drew near to his house, and he found his wife lying down feigning sickness.   She did not pour water upon his hands as was her custom, nor had she lit the lamp for him.   His house was in darkness, and she lay retching.   Her husband said to her, 'Who has had words with you ?'   Then she said to him, 'No one has quarrelled with me except your brother.   For when he came to fetch the seed for you, he found me sitting by myself.   He said to me, "Come, let us spend an hour sleeping together.   Bind up your ringlets."   So said he.   I would not listen to him.   "Lo, am I not your mother ?   And as for your elder brother, he is like a father."   So I said to him.   He was afraid, and he beat me that I should not tell you.   But if you allow him to live, I will kill myself.   Look to it when he comes at evening.   Do not listen to him.   For if I were to repeat this evil accusation, he would have treated it as an injury.'   [7]

Then his elder brother became like a leopard of Southern Egypt.[8]   He sharpened his spear.   He took it in his hand.   Then he stood behind the door of his byre in order to kill his younger brother when he came at evening to drive his cattle into the byre.

When the sun set he (the younger brother) loaded himself with all manner of field produce, as was his daily custom and came home.   The first cow entered the byre.   She said to her herdsman, 'Look, your elder brother standing in front of you, carrying his spear to kill you.   Flee from him.'   When therefore he heard what the first of his cattle said, and that the next one went in and said the same, he looked under the door of his byre.[9]   He saw the feet of his elder brother as he stood behind the door with his spear in his hand.   He laid down his burden on the ground, and took to speedy flight.   His elder brother went after him with his spear.

Notes

[1] *having her hair dressed.* Translators of this text have almost without exception rendered the Egyptian as meaning that Anupu's wife was herself arranging her hair. The verbal form in the original clearly implies that she was being assisted in this task. The coiffure of an Egyptian woman usually consisted of a large number of very small plaits, which required several hours to arrange. It may be noted that, when Anupu questioned his wife later in the story, she makes no mention of her hairdressing and claims to have been alone. The reader is left in no doubt that the woman was a liar as well as a would-be adulteress.

[2] *Three measures of wheat and two measures of barley.* A considerable load, about 600 lbs. in all.

[3] Cp. Gen. xxxix.7.

[4] Cp. Gen. xxxix.12.

[5] It is noteworthy that in the Egyptian story Bata refuses to comply with his sister-in-law's demand on the grounds of social impropriety. There is no reference to sin against God as in Gen. xxxix.9.

[6] The word *pdr* does not occur elsewhere in Egyptian. It has been compared with the Hebrew *peder* 'suet' (Lev. i.8, 12, viii.20 ; E.V. 'fat'). The suggestion has been made that Anupu's wife swallowed fat and suet to make herself sick. An objection to this interpretation is that the determinative sign after *pdr* is not that which would be expected after a word meaning a fatty substance. The sign used is a loop of cord. A possible comparison with the Hebrew *pāthīl*, meaning 'a cord', would lend some weight to the suggestion that the woman marked her body by means of fat and a twisted cord to simulate the weals of a beating.

[7] The meaning of this sentence is very uncertain.

[8] Cp. Gen. xxxix.19, where Potiphar is enraged on hearing his wife's false accusation against Joseph.

[9] The lower edge of the Egyptian door very rarely touched the sill. In most paintings in which the door is represented there is a considerable space between the lower edge and the ground level. It was therefore possible for Bata to see that his brother was concealed behind the door of the byre.

Bibliography

ERMAN, A. *The Literature of the Ancient Egyptians*, 1927, 150ff.

LEWIS, B. *Land of Enchanters*, 1948, 55ff. (The translation by BATTISCOMBE GUNN is especially good, accuracy and a lively and racy style being happily combined.)

MASPERO, G. *Popular Stories of Ancient Egypt* (Translated by Mrs. C. H. W. JOHNS), 1915, 1-20.

PEET, T. E. *A Comparative Study of the Literatures of Egypt, Palestine, and Mesopotamia* (Schweich Lectures 1929), 1931, 43ff.

PETRIE, W. FLINDERS. *Egyptian Tales* (Second Series. Based on a translation and notes by F. LL. GRIFFITH), 1924, 36ff.

WILSON, J. A., in *A.N.E.T.*, 23ff

J. M. PLUMLEY

The Teaching of Amenemope
(Plate 9)

THE literary remains of the ancient Egyptians reveal that didactic treatises containing wise maxims and proverbial truths were very greatly to their taste. It had long been suspected that for some, at least, of the Hebrew proverbs, models had been provided by this Wisdom Literature, but it was not until the publication of the 'Teaching of Amenemope' that definite evidence to support this conjecture was forthcoming. A number of passages in the Egyptian text were then seen to be so remarkable in resemblance to passages in the book of Proverbs that, even if it could not be proved that the Hebrew borrowed directly from the Egyptian, or *vice versa*, nevertheless there could be little doubt that both were essentially related. It has been suggested that an international, pan-oriental, common stock of proverbial literature existed in the ancient Near East. Certainly the resemblances between Amenemope's work and the book of Proverbs indicate that the proverbial literature of O.T. times knew no national boundaries.

The papyrus roll containing the 'Teaching of Amenemope' was secured for the British Museum in 1888 by the Egyptologist, Sir ERNEST WALLIS BUDGE, during his first mission to Egypt. It was not, however, until 1922 that he gave an account of the text with short extracts. In the following year the complete text was published by him in the *Second Series of Facsimiles of Egyptian Hieratic Papyri in the British Museum*. In this publication, and in a popular edition of the text printed in 1924, BUDGE drew attention to the resemblance of some passages in the 'Teaching' to verses in Proverbs. In the same year the German Egyptologist, ADOLF ERMAN, issued a revised translation, and communicated an important paper to the Prussian Academy in which he confirmed what BUDGE had been the first to point out. He further demonstrated that one section of Proverbs in particular (xxii.17-xxiv.22) was most closely paralleled by the text of Amenemope. He was able from the Egyptian to elucidate the meaning of a Hebrew word in Prov. xxii.20 which had puzzled translators since the time of the LXX, and had led to a number of conjectural interpretations. ERMAN showed that the Hebrew word *shilshōm*, translated in the R.V. 'excellent things' (margin 'heretofore'), means simply 'thirty'. He considered this to be a meaningless survival in its new context. But the explanation is that, just as Amenemope had arranged his 'Teaching' in thirty chapters, so the Hebrew writer of the third section of Proverbs retained the number in reference to the thirty subsections, of roughly four verses each, into which the section seems to be divisible.

The 'Teaching' is written in hieratic on the recto side of the British Museum Papyrus No. 10474. The text, which is complete, contains five hundred and fifty-one lines, divided into twenty-seven columns, each containing from nineteen to twenty-three lines of text. As noted above, Amenemope divided his 'Teaching' into thirty chapters. The number of lines in each chapter varies between six and thirty-six. All the chapters, with one exception, contain an even number of lines. The basic structure is the couplet, and, as in Hebrew, poetical effect is produced by parallelism. The couplets can often be grouped into larger divisions, the commonest being the quatrain, a form which, significantly, is characteristic of the section of Proverbs most closely resembling the 'Teaching'.

Translation of the 'Teaching' is difficult for several reasons, and, until Egyptian lexicography is further advanced, modern translations must be regarded as still provisional. The text abounds in rare and poetical words and idioms. The phraseology is concise. The sentences are short and disconnected, and the sense of many passages is not helped by inexact and unusual spellings. A short extract from the 'Teaching' exists on a wooden tablet at Turin. The unmistakable instances of scribal error in the sections preserved on this tablet provide a warning that modern translators must reckon with the probability of errors elsewhere in the text.

The date of the British Museum text is open to question. Suggested dates range from c. 1000 B.C. to c. 600 B.C. An unpublished ostracon in the Cairo Museum, which contains an extract from Amenemope, can be dated with some certainty to the latter half of the Twenty-first Dynasty (c. 1100-946 B.C.). The fact that part of the 'Teaching' was written on an ostracon, probably by a pupil-scribe, is good grounds for thinking that the 'Teaching' had already been in existence for some time. Possibly the original work was written at the end of the Eighteenth or the beginning of the Nineteenth Dynasty (c. 1300 B.C.), when contact between Egypt and Syria was particularly close. This date for the composition of the 'Teaching' gains some support from the fact that the work differs to a marked degree from earlier Egyptian didactic books which are almost entirely materialistic in outlook. In contrast, the 'Teaching' lays special emphasis on the practice of religious piety and moral rectitude, and at least one modern Egyptologist has ventured to state that, in spite of the instances of popular superstitions used by Amenemope to enforce his ideas, his theology is essentially monotheistic.

Amenemope has a special message to convey. Morality matters, and the source of true morality is religion. To the obedient reader of his book he promises both success in life and moral well-being. His ideal is tranquillity. The tranquil man, the truly silent man, is commended as being content with his lot, pious, and benevolent, whereas the hot-head, the passionate, vicious man is condemned for being noisy, unscrupulous, grasping, a nuisance to his fellows, and led into evil by his uncontrolled ambition.

The 'Teaching of Amenemope' has already resolved some of the difficulties in the text of Proverbs and has provided a basis for some possible, even likely, emendations. Indeed in some instances the Egyptian has confirmed some emendations suggested long before the 'Teaching' was known. With a growing understanding of Egyptian, especially in the field of lexicography, further valuable assistance may be reasonably expected in the elucidation of some of the difficulties in Proverbs which still remain unexplained.

The length of the 'Teaching' is such that only a selection of passages from it is possible here. Strictly, only those which bear directly upon the O.T. text should be quoted. But in order to avoid a patchwork appearance, which isolated maxims from the text would inevitably produce, several chapters are set out in full. From these the reader can gain some impression of the form and character of the 'Teaching'. Though, in the main, attention is drawn to comparisons between the Egyptian text and the book of Proverbs, reference is also made to general resemblances in other books of the O.T.

Text

PREFACE

The beginning of instruction on how to live,
Guidance for well-being ;
Every direction for consorting with elders,
Rules for a courtier ;
5 Ability to refute him who uttereth an accusation,
And to bring back a report to one who hath sent him.
To direct him to the path of life,
To make him prosper upon the earth ;
To let his heart go into its shrine,
10 Steering him clear of evil ;
To save him from the mouth of strangers,
Praised in the mouth of men.

Notes

This introductory section appears to consist of two stanzas of six lines, the first promising a guide to worldly prosperity, the second to moral well-being.

Lines 5f. Cp. Prov. xxii.21. On the basis of the Egyptian the M.T. may be emended to read : 'That thou mayest make known the truth to him that speaketh ; that thou mayest carry back reliable words to him that sent thee'.

Line 7. Cp. Prov. xxii.19b. The difficulty of the final words in the R.V., 'Even to thee', can be resolved if the M.T. is emended on the basis of the Egyptian to read : 'I have made thee know today the path of life'. Additional support for this emendation is provided by the LXX which has : 'And that thou mayest know the way'. The expression 'the way of life' occurs elsewhere in Proverbs (ii.14, v.6, xv.24).

Line 9. That is, to enable him to retain his composure. During the latter half of the New Kingdom the funerary scarab representing the heart was often placed in a shrine-shaped pectoral.

Text

HE SAYS : FIRST CHAPTER

Give thine ears, hear what is said,
Give thy mind to interpret them.
To put them in thy heart is beneficial ;
It is detrimental for him who neglecteth them.
5 Let them rest in the casket of thy belly,
That they may be a *pnat* in thy heart.
Even when there is a whirlwind of words,
They shall be a mooring-stake for thy tongue.
If thou spendest thy lifetime while this is in thy heart,
10 Thou wilt find it a success,
Thou wilt find my words a treasury of life ;
Thy body will prosper upon earth.

Notes

Lines 1ff. Cp. Prov. xxii.17-18a (also Ps. lxxviii.1). *mind . . . heart.* Amenemope uses two words, *heti* and *yib.* In the translation the former is rendered by 'mind' and the latter by 'heart'. In later forms of Egyptian, *heti* was used to mean both 'mind' and 'heart'.

Line 5f. *belly.* The meaning is 'inmost soul'. *pnat.* The meaning is uncertain. Suggested translations are 'threshold', 'key'.

Line 8. Cp. Prov. xxii.18b. On the basis of the Egyptian, 'together' of R.V. may be emended to mean '(as) a peg'.

Text

SECOND CHAPTER

Guard thyself against robbing the wretched
And against being puissant over the man of broken
    arm.
Stretch not forth thy hand to repel an old man,
Nor anticipate the aged.
5 Let not thyself be sent on a wicked mission,
Nor love him who hath performed it.
Cry not out against him whom thou hast injured,
Nor answer him back to justify thyself.

He who hath done evil, the river-bank abandons
  him,
10 And his flooded land carries him away.
  The north wind cometh down that it may end his
    hour ;
  It is united to the tempest ;
  The thunder is loud, and the crocodiles are evil.
  O hot-head, what is thy condition ?
15 He is crying out, his voice to heaven.
  O Moon, arraign his crime !
  Steer that we may ferry the wicked man across,
  For we shall not act like him—
  Lift him up, give him thy hand ;
20 Leave him (in) the hands of the god ;
  Fill his belly with bread that thou hast,
  So that he may be sated and may cast down his
    eye.

Notes

Lines 1f. Cp. Prov. xxii.22. *The man of broken arm*, i.e. helpless ; cp. a similar use in Hebrew in reference to the weakness of Pharaoh (Ezek. xxx.21f., 24) and of Moab (Jer. xlviii.25).

Line 4. *anticipate*, i.e. not allowing the aged to speak.

Line 9. *the river-bank abandons him*. Perhaps the meaning is that it crumbles away under his feet because it has been weakened by the inundation.

Line 16. *O Moon*. The moon was the symbol of Thoth, the Ibis-headed god who presided at the Judgement of the Dead when a man's heart was weighed against the feather of Truth. The scene is often depicted in copies of the Book of the Dead.

Lines 17-22. This remarkable passage is in striking contrast to the *lex talionis* of ancient times.

Line 18. Cp. Prov. xxiv.29.

Line 20. Cp. Deut. xxxiii.27.

Line 21f. Cp. Prov. xxv.21. *cast down his eye*, i.e. be ashamed.

Text

FOURTH CHAPTER

As for the hot-headed man in a temple,
He is like a tree growing in an enclosed space.
A moment completeth its loss of foliage.
Its end is reached in the *makherma*.
5 It is sunk far from its place ;
The flame is its burial shroud.
The truly silent man, he withdraweth himself
    apart.
He is like a tree growing in a plot.
It groweth green and doubleth its yield ;
10 It is before its lord.
Its fruit is sweet ; its shade is pleasant.
Its end is reached in the grove.

Notes

This Chapter of the 'Teaching' contains striking resemblances to Ps. i and Jer. xvii.5-8.

In spite of some difficulties of vocabulary the general meaning of the Chapter is clear. In two six-lined stanzas the fates of the man of unrestrained temper and the self-controlled man, both engaged in the service of the temple, are contrasted.

Lines 2-5. *enclosed space.* Perhaps the Egyptian should be emended to read 'forest', which would suit the comparison between a wild tree and one cultivated in a garden. *foliage.* The meaning is uncertain. The form of the Egyptian word suggests a Semitic original. *makherma.* Suggested translations are 'shipyard, dockyard'. The Demotic *mkhr* or *mkhy* meaning 'storehouse' may, however, be compared. *It is sunk*, perhaps in the sense of waterlogged and floated away.

Line 8. *plot.* The meaning is uncertain. In Egypt trees were planted in pits surrounded by raised rims to retain water. Possibly such a pit is meant.

Line 10. Cp. line 5, where the tree is lost *far from its place.*

Line 12. *the grove.* The underlying idea is the garden of trees in the realm of the blessed dead. In contrast to line 6, where the burial shroud of the hot-headed man is the destroying flame, the self-controlled man may expect after death revivification in the garden of the gods. The Egyptian word, here translated 'grove', implies a number of meanings all associated with a goodly burial in contrast to the miserable end of the man of unrestrained passion.

Text

SIXTH CHAPTER

Remove not the landmark at the boundaries of
    the arable land,
Nor disturb the position of the measuring-cord ;
Covet not a cubit of land,
Nor throw down the boundaries of a widow . . .
5 Beware of throwing down the boundaries of the
    fields,
Lest a terror carry thee off . . . .
Better is poverty in the hand of the god
Than riches in a storehouse ;
Better is bread, when the heart is happy,
10 Than riches with vexation.

Notes

Lines 1-4. Cp. Prov. xxiii.10 (also xxii.28).
Lines 5f. Cp. Prov. xxiii.11.
Lines 7-10. Cp. Prov. xv. 16f., xvii.1.

Text

SEVENTH CHAPTER

Cast not thy heart after riches ;
There is no ignoring Shay and Renent.
Place not thy heart upon externals ;
Every man belongeth to his hour.
5 Labour not to seek for increase ;
Thy needs are safe for thee.
If riches are brought to thee by robbery,
They will not spend the night with thee ;
At daybreak they are not in thy house :
10 Their places may be seen, but they are not.
The ground has opened its mouth—'Let him enter
    that it may swallow',
They sink into the underworld.
They have made for themselves a great breach
    suitable to their size
And are sunken down in the storehouse.

15 They have made themselves wings like geese
And are flown away to heaven.
Rejoice not thyself (over) riches (gained) by
    robbery,
Nor groan because of poverty.

Notes

Line 2. *Shay and Renent* were deities of fortune. Perhaps 'Fate and Fortune'
is the best translation.

Line 4. *his hour*. This is possibly a reference to a man's horoscope.

Lines 5-16. Cp. the remarkable parallel in Prov. xxiii.4f.

Line 11. '*Let him enter . . . swallow*' is a descriptive epithet of the devouring
mouth of the earth.

Line 15. *geese*. In the book of Proverbs it is the soaring eagle which is the
simile of the flight of wealth (xxiii.5). Palestine is remarkable for the number
of birds of prey. Geese, not mentioned in the O.T., were extensively bred in
Egypt. But perhaps Amenemope was here thinking of the annual migratory
flight of the wild geese northwards. In a Late Egyptian story (*c.* 1000 B.C.),
Wenamun, the chief character in the tale, relates how, stranded and friendless
in Syria, he stands on the seashore and watches the birds winging their way
back to Egypt from the North.

Text

NINTH CHAPTER

Associate not with the hot-head,
Nor become intimate with him in conversation . . . .
Leap not to cleave to such a one,
Lest a terror carry thee off.

Notes

The Ninth Chapter, consisting of thirty-six lines, contains advice to avoid
the passionate man and his ways. The first and last couplets, given here, are
paralleled by Prov. xxii.24f.

Line 1. *hot-head*. Literally 'the heated man' ; R.V. 'the wrathful man'.
There is an interesting parallel between the Egyptian and the Hebrew, both
of which use a word meaning 'to be hot' and almost certainly derived from the
same root. The Hebrew '*īsh chēmōth* 'man of hotness' is very near to the
Egyptian.

Text

TENTH CHAPTER

Salute not thy hot-headed (opponent) perforce,
And hurt thine own heart (thereby).
Say not to him : 'Hail to thee !' falsely,
While there is dread in thy belly.

Notes

With the first four lines of this Chapter, cp. Prov. xxvii.14. On the basis
of the Egyptian an attractive and simple emendation of the M.T. results in the
translation 'he that blesseth an evil man'. The phrase 'rising early in the
morning' should probably be omitted.

Line 1. *perforce*, i.e. in the sense of forcing oneself, so 'insincerely'. Cp. the
R.V. 'with a loud voice'.

Text

ELEVENTH CHAPTER

Covet not the property of an inferior person,
Nor hunger for his bread.
As for the property of an inferior person, it is an
   obstruction to the throat,
It maketh a vomiting in the gullet.
5 By false oaths he hath produced it,
His heart being perverted in his body. . .

Notes

With this Chapter cp. Prov. xxiii.6, 8.

Line 1. *inferior person* elsewhere in the 'Teaching' is contrasted with the
'nobleman'. Perhaps the word had acquired an adverse moral significance
like 'mean'. The Hebrew parallel has 'him that hath an evil eye'.

Line 3f. *obstruction*. An alternative translation would be 'rainstorm'. The
original text would appear to have combined two similar sounding words in a
composite written form, thus making the kind of pun which the Egyptians
were fond of using. On the basis of the alternative translation it has been
proposed, instead of R.V. 'as he reckoneth', to read 'as a storm'. It may be
noted that the consonants of the Hebrew word may be vocalised in a variety
of ways to convey a number of meanings, among them 'hair', which is the
rendering of the LXX. *vomiting*, or possibly 'irritation'.

Text

THIRTEENTH CHAPTER

Injure not a man, [with] pen upon papyrus—
O abomination of the god !
Bear not witness with lying words,
Nor seek another's reverse with thy tongue.
5 Make not a reckoning with him who hath nothing,
Nor falsify thy pen.
If thou hast found a large debt against a poor man,
Make it into three parts,
Forgive two, and let one remain,
10 In order that thou shalt find thereby the ways of
    life.
Thou wilt lie down—the night hasteneth away—
    (lo !) thou art in the morning ;
Thou hast found it like good news.
Better is praise for one who loves men
Than riches in a storehouse ;
15 Better is bread, when the heart is happy,
Than riches with contention.

Notes

Line 6. Cp. Jer. viii.8.

Line 7-10. It has been suggested that the difficult parable of the Unjust
Steward, recorded in St. Luke's Gospel, but absent from the other Gospels,
may be a reminiscence of these lines (Luke xvi. lff.).

Lines 13f. Cp. Prov. xvi.8.   Lines 15f. Cp. Prov. xvii.1.

Text

SIXTEENTH CHAPTER

Tamper not with the scales nor falsify the weights,
Nor damage the fractions of the measure.
Desire not the agricultural measure,
And neglect those of the Treasury . . . .

Plate 8   ' Israel Stele ' of Merenptah

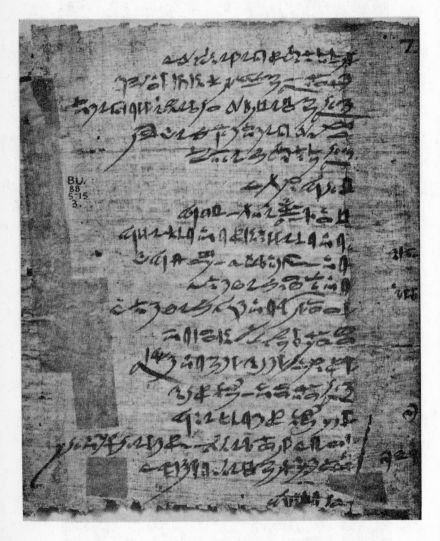

Plate 9   The Teaching of Amenemope : Papyrus Roll

Notes

With these lines cp. Prov. xi.1, xx.23.

Lines 3f. The meaning seems to be a warning against measuring the harvest carefully, but falsifying the amount due to the Treasury.

Text

EIGHTEENTH CHAPTER

Lie not down at night being fearful of the morrow.
When the day breaks, what is the morrow like ?
Man knoweth not what the morrow is like.
God is (ever) in his success,
5 Whereas man is in his failure ;
One thing are the words which men have said,
Another is that which the god doeth . . . .

Notes

Lines 1ff. Cp. Prov. xxvii.1 and the saying of Jesus in the Sermon on the Mount (Matt. vi.34).

Lines 6f. Cp. Prov. xvi.9, xix.2. From these verses is derived the maxim *Homo proponit sed Deus disponit* (Thomas à Kempis, *De Imitatione Christi* 1.19).

Text

TWENTY-FIRST CHAPTER

Empty not thine inmost self to everybody,
And so damage thine influence.
Spread not thine utterances to the common people,
Nor associate with thyself the over-communicative.
5 Better is a man who concealeth his report in his
　　inmost self
Than he who speaketh it out injuriously.

Notes

Line 4. Cp. Prov. xx.19.　　　　　Lines 5f. Cp. Prov. xii.23.

Text

TWENTY-THIRD CHAPTER

Eat not bread in the presence of a noble,
Nor apply thy mouth at the beginning.
If thou art satisfied—false chewings
Be a diversion for thy saliva !
5 Look at the cup which is in thy presence
And let it serve thy needs.

Notes

There is here a general resemblance to Prov. xxiii.3, though the ideas are
completely changed. The meaning of the Egyptian seems to be that the truly
silent man will abstain from the food which would be offered in an interview
with a great man.

Text

TWENTY-FIFTH CHAPTER

Laugh not at a blind man nor tease a dwarf,
Nor injure the plans of the lame.
Tease not a man who is in the hand of the god,
Nor be furious against him when he hath erred.
5 As for man, clay and straw,
The god is his builder.
He teareth down and buildeth up every day.
He maketh a thousand poor men at his will,
(Or) he maketh a thousand men as overseers,
10 When he is in his hour of life.
How joyful is he who hath reached the West,
Being safe in the hand of the god.

Notes

Line 1. Cp. Lev. xix.14 ; Deut. xxvii.18.

Line 2. The probable meaning is to play a malicious joke so as to hinder the
movements of the lame.

Line 3. *in the hand of the god,* i.e. mad or ill. It was a common belief that the
imbecile was under the special protection of God (cp. 1 Sam. xxi.10—xxii.1).

Line 5. Cp. Job xxxiii.6. Clay and straw were the materials from which bricks were made.

Lines 7ff. Cp. Ps. lxxv.8.

Lines 11f. A couplet in praise of death. For the Egyptian the West was the region of the departed.

Text

THIRTIETH CHAPTER

See for thyself these thirty chapters :
They give pleasure ; they instruct ;
They are the foremost of all books ;
They instruct the ignorant.
5 If they are read out in the presence of the ignorant,
Then he will be cleansed by reason of them.
Fill thyself with them ; put them in thy heart,
And be a man who can explain them,
Interpreting them as a teacher.
10 As for the scribe who is experienced in his office,
He shall find himself worthy to be a courtier.

COLOPHON

It has come to its end
In the writing of Senu, son of the God's Father
Pa-miu.

Notes

Line 1. Cp. Prov. xxii.20.

Lines 10f. Cp. Prov. xxii.29.

Lines 12f. The colophon records the successful completion of the copying of the text and gives the name of the copyist. Egyptian books were normally concluded in this way. *the God's Father* was a title given to a class of elder temple priests.

Bibliography

GRESSMANN, H. 'Die neugefundene Lehre des Amen-em-ope und die vor-exilische Spruchdichtung Israels', *Z.A.W.* N.F. i (1924) 272-96.

—— *Israels Spruchweisheit im Zusammenhang der Weltliteratur*, 1925.

GRIFFITH, F. Ll. 'The Teaching of Amenophis', *J.E.A.* xii (1926) 191-231.

LANGE, H. O. *Das Weisheitsbuch des Amenemope*, 1925 (The most convenient transcription of the text. It needs, however, to be corrected in a few instances by reference to GRIFFITH, *q.v.*)

OESTERLEY, W. O. E. *The Wisdom of Egypt and the Old Testament*, 1927.

—— 'The "Teaching of Amen-em-ope" and the Old Testament', *Z.A.W.* N.F. iv (1927) 9-24.

—— *The Book of Proverbs (WC)*, 1929, xxxiii-lv.

SIMPSON, D. C. 'The Hebrew Book of Proverbs and the Teaching of Amenophis', *J.E.A.* xii (1926) 232-9. (This article, and GRIFFITH's article, *q.v.*, are still the best work on the subject in English, and are indispensable for the student of the book of Proverbs.)

WILSON, J. A., in *A.N.E.T.*, 421-5.

J. M. PLUMLEY

Love Songs

SEVERAL collections of love songs have come down to us from the later Egyptian Empire (*c.* 1300-1100 B.C.). As nothing of like kind has survived from the earlier periods of Egyptian history, there is reason for believing that they are a particular product of the later Empire. The poems breathe a strong love of nature and depend for their effect on the comparison between the beauties of the beloved one and those of natural objects, more especially of trees, flowers and gardens. They are mostly short songs and were probably intended to be sung to the accompaniment of a musical instrument. Owing to the nature of Egyptian writing—the vowels were not represented—it is impossible to state what form of metre was employed. However, if comparison be made with poetry produced by the Egyptians in the Christian period when, in the form of the language known as Coptic, the vowels were written in full, it is not unreasonable to assume that in the older poetry also every word or word-complex had only one strongly accented syllable. Furthermore, as in Hebrew, each line of verse had a number of stressed syllables, so that free rhythm and not rigid metre was the characteristic of Egyptian poetry.

The general resemblance of the four extracts from the collections of Egyptian love songs to the Song of Songs will at once strike the reader. A most striking similarity in detail is the use by the lovers of the titles 'brother' and 'sister' when speaking of one another.

In the story of Wenamun (*c.* 1000 B.C.) mention is made of an Egyptian female singer at the court of the prince of Byblos. It is not hard to see by what road the lyric poetry of Egypt came into Palestine. It is significant that literally nothing of this kind of literature has come down to us from Babylonia. It has been observed that, 'if the Egyptians were the inventors of the love-poem, and it is not unlikely that, with their love of brightness and gaiety, they were, we may well regard it as one of their chief contributions to literature' (T. E. PEET, p. 97).

The first poem is taken from the Papyrus Harris 500 (B.M.

10060) recto iv.1-7 ; the second from the same papyrus, recto v.6ff. ; the third from an ostracon in the Cairo Museum, No. 25218, lines 6-10 (the hieratic writing of this ostracon is particularly ill-formed and difficult to read ; there is little doubt that it was written by a pupil scribe) ; and the fourth from the Papyrus Chester Beatty I, verso C ii.4-9.

Text

The beginning of the beautiful songs of entertainment of thy sister, the beloved one of thy heart, as she comes from the meadow.

> My brother, my beloved,
> My heart follows the love of thee.
> All has been created for thee.
> I say to thee, 'See what I do'.
> 5 I have come from setting my trap with my hand,
> My cage in my hand together with my snare.
> All the birds of Punt, they alight in Egypt,
> Anointed with myrrh.
> The one that comes first takes my worm.
> 10 Its fragrance is brought from Punt,
> Its claws are full of resin.
> My desire for thee is that together we might set
>   them free,
> I alone with thee ;
> That I might cause thee to hear the shrill voice
> 15 Of my myrrh anointed one.
> Lovely for me is thy being with me while I set the
>   trap.
> Lovely is the going to the meadow
> To him who is beloved.

Notes

Line 7. *Punt*. This was a land, probably on the coast of Somaliland, which was famous for gums and perfumes, highly prized at all times by the ancient Egyptians. A number of records exist of expeditions despatched by various Pharaohs to Punt. The most famous of these expeditions was that sent by Queen Hatshepsut, *c.* 1500 B.C. Scenes of this expedition were carved on the walls of her mortuary temple at Deir el-Baheri near the city of Thebes. The

Egyptians believed that their ancestors originally came from Punt and named it 'The God's Land'. The proposed identification of Punt with Put, which is mentioned several times in the O.T. (e.g. Gen. x.6 ; Jer. xlvi.9 ; Ezek. xxvii.10, xxx.5, xxxviii.5) is, on phonetic grounds, improbable.

Line 8. *myrrh*. Myrrh and spices are frequently referred to in Song ivf.

Text

   The voice of the swallow speaks, saying,
   'The land is bright.   What of thy way ?'
   Prithee, do not, O bird, scold me.
   I have found my brother in his bed,
5 And my heart is pleased even more.
   We have said (to one another),
   'I shall not go far away
   While my hand is in thy hand.
   I shall stroll about
10 Being with thee in every beautiful place'.
   He has made me the chief of his lovely women
   Lest he should wound my heart.

Notes

Line 1. Cp. Song ii.12.

Line 2. The meaning would appear to be, 'The dawn has come. Why dost thou not stir and come forth from the house ?'

Line 6. The papyrus is damaged here. The reading given here is therefore open to question, but the translator ventures to think that the interpretation of the following four lines as a mutual conversation between the lovers is both natural and possible.

Text

   The love of my sister is on yonder side
   Of the stream in the midst of the fish.
   A crocodile stands on the sandbank ;
   Yet I go down into the water.
5 I venture across the current ;
   My courage is high upon the waters.
   It is thy love which gives me strength ;
   For thou makest a water-spell for me.
   When I see my sister coming,

10 Then my heart rejoices.
My arms are open wide to embrace her ;
My heart is glad in its place
Like . . . . eternally
When my mistress comes to me.

Notes

Song viii.7 may be recalled in connection with this poem.

Line 2. There is little doubt that the passage as it stands is corrupt. We should expect a reading like, 'A stream is between us'.

Line 8. The spell is intended to protect the lover against the attack of the crocodiles. In tomb scenes from the Old Kingdom (*c.* 2778-2423 B.C.) there are representations of herdsmen ferrying cattle across stretches of water and making a particular gesture with their fingers which was supposed to keep off crocodiles.

Line 12. According to the Egyptian conception the heart rested upon a support and was only happy so long as it remained there.

Line 13. The writing is mostly obliterated.

Text

Seven days to yesterday I have not seen my sister.
Sickness has entered into me.
I have become heavy of body,
Forgetful of my own self.
5 If the greatest physicians come to me,
My heart will not be contented with their remedies.
The lector-priests—there is no way in them ;
My sickness will not be discerned.
To say to me, 'She is here', that is what will
revive me.
10 Her name is that which will lift me up.
The coming and going of her messengers is that
which will revive my heart.
My sister is more beneficial for me than all the
medicines ;
She is more to me than the collection of medical lore.
My health is her coming in from without.
15 To see her—then health.
Let her but open her eye—my body is young again.

To speak with her—then I am reinvigorated.
When I embrace her, she drives evil away from me.
[But] she has gone forth from me for seven days.

Notes

Line 2. *Sickness has entered into me.* Cp. Song ii.5, v.8.

Line 7. *The lector-priests.* Literally 'the holders of the ritual book'. The practice of medicine in ancient Egypt involved both the application of material remedies and the use of magical incantations.

Bibliography

ERMAN, A. *The Literature of the Ancient Egyptians*, 1927, 242-51.

GARDINER, ALAN H. *The Library of A. Chester Beatty. The Chester Beatty Papyri No.* 1, 1931, 27-38. (This collection of Love Songs contains an introduction, translations of the texts and notes.)

MULLER, W. MAX. *Die Liebespoesie der alten Aegypter*, 1899. (Contains all the Love Songs, except the Chester Beatty collection. The texts are reproduced in the original hieratic with transcriptions into hieroglyphs and translations. The extensive notes and full introduction, though written half a century ago, are still useful.)

PEET, T. E. *A Comparative Study of the Literatures of Egypt, Palestine, and Mesopotamia* (Schweich Lectures 1929), 1931, 92-7.

WILSON, J. A., in *A.N.E.T.*, 467ff.

J. M. PLUMLEY

A Moabite Document

The Moabite Stone

The Moabite Stone

(Plate 10)

THE stone was discovered in 1868 by a missionary, F. A. KLEIN, at Diban (O.T. Dibon), some thirteen miles east of the Dead Sea. It was later broken by Bedouins, but, fortunately, only after a squeeze of the inscription had been obtained. Since 1873 the reconstructed monument has been in the Louvre. The inscription on the stone commemorates the victories of Mesha, king of Moab, over Israel (2 Kings iii.4). Its great importance, historical, religious, and linguistic, lies in its close connection with the O.T. narrative. The authenticity of the stone has not infrequently been disputed, but there remain no grounds for doubt. The date of the monument must be fixed towards the end of Mesha's reign, *c.* 830 B.C.

Israel and Moab were closely related tribal confederations. In the narrative in Genesis, Moab is mentioned as a son of Lot (Gen. xix.37), and Lot was, of course, Abraham's nephew. Moab settled in the territory to the east of the southern reaches of the Jordan and the northern half of the Dead Sea. During the reigns of Saul and David, Israel fought against the land of Moab, and David finally succeeded in subjugating it (2 Sam. viii.2). In the days of Omri and his son Ahab, Moab was still 'oppressed' by Israel, as we know from the testimony of the Moabite stone (lines 5ff.) as well as from the O.T. (2 Kings iii.4). Mesha's successful rebellion against Israelite oppression is likewise corroborated by the O.T. (2 Kings iii. 5ff.). Whereas, however, according to 2 Kings iii.5 (cp. i.1), Mesha's revolt occurred after Ahab's death, the inscription makes it clear that the revolt took place in the latter years of Ahab's reign. Such discrepancies as may exist between the account given on the Moabite stone and that in 2 Kings iii are no doubt due to the inclination of each side to lay stress on the victories rather than the setbacks. The Moabite stone is thus a historical document of the first order, both confirming and slightly contradicting the Biblical narrative, to whose style and genre it is most closely related.

Chemosh, referred to several times in the inscription, was the national god of Moab in very much the same way in which Yahweh was the national god of Israel. Chemosh, like Yahweh, is apt to be angry with his people, to forsake them and to deliver them to their enemies (line 5), yet to save them in the end. The inscription reads, in fact, like a chapter from the O.T. with its alternation of punishment and salvation. Chemosh speaks to Mesha (lines 14, 32) in exactly the same words as Yahweh does to Saul or David (1 Sam. xxiii.4, etc.). The rite of *chērem*, that is, consecration to destruction, occurs both on the stone (line 17) and in the O.T. (cp. 1 Sam. xv.). The sanctuaries are situated at high places, and the worship of Chemosh is connected with one place in particular, viz. Qrchh (line 3); cp. also the position in South Arabia (G. RYCKMANS, *Religions Arabes Préislamiques*, 1951, 42).

Moabite and Hebrew were almost certainly mutually intelligible, and the language of the stone differs only slightly—in grammar, syntax, and vocabulary—from that of the O.T. It is not possible to say to what extent that proximity applied to the phonology as well. There are only a few words which are either not attested at all in the O.T. or in slightly varying shades of meaning.

Text

I am Mesha, son of Chemosh- . . ., king of Moab, the Dibonite. My father was king over Moab thirty years and I became king after my father. And I made this sanctuary for Chemosh at Qrchh, [a sanctuary of] salvation; for he saved me from all the kings and let me see my desire upon my adversaries. Omri, (5) king of Israel, he oppressed Moab many days, for Chemosh was angry with his land. And his son succeeded him and he too said, 'I will oppress Moab.' In my days he spoke (thus), and I saw my desire upon him and upon his house, when Israel perished utterly for ever. And Omri had taken possession of the land of Medeba and [Israel] dwelt in it his days and half the days of his son, forty years; but Chemosh dwelt in it in my days. And I built Baal-meon and made in it the reservoir, and I built (10) Qaryaten. And the men of Gad had long dwelt in the land of Ataroth, and the king of Israel had built Ataroth for himself. But I fought against the town and took it and I slew all the people of the town, a spectacle for Chemosh and Moab. And I brought back from there the altar-hearth of David and I dragged it before Chemosh at Qeriyoth. And I settled there the men of Sharon and the men of Mchrt. And Chemosh said to me, 'Go, take Nebo against Israel.' And I (15) went by night and fought against it from the break of dawn till noon ; and I took it and slew all : seven thousand men, boys, women, and [girls] and female slaves, for I had consecrated it to Ashtar-Chemosh. And I took from there the vessels of Yahweh and dragged them before Chemosh. And the king of Israel had built Jahaz and he dwelt in it while fighting against me. But Chemosh drove him out before me. And (20) I took from Moab two hundred men, all of them leaders, and led them up against Jahaz and took it to annex it to Dibon. I built Qrchh, the walls of the parks and the walls of the mound ; and I built its gates and I built its towers ; and I built the king's house ; and I made both the reservoirs for water inside the town. And there was no cistern inside the town at Qrchh, so I said to all the people, 'Make (25) yourselves each one a cistern in his house.' And I had ditches dug for Qrchh by prisoners of Israel. I built Aroer and I made the road by the Arnon. I built Beth-bamoth, for it was destroyed ; I built Bezer, for it was in ruins, with fifty men of Dibon, for all Dibon is under my authority. And I reigned [over] hundreds of towns which I had annexed to the country. And I built (30) . . . Medeba and Beth-Diblathen and Beth-Baal-Meon, and I led up there the breeders of the sheep of the land. And as for Hauronen, there dwelt in it . . . Chemosh said to me, 'Go down, fight against Hauronen.' And I went down . . . [and there dwelt] in it Chemosh in my days . . . from there . . . and I . . .

Notes

Lines 1-4. For the name *Mesha*, cp. other names derived from the same Semitic root (meaning 'to help, save'), e.g. Hosea, Joshua. *Chemosh* was the national god of the Moabites, and the name of Mesha's father, of which the last two (?) letters are missing, is a composite name comparable to O.T. names incorporating Yahweh, e.g. Isaiah, Jehoash, etc. *Dibonite*—of the town of Dibon. For this and other Moabite towns mentioned in the inscription, cp. Jer. xlviii. *Sanctuary*, or high place, so called because it was usually built on a hill (cp. 1 Kings xi.7). *Qrchh* (cp. lines 21, 24ff.), of uncertain vocalisation, was probably situated in the district of Dibon ; it was particularly associated with the worship of Chemosh. *see my desire upon.* This idiom (cp. line 7) occurs also in the O.T., e.g. Pss. lix.11, cxviii.7. *Omri* (1 Kings xvi.16ff.) reigned *c.* 887-876 B.C.

Lines 5-9. *his son*, i.e. Ahab (1 Kings xvi.28ff.) who reigned *c.* 876-853 B.C. *Medeba* (cp. Num. xxi.30, etc.) was situated to the east of the northern tip of the Dead Sea. It is the modern Madeba. *dwelt in it.* Or perhaps 'restored it'. *Baal-Meon* (cp. Num. xxxii.38, etc. and line 30), the modern Ma'in, lay south-west of Medeba. *reservoir.* The Moabite word (*'shwch*) has its Hebrew counter-part in *shūchāh* 'pit' (Jer. xviii.20). A similar word occurs later in Mishnaic Hebrew ; cp. also Ecclus. l.3 (in R. H. CHARLES, *The Apocrypha and Pseudepi-grapha of the Old Testament in English*, 1 (1913) 507).

Lines 10-14. *Qaryaten.* The vocalisation is conjectural. The name Kiriathaim (modern el-Qereiyat) occurs in Jer. xlviii.1, etc. *Ataroth* (cp. Num. xxxii.34, etc.), the modern 'Attarus, is situated north-west of Dibon. *altar-hearth of David.* The phrase probably means 'lion-figure of David'. A possible meaning is 'Arel its chieftain', a meaning based apparently on the word *dawidum*, a title or dignity, which is found in the documents from Mari (Tell el-Hariri) on the Middle Euphrates. The translation 'altar of Dod(o)' is most unlikely. *Qeriyoth* is the O.T. Kerioth (cp. Jer. xlviii.24 ; Amos ii.2). The exact site is not known. *Sharon.* Cp. 1 Chr. v.16. *Mc̣hrt* is not found in the O.T. *Nebo* (cp. Jer. xlviii.1, etc.), probably the modern Chirbet el-Muchayyit, lies near mount Nebo (today Jebel Neba).

Lines 15-19. *boys.* The reading is uncertain. 'Strangers' is possible. *girls.* The reading is uncertain. *female slaves.* Literally 'damsels', as in Jud. v.30. *consecrated it,* i.e. the town (cp. Num. xxi.2). *Jahaz* (cp. Num. xxi.23, etc.) is situated between Dibon and Medeba ; the exact site is uncertain.

Line 22. *mound.* Cp. Neh. iii.27, etc.

Lines 25-9. *Aroer* (cp. Jer. xlviii.19), the modern 'Ara'ir, is south of Dibon. *Arnon* (cp. Jer. xlviii.20) is a Moabite river (modern Wadi el-Mojib). *Beth-bamoth* may be identical with Bamoth in Num. xxi.19. *Bezer* (cp. Deut. iv.43, etc.) may lie to the north of Medeba and may be identical with Bozrah (cp. Jer. xlviii.24). *of towns.* Literally 'among towns'.

Lines 30-4. *Beth-Diblathen.* Cp. Jer. xlviii.22. *breeders.* This is partly supplied, but authority for it can be found in 2 Kings iii.4. *Hauronen* is the O.T. Horonaim (cp. Jer. xlviii.3) ; the site is uncertain.

Bibliography

ALBRIGHT, W. F. 'Is the Mesha Inscription a Forgery?' *J.Q.R.* xxxv (1945) 247-50.

—— *A.N.E.T.*, 320f.

COOKE, G. A. *A Text-Book of North-Semitic Inscriptions*, 1903, 1-14.

DIRINGER, D. *The Alphabet*, 1949, 243f. *et passim.*

DUSSAUD, R. *Les monuments palestiniens et judaïques* (*Musée du Louvre*), 1912, 4-22.

GRESSMANN, H. *Altorientalische Texte zum Alten Testament*, second ed., 1926, 440ff.

YAHUDA, A. S. 'The Story of a Forgery and the Mesha Inscription', *J.Q.R.* xxxv (1944) 139-63.

E. ULLENDORFF

Plate 10 The Moabite Stone

Hebrew Documents

The Gezer Calendar
Inscribed Potsherds from Samaria
The Siloam Inscription
Letters from Lachish
Seals
Weights
Coins

The Gezer Calendar

(Plate 11)

IN 1908 at Gezer, twenty miles west-north-west of Jerusalem, R. A. S. MACALISTER discovered the small inscribed limestone tablet now called the Gezer calendar. $4\frac{1}{4}''$ high, $2\frac{3}{4}''$ broad and $\frac{5}{8}''$ thick, its oblique and irregular bottom edge implies that at some time a portion of it was broken off; when that happened a study of the inscription itself may help to determine. A rectangular hole at the bottom suggests that the tablet was kept suspended from a wall-hook, and the roughness of the writing and the varying forms of the repeated letters indicate that the tablet was not an official one, but was used for writing exercise by an inhabitant of Gezer practising his skill or instructing others. The tablet was first dated in the sixth century B.C. Recently, however, it has been attributed to the eleventh, tenth or ninth century B.C., and it may be regarded, on linguistic and palæographic grounds, as the most ancient inscription in Early Hebrew writing, as old as the age of Saul or David. Certain vestigial marks and strokes which appear in some cases to be letters of a former inscription imperfectly erased make the tablet technically a palimpsest and add to the difficulties of decipherment.

Text

Two months of ingathering. Two months of sow-
ing. Two months of late sowing (*or* spring growth).
Month of pulling flax.
Month of barley harvest.
Month when everything [else] is harvested.
Two months of pruning [vines].
Month of summer fruit.

Notes

The main problem of decipherment is the form and meaning ('month' or 'two months') of the Hebrew word *yrchw* in lines 1f., 6. If the final letter is *h*, the meaning is 'month'; if it is *n*, a dual ending, 'two months' is the meaning;

but orthographically the final letter is undoubtedly *w*. As such, it may have only syntactical value ('month'), or it may be the conjunctive 'and' ('month and') ; but recently it has been adjudged a nominative dual ending ('two months'). The meaning 'his two months' has also been proposed.

Other problems of decipherment are of minor importance, e.g. the choice between 'sowing' and 'planting' in lines 1f., or the proper association of the final letter of the word for barley in line 4, where it is written vertically off-line ; in neither case is the meaning affected. In line 5 we might expect reference to a particular crop, but a proposal that the letters written vertically at the bottom of the tablet, and usually regarded as part of the writer's name or signature, should be attached to the line to make it mean 'month when all the spring fruits are harvested', is ruled out by the remoteness of these letters from line 5.

The inscription is an agricultural calendar. The fact that it catalogues the agricultural operations for the twelve months of the year implies that the tablet had its present form when the calendar was written on it. The *ingathering* (line 1), the storage of grain and wine at the beginning of the year (Sept./Oct.), had to be completed before the first rains came (cp. Exod. xxiii.16, xxxiv.22) ; the *sowing* (Nov./Dec.) could be done only after these rains had softened the surface of the soil, hard baked by the summer heat (cp. Jer. xiv.1-6 ; Hos. ii.21f.). For prayers for rain at this season, see N. H. Snaith, *The Jewish New Year Festival*, 1947, 62ff. ; the prosperity of the country depended on them (cp. Deut. xi.14 ; Jer. v.24 ; Hos. vi.3 ; Joel ii.23). The *late sowing* (Jan./Feb.) came after the winter rains and depended for its success on the later rains of March./Apr. The *flax* was pulled (or harvested) during March (cp. Josh. ii.6) ; seldom mentioned in the O.T., it may nevertheless have been an important crop near Gezer. *barley harvest* (cp. Ruth i.22, ii) was in April, and the rest of the harvest in May (lines 5f.). It is noteworthy that there is no specific mention of wheat or olives and only an implicit reference to vines, although corn, wine, and oil were the staple products of Palestine (cp. Deut. vii.13, xi.14, etc.). The *pruning* of the vines must have meant cutting off excessive foliage to fill out the grapes, or a normal trimming after an early vintage (June/July). *summer fruit*, mostly figs, was gathered in August, and the word used for it was associated with the end of the agricultural year (2 Sam. xvi.1 ; Amos viii.1f. ; Jer. viii.20, xl.10, 12 ; Mic. vii.1).

Bibliography

Albright, W. F. 'The Gezer Calendar', *B.A.S.O.R.* No. 92 (1943) 16-26.

—— *The Archæology of Palestine* (Pelican Books), 1949, 132.

—— *A.N.E.T.*, 320.

Cook, S. A. 'The Old Hebrew Alphabet and the Gezer Tablet', *P.E.F.Q.S.*, 1909, 284-309.

Daiches, S. 'Notes on the Gezer Calendar and Some Babylonian Parallels', *P.E.F.Q.S.*, 1909, 113-18.

Dalman, G. 'Notes on the Old Hebrew Calendar-Inscription from Gezer', *P.E.F.Q.S.*, 1909, 118f.

DIRINGER, D. *Le Iscrizioni Antico-Ebraiche Palestinesi*, 1934, 1-20 (an extensive bibliography is given).

DRIVER, G. R. *Semitic Writing : From Pictograph to Alphabet* (Schweich Lectures 1944), revised ed. 1954, 108ff.

—— 'Brief Notes', *P.E.Q.*, 1945, 5-9.

DRIVER, S. R. *Notes on the Hebrew Text and the Topography of the Books of Samuel*, 1913, viif.

LIDZBARSKI, M. 'The Old Hebrew Calendar-Inscription from Gezer', *P.E.F.Q.S.*, 1909, 194f.

LIDZBARSKI, M., BUCHANAN GRAY, G., PILCHER, E. J. 'An Old Hebrew Calendar-Inscription from Gezer', *P.E.F.Q.S.*, 1909, 26-34.

MACALISTER, R. A. S. 'Report on the Excavation of Gezer', *P.E.F.Q.S.*, 1909, 87-92.

—— *The Excavation of Gezer*, II, 1912, 24-8.

RONZEVALLE, S. 'The Gezer Hebrew Inscription', *P.E.F.Q.S.*, 1909, 107-12.

VINCENT, H. 'Un Calendrier Agricole Israélite', *R.B.* vi, 1909, 243-69.

J. MAUCHLINE

Inscribed Potsherds from Samaria

An expedition from Harvard University, excavating at Samaria in 1908-10, discovered sixty-five inscriptions written on pottery with a reed pen in black carbon ink, and others have been found since. They were found in the lowest part of the debris in a room of the great west court of the palace assigned by the excavators to the reign of Ahab (c. 876-854 B.C.). The room may have been a store room of the type built by Hezekiah for corn and wine and oil (2 Chr. xxxii.28). In the same stratum was found an alabaster vase of Osorkon II, king of Egypt (c. 874-853 B.C.), but the room, with alterations, continued to be used until the fall of Samaria in 722 B.C., and more recent excavations in 1931-35 produced evidence to suggest that the ostraca could be dated in the reigns of Jehu (c. 842-815 B.C.), or Jehoahaz (c. 814-798 B.C.), or even Jeroboam II (c. 784-744 B.C.). Two short inscriptions are labels written on jars, but the remaining potsherds came from five different kinds of jar which had already been broken into their present shapes before being used for writing; in three cases two different pieces fit together as part of the same vase.

The writing is clear and flowing, the work of skilled writers, and it is evident that writing had long been practised in Israel for ordinary private purposes, for the ostraca are temporary, rough, records or invoices. Words are divided by dots or strokes, the script is ancient Hebrew, like that of the Moabite stone and the Siloam inscription, and the language is Hebrew. No vowels are indicated, and the pronunciation, especially of proper names, is never certain.

From the contents we can divide the ostraca into four groups. Each ostracon is dated, by reference probably to a king's reign, to the ninth, tenth, and either the fifteenth and seventeenth, or perhaps the eleventh and thirteenth, year; nine and ten are denoted by words, but the other numerals are denoted by figures, and the meaning is not certain. All the ostraca are concerned with the delivery of jars of old wine or purified olive oil. In the first group no persons are mentioned, but only the place or estate from which the delivery came; the second group contains place names, and the names of the recipients and of those by whom, or on behalf of whom, the produce was given ; the third is similar but makes no mention of the goods delivered ; the fourth has the names of persons and place and the number of gifts, but does not state whether they consist of oil or wine.

Twenty-seven places from which the wine and oil came are mentioned, but only one is known as a place name from the O.T., viz. Shechem ; two others are preceded by the word *kerem*, the Hebrew word for 'vineyard', and are probably the names of particular vineyards. Six other places are identical with the names of clans or sub-divisions of the tribe of Manasseh in Num. xxvi.29 and Josh. xvii.2, viz. Abiezer, Helek, Shechem, Shemida, Noah, Hoglah ; and they may represent the district where the clan lived or the contribution of the clan. The fact that Abiezer seems to be a personal name would militate against the theory that original place names were used by O.T. writers in compiling tribal lists. Attempts have been made to identify the various places or districts mentioned, but few can be certainly located. An interesting suggestion is that all the names refer to places within eleven kilometres of Samaria, and that all of them were vineyards or gardens of the royal estates grouped round the palace at Samaria, comparable with those around the palace at Jezreel (1 Kings xxi.1). Many of the personal names are mentioned in the O.T., some are different forms of an O.T. name, and others are Phoenician names. In addition to those cited in the texts below, O.T. names found in the ostraca are Abimelek, Ahinoam, Ela, Baalmeoni, Gera, Helez, Hanan, Joash, Nathan, Rapha, Shemida, and Gomer.

That the ostraca were found in the royal palace makes it probable that they were invoices or labels sent with oil and wine due to the king, but the limited list of places, and the fact that wine and oil only are mentioned, suggests that we are not dealing with annual tribute such as Solomon demanded (1 Kings iv.7, 22f.), for he included flour, meal and animals, and omitted oil and wine. A comparison of the ostraca with similar writings found on jars in Egypt suggests that the produce came from crown property round Samaria, that it was paid by royal tenants of vineyards and gardens to district overseers mentioned as recipients, and that these officials forwarded it to the king's steward at the palace. If so, the ostraca throw light on the extent of the royal property rather than on the fiscal organisation of the northern kingdom.

The religious significance of the ostraca is great. There are here, as in the O.T., names compounded with Ab (Hebrew *'ābh* 'father') Ah (Hebrew *'āch* 'brother') and Am (Hebrew *'am* 'people'), but also with divine names. El, the general Semitic name for God, occurs in three names—Elisha, Eliba, Elmattan ; six names have Baal in them, viz. Abibaal, Baalzamar, Bålmeoni, Baalazakar, Meribbaal, Baala ; and nine are compounded with *yau*, a shorter form of Yahweh, viz. Abiyau, Bediyau, Gaddiyau, Jediyau, Marnayau, Egelyau, Shemaryau, Yauyoshib, Obedyau (in the O.T. the corresponding names have usually *iah* for *yau*) ; while, in addition, 'to Yah' is found inscribed on the rim of a jar. Of these names Egelyau is of particular interest as combining the word for 'calf' or 'young bull' (*'ēgel*) with *yau*, thus supporting evidence from other sources that in northern Israel the calf was a Yahweh symbol comparable with the ark in the south. If the ostraca are dated in the reign of Ahab, the personal names give no indication of religious conditions during his reign, as all the men were born and named earlier, but if they belong to the time of later kings, they testify—as do the names given by Ahab to his own children—to the continuity of Yahweh worship in the north, despite the reputation given to Ahab by some O.T. writers.

Text

In the tenth year. To Shemaryau . From Beeryam.
Bottle of old (wine).

Raga son of Elisha	2
Uzza son of Q-bsh	1
Eliba ?	1
Baala son of Elisha	1
Jedayau	1

Notes

Beeryam, the place from which the produce came, is compounded of the Hebrew word *be'ēr* 'well' and *yām* 'sea', the second element differentiating it from other places called Beer ; cp. Beersheba and Beer (Jud. ix.21). *Yam* possibly refers to the Sea of Galilee and denotes a Beer within sight of the lake, perhaps the modern El Birah, north of Beisan. The recipient *Shemaryau* has a name corresponding to the O.T. form Shemariah (2 Chr. xi.19, xvii.8 ; Ezra x.32), compounded of the verb 'keep' and the divine name Yahweh, just as *Jedayau* is compounded of this divine name and the verb 'know' or 'care for'.   Of the personal names of the men from whom the wine came, *Elisha*, the name of the northern prophet, *Uzza* and *Jedayau* (in the form Jedaiah) are often found in the historical books of the O.T. ; *Raga* is connected with a common Hebrew stem, but does not occur as a personal name in the O.T. ; *Baala* is an Aramaic form of the divine name Baal ; *Eliba* is another compound name containing the Semitic word for God, El.   The adjective *old*, used in many other ostraca to qualify *wine*, which must be supplied here, is never used of wine in the O.T.   In the Holiness Code it is used of old produce as opposed to new (Lev. xxvi.10 ; cp. Song vii.13), and of old harvest that had to be eaten during the eighth year, after the land had lain fallow in the seventh year (Lev. xxv.22 ; cp. Neh. iii.6, xii.39, of an old gate ; Is. xxii.11, of an old pool ; Deut. iv.25, of growing old in the land ; Lev. xiii.11, of an old leprosy) ; the meaning of the stem appears to be 'to be inactive, sleeping', and hence 'old' as distinct from 'new'.

Text

In the tenth year. To Gaddiyau. From Azah.

Abibaal	2
Ahaz	2
Sheba	1
Meribbaal	1

Notes

Here no mention is made of the produce supplied, but otherwise the form is the same as in the previous text.   If the place of origin is vocalised *Azah*, it may be the modern Zawata, between Sebaste and Nablus ; but it is possible that it should be Azzah, identifiable with Inzata of the Egyptian lists and possibly the modern Anzah, south of Jenin.   The recipient *Gaddiyau* has a name corresponding to an O.T. form Gedaiah which, however, does not occur in the O.T. (cp. however, Gaddiel, Num. xiii.10, where the divine name El is used instead of Yahweh).   The name combines Yahweh with Gad 'Fortune' (Is. lxv.11).   Gaddiyau appears to have been an important official ; he is mentioned as recipient on ten ostraca from four different places in the ninth and tenth years, and a man Helez, son of Gaddiyau, is a recipient in the fifteenth (or eleventh) year on four ostraca.   Of the other personal names *Abibaal* combines the word 'father' and the divine name Baal.   In the O.T. Abiel occurs in 1 Sam. xi.1, xiv.51, and 1 Chr. xi.32, and Abijah is often found in both the earlier and later historical books, but Abibaal is not found.   *Ahaz* is well known, and *Sheba* occurs in 2 Sam. xx and Josh. xix.2.   *Meribbaal* 'one who contends for Baal' or 'Baal contends', is found in 1 Chr. ix.40 and viii.34 as the name of the son of Jonathan, but in 2 Sam. iv.4, ix.6ff. it has been altered to Mephibosheth, where *bōsheth* 'shame' replaces the name of the god Baal. In some ostraca the preposition 'to' occurs before the names of the senders, and there it probably has the meaning 'to be credited to'.

Bibliography

ALBRIGHT, W. F., in *A.N.E.T.*, 321.

CROWFOOT, J. W., KENYON, K. M., and SUKENIK, E. L.   *The Buildings at Samaria*, 1942, 5-9, 24-7.

DIRINGER, D.   *Le Iscrizioni Antico-Ebraiche Palestinesi*, 1934, 21-68.

DUSSAUD, R.   'Samarie au temps d'Achab', *Syria* vi (1925) 314-38, and vii (1926) 9-29.

GRESSMANN, H.   'Die Ausgrabungen in Samaria', *Z.A.W.* xliii (1925) 147-50.

JACK, J. W.   *Samaria in Ahab's Time*, 1929, 37-64.

MAISLER, B.   'The Historical Background of the Samaria Ostraca', *J.P.O.S.* xxi (1948) 117-33.

MOSCATI, S.   *L'Epigrafia Ebraica Antica 1935-1950*, 1951, 27-39.

NOTH, M.   'Das Krongut der israelitischen Könige und seine Verwaltung. Die samarischen Ostraka', *Z.D.P.V.* l (1927) 211-44

REISNER, G. A., FISHER, C. S., and LYON, D. G.   *Harvard Excavations at Samaria 1908-1910*, 1924, 227-46.

J. N. SCHOFIELD

The Siloam Inscription

(Plate 11)

THE inscription was found in 1880 by a boy who had been bathing in the Pool of Siloam. It is five feet up on the south side of a tunnel, about nineteen feet from the Siloam end. This tunnel connects the Virgin's Spring with the Pool of Siloam, and it is in the south-east spur of the Temple Mount. The tunnel is 1,777 feet long according to H. VINCENT, though some authorities estimate it as much as seventy feet shorter. The distance from one end of the tunnel to the other in a direct line is about 1,090 feet. There are many changes of direction. Starting from the Spring, it runs due east for 250 feet, following an old working, one of many tunnels which were cleared by Captain PARKER in 1909-11 (they are fully described by VINCENT). The excavation then turns due south. The gang which started from the Pool, at the other end, began in a north-easterly direction. They then turned south-east until they reached approximately the north-south line which the Spring-party were following, when they turned due north to meet them. The changes in direction seem in the main to have been deliberate, possibly, as has been suggested, to avoid the tombs of the kings, but there are many deviations, as though the workers were not always sure of their direction. Finally, as the inscription states, the two gangs were working away in opposite directions but separated by four and a half feet. As they were passing each other, they heard a shout, with the result that both parties turned sharply to the right, and the tunnel was complete.

The tunnel, which was made by use of hammer, wedge and pickaxe, is undoubtedly that which was made by Hezekiah, king of Judah, who 'made the pool, and the conduit, and brought the water into the city' (2 Kings xx.20). According to 2 Chr. xxxii. 30, 'This same Hezekiah also stopped the upper spring of the waters of Gihon, and brought them straight down on the west side of the city of David'. Also in Is. xxii.11 there is a reference to the original diggings which were used: 'Ye made also a reservoir between the two walls for the water of the old pool:

but ye looked not unto him that had done this, neither had ye respect unto him that fashioned it long ago'. Ben Sirach also mentions this notable feat of engineering in Ecclus. xlviii.17 : 'Hezekiah fortified his city, and brought in water into the midst of them : he digged the sheer rock with iron, and builded up wells for waters.'

The tunnel was completed before 701 B.C., possibly not long before, when Sennacherib of Assyria besieged Jerusalem, but presumably after the capture of Samaria by Sargon of Assyria in 722 B.C. It was probably part of the considerable preparations which Hezekiah made for the general revolt of the West against the Assyrian overlordship. This revolt took place at the end of the century and Hezekiah took a leading part in it.

The inscription, which is now preserved in the Museum of the Ancient Orient at Istanbul, is in the Early Hebrew script, and the style is good classical Hebrew. Some of the characters have been worn away by flowing water. Above the inscription the surface of the tunnel is smooth, and has been dressed for more writing or for a relief. It has been suggested, probably correctly, that it contained the first half of the original inscription.

Text

(? the completing of) the piercing through. And this is the story of the piercing through. While (the stone-cutters were swinging their) axes, each towards his fellow, and while there were yet three cubits to be pierced through, (there was heard) the voice of a man (3) calling to his fellow, for there was a crevice (?) on the right . . . And on the day of the piercing through, the stone-cutters struck through each to meet his fellow, axe against axe. Then ran the water from the Spring to the Pool for twelve hundred cubits, and a hundred cubits was the height of the rock above the head of the stone-cutters.

Notes

Line 1. Two or three characters are illegible at the beginning of the line. The best conjecture is *tm*, read as *tōm* ('the completing of '). Many characters at the end of the line are illegible, but there is a general consensus of opinion concerning the probable original.

Line 3. *crevice*. The word *zdh* (? *zādāh*, *ziddāh*), which does not occur in the O.T., is of uncertain meaning. A meaning 'excess, overlap' has been suggested but would the workmen be able to hear each other's voices through four and a half feet of solid rock ? The alternative is 'cleft, fissure, rift, crevice'. Instead of *zādāh, ziddāh*, a reading *zewāʿāh* 'quivering' has been proposed. After *on the right* there is a worn space which contained about six characters. Most scholars suggest 'and on the left', but this can scarcely be correct because the crevice (? overlap) was to the right of both gangs of workmen.

Bibliography

ALBRIGHT, W. F., in *A.N.E.T.*, 321.

COOKE, G. A. *A Text-Book of North-Semitic Inscriptions*, 1903, 15ff.

DIRINGER, D. *Le Iscrizioni Antico-Ebraiche Palestinesi*, 1934, 81-102.

DUNCAN, J. G. *Digging up Biblical History*, II, 1931, 126f.

FINEGAN, J. *Light from the Ancient East*, 1946, 158ff.

MOSCATI, S. *L'Epigrafia Ebraica Antica 1935-1950*, 1951, 40-3.

SMITH, G. A. *Jerusalem*, I, 1907, 94ff.

VINCENT, H. *Jérusalem sous Terre. Les récentes fouilles d'Ophel*, 1911.

N. H. SNAITH

Letters from Lachish

In 1935 eighteen ostraca with inscriptions in ancient Hebrew written upon them were discovered by the Wellcome Archæological Research Expedition to the Near East in the ruins of a small room under the gate-tower which formed part of the main defences of Tell ed-Duweir, now generally identified with the ancient fortress city of Lachish. In 1938 three others, short and fragmentary, and of uncertain date, were unearthed. Of those discovered in 1935, only some are legible enough to admit of intelligible translation. The three here selected for treatment are on the whole well preserved, but problems of decipherment still remain.

The ostraca unearthed in 1935 may be dated *c.* 590 B.C. They belong to the close of Zedekiah's reign, to the time when the Hebrew monarchy was nearing its end, 'when the king of Babylon's army fought against Jerusalem, and against all the cities of Judah that were left, against Lachish and against Azekah ; for these *alone* remained of the cities of Judah *as* fenced cities' (Jer. xxxiv.7). For the most part the ostraca are letters. In those in which the recipient is named he is Yaosh, the military governor of Lachish. In only one of them, namely Ostracon III (see below), is the sender of the letters mentioned. He is Hoshayahu, a subordinate officer of Yaosh, in charge of an outpost, which may have been located at Mareshah (Tell Sandahannah), four miles or so north-east of Lachish and eight miles south of Azekah (Tell Zakariyeh), or Debir (Tell Beit Mirsim), twenty miles or so from Azekah. Though Hoshayahu is mentioned only once in the letters, some, but not necessarily all, of the other letters will probably have been sent by him to Yaosh.

These ostraca from Lachish enable us to know with certainty the kind of Hebrew language and script Judaeans were using in the age of Jeremiah. The language is in all essentials identical with the Hebrew of the Old Testament. The script, written in ink with a wooden or reed pen, is the Early Hebrew script in common use in Israel in pre-exilic days. In this script part of the O.T.—the historical books and large parts of the prophetical books—will have been originally written, on papyrus or leather. The ostraca have an importance too for the study of Hebrew epistolary style—of which there are but few examples in the O.T.—and of Hebrew proper names in Judah in the last days of the monarchy. They are no less important for the textual criticism of the O.T. For example, the irregular use of a dot as a word divider, and the splitting of words at the end of a line, illustrate how some kinds of textual error in the M.T. may have arisen.

In the notes which accompany the translations, attention is drawn to certain contacts between these ostraca and the book of Jeremiah. It is to be emphasised that such contacts are indirect, not direct. Direct contact still awaits proof.

Text

OSTRACON I

Gemaryahu son of Hitsilyahu
Yaazanyahu son of Tobshillem
Hagab son of Yaazanyahu
Mibtahyahu son of Yirmeyahu
Mattanyahu son of Neriyahu

Notes

This ostracon, like the others to which reference is made, is numbered in accordance with TORCZYNER's edition. The significance of the names in this list can only be guessed at. They may be the names of soldiers, or of officials, or of messengers who were registered on arrival at the guard-room at Lachish.

Of the nine different names appearing on this ostracon, five are typical of the age of Jeremiah. They are *Gemaryahu* 'Yahu has accomplished' (Jer. xxix.3, xxxvi.10ff., 25), *Yaazanyahu* 'Yahu hears' (Jer. xxxv.3, xl.8, xlii.1), *Yirmeyahu* (of uncertain meaning ; Jer. xxxv.3, lii.1), *Mattanyahu* 'Gift of Yahu' (2 Kings xxiv.17), and *Neriyahu* 'My lamp is Yahu' (Jer. xxxii.12, xxxvi.14, 32, li.59). These persons do not bear any relation to anyone mentioned in the O.T. The name *Hitsilyahu* 'Yahu has delivered' is not found in the O.T. ; nor is *Tobshillem* 'Good is (the god) Shalem', a name similar in form to Tobyahu 'Yahu is my good', which occurs in Ostracon III (see below) and several times in the O.T. (e.g. 2 Chr. xvii.8 ; Zech. vi.10, 14), and Tabrimmon 'Good is (the god) Ramman' (1 Kings xv.18) ; nor is *Mibtahyahu* 'Yahu is confidence', though this name occurs in the Aramaic papyri from Elephantine. The name *Hagab* 'locust' (cp. Ezra ii.46) is especially interesting in the light of the nearly contemporary animal names Shaphan 'rock badger', Achbor 'mouse', and Huldah 'mole', all mentioned together, in the reign of Josiah, in 2 Kings xxii.14.

Text

OSTRACON III

(Plate 12)

Thy servant Hoshayahu hath sent to inform my lord : May Yahweh bring thee peaceful tidings ! And now [thou hast sent a letter but my lord did not] enlighten thy servant concerning the letter which my lord sent to thy servant yesterday. For the heart of thy servant hath been sick since thou didst send to thy servant. And now when my lord saith, 'Thou dost not know how to read a letter ! ' as Yahweh liveth, no one has ever tried to read a letter to me, and indeed any letter which may have ccme to me, I have certainly not read it . . . at all.

And thy servant hath been informed, saying, 'The commander of the army, Konyahu, son of Elnathan, hath gone down on his way to Egypt, and Hodawyahu, son of Ahiyahu, and his men hath he sent to obtain . . .'

And as for the letter of Tobyahu, servant of the king, which came to Shallum, son of Yaddua, through the instrumentality of the prophet, saying, 'Take care ! ' thy servant hath sent it to my lord.

Notes

The situation in the first part of the letter appears to be that Yaosh sent a letter to Hoshayahu of which the latter emphatically, and with some anxiety —his *heart* is *sick* (cp. Jer. viii.18 ; Lam. i.22, v.17)—disclaims all knowledge. *Hoshayahu* 'Yahu has saved' is another name typical of the Jeremian period (Jer. xlii.1, xliii.2). *Yaosh* 'May (Yahweh) give', or perhaps 'May (Yahweh) heal', is a shortened form of the name Josiah. *as Yahweh liveth*—a frequent phrase in the O.T. (e.g. 1 Sam. xx.3 ; 2 Kings ii.2, 4, 6). The ostraca from Lachish provide the earliest external Israelite witness for the full form of the Tetragrammaton (YHWH = YAHWEH). This form occurs in them about ten times. The free use of the Tetragrammaton in a military correspondence is highly noteworthy.

Konyahu 'Yahu is firm' and *Elnathan* 'God has given' are both 'Jeremian' names (Jer. xxii.24, 28, xxvi.22, xxxvi.12, 23, xxxvii.1). The text is silent as to the object of Konyahu's expedition to Egypt. It may have gone to appeal for help against the Babylonians, or to join up with an Egyptian army with a view to a combined operation against the Babylonians. Other suggestions are that Konyahu went to fetch supplies, or merely to take refuge in flight. The most that can be said with any confidence is that it would not be surprising if a Judaean officer of high rank went at this time to Egypt, the hope of the royal court, and doubtless of the army leaders, for military talks. The expedition

The Gezer Calendar

The Siloam Inscription

Plate 11

Plate 12   Lachish Letter III : Reverse

here referred to is quite a different one from that mentioned in Jer. xxvi.20ff. There is no connection between the two events. *Hodawyahu.* Cp. the name Hodaviah in 1 Chr. iii.24. Probably the name should be read Hoduyahu 'Give thanks to Yahu'. *Ahiyahu.* This name appears frequently in the O.T. before and after the Jeremian period (e.g. 1 Sam. xiv.3 ; Neh. x.27), but not in the Jeremian period itself. The object of *to obtain* is perhaps 'supplies'. The Hebrew letters can, however, be read so as to mean 'from here'.

On *Tobyahu,* see on Ostracon I above. *servant of the king.* The phrase indicates that Tobyahu was a court official at Jerusalem. *Shallum* is a name current in the age of Jeremiah (2 Kings xxii.14 ; Jer. xxii.11, xxxii.7, xxxv.4). *Yaddua.* Cp. Neh. x.21, xii.11f.

The prophet. This is the first occurrence in non-Biblical texts of the common Hebrew word for prophet (*nābī'*). The prophet has been identified with Uriah, son of Shemaiah, of Kiriath-jearim, whose flight into Egypt and subsequent fate at the hands of Jehoiakim are related in Jer. xxvi.20ff. ; and again with Jeremiah, the ostraca reflecting, so it is believed, the conflict between the pro-Babylonian and pro-Egyptian elements in Judah at the time of the Babylonian invasion. Ostracon VI especially has been thought to reflect this conflict. It is, however, badly preserved, and much in it remains uncertain. So far as it can be translated, the contents of it do not seem to be any more applicable to Jeremiah than to any political agitator of the time (cp. Jer. xxvii.14ff.). Neither Uriah nor Jeremiah is mentioned by name in the ostraca, and the attempts to identify the prophet with one or the other have not been successful. The evidence does not in fact make any identification possible. All that is known from Ostracon III is that the prophet acted as a messenger, passing on a letter from Tobyahu to Shallum, perhaps in concert with the military authorities. There is nothing unusual in the active participation of a prophet in a military situation (cp. 2 Kings iii.6ff., where Elisha is called upon to find a solution when Jehoram and Jehoshaphat ran short of water during their attack on Moab). Perhaps the prophet was a wandering holy man—a type of dervish—a suitably reliable person to whom to hand over a letter for safe delivery, The letter passed on may, as perhaps also the ostraca themselves, have been accompanied by a verbal message which was given at the time of delivery by the bearer of it. The prophet will then have been not only a messenger, but spokesman also on behalf of the sender of the letter (cp. Exod. vii.1, where Aaron is described as the prophet (*nābī'*) of Moses—he is spokesman for Moses ; cp. further iv.14ff.). There were many prophets contemporary with Jeremiah whose names are known, for example, Hananiah (Jer. xxviii.1ff.), Zedekiah (Jer. xxix.21), and Shemaiah (Jer. xxix.31). There will no doubt have been others whose names are not known. Anonymous prophets could be counted in ancient Israel by the hundred (cp. 1 Kings xviii.4, 13), and they are referred to as individuals in some other passages (e.g. Jud. vi.8 ; 1 Kings xx.13). The prophet of the ostracon is likewise to be regarded as anonymous. *Take care !* The significance of this warning is not clear.

Text

OSTRACON IV

May Yahweh bring my lord this very day good tidings! And now, in accordance with all that my lord hath written, so hath thy servant done. I have written on the door in accordance with all that [my lord] hath directed me. And with regard to what my lord hath written about Beth-haraphid, there is nobody there. And as for Semakyahu, Shemayahu hath taken him and brought him up to the capital, and thy servant . . . send thither. . . . And [my lord] will know that we are watching for the signals of Lachish, according to all the signs which my lord hath given, for we cannot see Azekah.

Notes

written on the door. The meaning of this phrase is uncertain. The Hebrew word translated 'door' is *deleth*, the word which is translated 'leaves' in Jer. xxxvi.23 (cp. the Greek *delta* 'writing tablet'). Perhaps a papyrus sheet is meant. Or the phrase may mean to put a notice on the door, or to inscribe words on the door itself (cp. Deut. vi.9, xi.20). Or again, it may be an idiomatic expression equivalent to 'make a note of it'. It has been suggested that *deleth* should be read *dallōth*. The phrase would then mean 'I have written concerning the poor ones' (cp. 2 Kings xxiv.14, xxv.12 ; Jer. xl.7, lii.15f.). *Beth-hārāphīd* means, according to some, 'a sleeping house' (a village rest-house). More likely, however, it is a place name (cp. Rephidim, Exod. xvii.1). But the letter *d* is by no means certain. *there is nobody there.* Beth-hārāphīd may have already been evacuated. *Semakyahu* 'Yahu has sustained' (cp. 1 Chr. xxvi.7). *Shemayahu* 'Yahu has heard' is a 'Jeremian' name (Jer. xxvi.20, xxix.31f.). *the capital.* Literally, 'the city', that is, Jerusalem, which is not mentioned by name in the ostraca. In the O.T. the capital of the northern kingdom is referred to as 'the city' in 1 Kings xxii.26 and 2 Kings x.5. The capital of the southern kingdom is likewise called 'the city' in Is. lxvi.6 and Ezek. vii.23.

the signals of Lachish. This ostracon supplies important external evidence for the use of fire signals in ancient Israel. The Hebrew word used here is the same as that used in Jer. vi.1 (cp. Jud. xx.38, 40), namely, *masēth*. At Mari (Tell el-Hariri) on the middle Euphrates, fire signals were used as early as 2000 B.C. at times of military and political crisis, and on important occasions. The number of the signs and their movement, combination and direction together made up a code. It may be that at Lachish *masēth* was used of the signal system as a whole, whereas the *signs* (Hebrew *'ōthōth*) constituted the code or key to the system. Lachish is mentioned only here in the ostraca. *for we cannot see Azekah.* These words have been taken to mean that the Babylonians had already captured Azekah. This conclusion is not, however, necessary, for the signals of Azekah may not have been visible for other reasons—for example, the climatic conditions may not have been good, or again, Azekah may have been too far away. Lachish and Azekah are mentioned together, and in this order, in Jer. xxxiv.7 and Neh. xi.30.

Bibliography

ALBRIGHT, W. F., in *A.N.E.T.*, 321f.

—— 'The Oldest Hebrew Letters: the Lachish Ostraca', *B.A.S.O.R.* No. 70 (1938) 11-17.

—— 'A Re-examination of the Lachish Letters', *B.A.S.O.R.* No. 73 (1939) 16-21.

—— 'The Lachish Letters after Five Years', *B.A.S.O.R.* No. 82 (1941) 18-24.

HEMPEL, J. 'Die Ostraka von Lakiš', *Z.A.W.* xv (1938) 126-39.

JACK, J. W. 'The Lachish Letters: their Date and Import', *P.E.Q.*, 1938, 165-87.

REIDER, J. 'The Lachish Letters', *J.Q.R.* xxix (1939) 225-39.

THOMAS, D. WINTON. 'The Lachish Letters', *J.T.S.* xl (1939) 1-15.

—— 'The Site of Ancient Lachish: The Evidence of Ostracon IV from Tell ed-Duweir', *P.E.Q.*, 1940, 148f.

—— *The Prophet in the Lachish Ostraca*, 1946.

—— 'The Lachish Ostraca: Professor Torczyner's Latest Views', *P.E.Q.*, 1946, 38-42.

—— 'Jerusalem in the Lachish Ostraca', *P.E.Q.*, 1946, 86-91.

—— 'Ostracon III: 13-18 from Tell ed-Duweir', *P.E.Q.*, 1948, 131-6.

—— 'The Age of Jeremiah in the Light of Recent Archæological Discovery', *P.E.Q.*, 1950, 1-5.

—— 'Ostraca XIX-XXI from Tell ed-Duweir (Lachish)', in *Essays and Studies presented to Stanley Arthur Cook* (ed. D. WINTON THOMAS, 1950, 51-8).

—— 'Again "The Prophet" in the Lachish Ostraca', in *Von Ugarit nach Qumran, Festschrift für Otto Eissfeldt* (ed. J. HEMPEL and L. ROST, 1958, 244-9).

TORCZYNER, H. *The Lachish Letters*, 1938.

DE VAUX, R. 'Les Ostraka de Lâchis', *R.B.* xlviii (1939) 181-206.

A full bibliography, covering the years 1938-50, may be found in *Lachish III* (*Tell ed-Duweir*) *The Iron Age* (*Text*), 1953, by O. TUFNELL and others (pp. 21-3). On pp. 331-9 D. DIRINGER gives his reading of the twenty-one ostraca, together with translations where the readings are generally agreed.

D. WINTON THOMAS

Seals

INSCRIBED seals constitute one of the most important groups of Early Hebrew inscriptions. About one hundred and fifty of them are known.

In O.T. times seals were used for the sealing of documents and as marks of ownership in exactly the same way—though probably much more frequently—as they are used today. Herodotus (I, 195) and Strabo (XVI, 513) remark of the Babylonians that every man (i.e. of standing) bore a staff and a seal. To judge from Gen. xxxviii.18 something similar may have obtained in ancient Israel. All documents had to be authenticated by affixing a seal (Is. viii.16, xxix.11 ; Jer. xxxii.10ff. ; cp. 1 Cor. ix.2 ; Jn. iii.33, vi.27) ; letters too were sealed with a seal (1 Kings xxi.8).

The earliest extant inscribed Hebrew seals belong to the ninth or eighth century B.C. ; the latest Early Hebrew inscribed signets may be attributed to the fourth century B.C. The seals exhibit a great variety of shapes, though they are mainly oval-shaped or scaraboid (the back being slightly vaulted). They were made either of semi-precious, hard stone, such as cornelian, chalcedony, jasper, agate, onyx ; or of rock crystal, hæmatite, jade, opal, amethyst ; or, rarely, of soft material, such as steatite. The fact that some were made of limestone suggests that seals were also widely used among the common people. Most of the Early Hebrew seals extant are pierced longitudinally (as they were worn on a string ; Gen. xxxviii.18 ; Jer. xxii.24 ; Song viii.6). Others were set in rings, which were also worn on a cord. Some in fact have been found in their original rings (see No. VI).

The seals are of particular interest both for their inscriptions and their representations. This representational art did not give offence to Hebrew religious feeling (especially is this true of the period before the seventh century B.C.). The predilection for winged, composite creatures, such as cherubim and seraphim (Gen. iii.24 ; 1 Sam. iv.4 ; Is. vi.2, 6, etc.) is clearly evidenced from the seals, on which winged lions with human heads, or winged sphinxes also with human heads (cherubim) or with a falcon's head (griffins), or the winged uræus-snake are frequently portrayed. Various Egyptian motifs are found, such as the last mentioned, or the griffin wearing the double crown of Upper and Lower Egypt, or the lotus flower, or the 'child Horus', or the Egyptian sign of life known as *ankh*. Lions, serpents, birds, etc., too, are found, and also scenes of adoration and sacrifice. However, many of the Early Hebrew seals belonging to the seventh and later centuries B.C. bear an inscription only and no pictorial representation. It has been suggested that these reflect the growing consciousness of the Mosaic prescriptions following the religious reformation in the time of Josiah (621 B.C.), and, in later times, the more rigorous application of the Law after the return from the Exile. Practically all these seals are oval in shape ; the engraved face, surrounded by an oval line, contains two zones separated by a double line, which in some seals is skilfully ornamented. The inscription is divided between two zones, and in several cases in which the inscription contains the Hebrew word *bn* (i.e. *ben* 'son'), the *b* ends the first line and the *n* begins the second line.

I JAR HANDLE SEAL IMPRESSIONS

Over five hundred jar handles have been unearthed containing impressions of seals or sealings. These jar handle stamps are probably trade marks of pottery factories. Some bear private names, being the names of the owners of the factories, and have the form of the common Early Hebrew oval seal divided horizontally by double lines, one line of inscription being above and another below. These names—as indeed the names on seals in general—not only increase our knowledge of Early Hebrew nomenclature, but also enable us to gain a deep insight into the religious beliefs of the period to which the jar handles belong, i.e. the seventh and sixth centuries B.C. In fact, several names (Shebenyahu, 'Azaryahu, Hitsilyahu, Yophiyahu, and many others) give expression to parental sentiment and to a pious devotion to Yahweh.

The great majority of the jar handle seal impressions are known as 'royal' jar handle stamps. They contain either a four-winged symbol (representing the flying scarabæus, or sacred beetle) or a two-winged symbol (which seems to represent a flying scroll, or winged scroll, or else a crested bird) and a short inscription. This consists of two lines, one above the symbol and the other below. The upper line contains the word *lmlk* '(belonging) to the king', 'royal'. The lower line contains one of the following words—*chbrn,zp* or *zyp,shkwh, mmsht*. The first three are respectively the names of the cities Hebron, Ziph and Socoh ; the fourth is an unknown place name. It is very probable that these jar handle stamps belonged to jars which were made in the royal factories mentioned in 1 Chr. iv.23.

II   THE SEAL OF SHEMAʿ

(Plate 13)

The most remarkable of all Early Hebrew seals is that which was found in 1904 at Tell el-Mutesellim (ancient Megiddo). It was at one time preserved in the private treasury of the Sultan at Constantinople, and later it passed to the Museum of Antiquities there. Unfortunately it now seems to be lost. It is a finely worked semi-precious hard stone (jasper) in scaraboid form. The engraved face is surrounded by an oval line, and a single line separates the lower part of the inscription and serves as a kind of platform for the lion. The roaring lion is most vividly represented.

The lion was a favourite animal motif in ancient oriental art. It appears on other Early Hebrew, as well as on Phoenician and Aramaic, seals ; and at Megiddo, several stone models of lions were discovered. No wild animal is so frequently mentioned in the O.T. as the lion, and none is known by a greater variety of names. It was the symbol of strength (Jud. xiv.18), of cruelty (Ps. vii.2), of 'majesty in going' (Prov. xxx.30), etc. It was the symbol of the tribe of Judah (Gen. xlix.9) and of Dan (Deut. xxxiii.22). In Prov. xix.12 the king's wrath is compared to the roaring of a lion. Lion decoration adorned the Temple at Jerusalem (1 Kings vii.29), and, in accordance with oriental usage, lions guarded the throne of Solomon (1 Kings x.19f.). It has been suggested that the motif of the lion on the Megiddo seal was derived from Mesopotamian art. The seal also contains the Egyptian *ankh*-symbol, behind the lion, and the tree of life or a palm tree in front of it. These symbols are lightly painted, not engraved. A suggestion has been made that they were drawn at the time of the drawing of the lion, but for some

unknown reason their engraving was never executed. This
theory is untenable because the colour would doubtless have
disappeared with the use of the seal. It is more likely that these
symbols were added by a later owner of the signet, which may
then have been used as an amulet.

The inscription consists of two lines, one above and one
below the lion. It gives the name of the owner of the signet, and
it reads :

> *lshm'*   '(belonging) to Shema'
> *'bdyrbm*   servant of Jeroboam'

The word *'bd* (*'ebed*) literally means 'slave', but there is no doubt
that in this connection the term does not apply to a slave or a
servant, but to a minister or high official. This term occurs on
several other seals, and the title *'bd hmlk* 'servant of the king'
is also to be found. It may be observed that there is an Early
Hebrew seal (DIRINGER, Seal No. 71) bearing the inscription
lshm' 'bd hmlk '(belonging) to Shema', servant of the king',
and it is possible that we are here dealing with the same person
as in the case of the Megiddo signet. The designation *'ebed ha-
melek* 'servant of the king' is well known from the O.T. (e.g.
2 Kings xxii.12) ; in 2 Kings xvi.7, King Ahaz styles himself as
servant and son of the Assyrian King Tiglath-pileser. The designation 'son' (Hebrew *ben*) occurs on another Early Hebrew seal
(DIRINGER, Seal No. 72 ; *l'lshm' bn hmlk* '(belonging) to Elishama',
son of the king'). For the allied designation *na'ar*, see notes on
No. IV below.

The name Jeroboam only occurs in the O.T. as the name of
two kings of the Northern Kingdom. This, of course, does not
necessarily mean that it could not have been also a private name.
At any rate there is hardly any doubt that in the present case it
does refer to the name of a king. We have, however, no direct
means of knowing whether the Jeroboam referred to was Jeroboam I (1 Kings xii.12ff.), who reigned *c.* 930-914 B.C., or
Jeroboam II (2 Kings xiv.23ff.), who reigned *c.* 786-746 B.C.
Indirect evidence, however, would point to the latter, and it is
generally agreed that the owner of the signet was a minister of
Jeroboam II.

III   THE SEAL OF JAAZANIAH
(Plate 13)

The designation 'servant of the king' also appears on a beautiful signet discovered in 1932 at Tell en-Nasbeh (probably ancient Mizpah), which is preserved in the Palestine Archæological Museum at Jerusalem. It is a black and white banded onyx scaraboid, and is to be dated *c*. 600 B.C.

The engraved face is divided into three zones, separated by double lines. The two upper zones contain the inscription, while in the lower zone there is an extremely interesting representation of a fighting cock. Not only is it the earliest Palestinian representation of this fowl, but it fills a gap in our knowledge of the life of the ancient Israelites. For, since cocks are not mentioned in the O.T., it has hitherto been believed that they were not known in ancient Palestine.

The inscription is in beautiful, characteristic Early Hebrew characters. The letters *he, zayin, kaph, mem, nun*, the ligature *he-waw*, and the interesting ligature of three letters, *beth-daleth-he*, may be especially noted. It reads :

> *ly'znyhw*   '(belonging) to Jaazaniah
> *'bdhmlk*   servant of the king'

The Hebrew name *Yaazanyahu* 'God hears' appears with the same spelling in 2 Kings xxv.23 ; in Jer. xl.8 the same person's name is spelt Yezanyahu. Another person with the same name is referred to in Ezek. viii.11, whereas the same name borne by two other people—all four being contemporary—is spelt Yaazanyah (Jer. xxxv.3 ; Ezek. xl.1). The latter name also appears on a seal as that of the father of its owner (DIRINGER, Seal No. 21) ; and a parallel name Yezanel appears on another Early Hebrew seal (DIRINGER, Seal No. 28). Yaazanyahu is a theophorous name, being compounded of the Hebrew root *'āzan* 'hear' and Yahu (Yahweh). It is generally held that the owner of the seal is the person mentioned in 2 Kings xxv.23 and Jer. xl.8, who was one of the captains of the Judaean army in the time of Gedaliah. This identification, though highly probable, is, however, not beyond all doubt.

IV   THE SEAL IMPRESSION OF GEDALIAH

(Plate 13)

It is an extremely fortunate coincidence that a seal impression bearing the name of Gedaliah—most probably identifiable with the person just referred to—should also have been discovered. It was unearthed in 1935 at Tell ed-Duweir (ancient Lachish), and is now preserved in the Institute of Archæology, University of London.

This clay seal impression, like a great number of Early Hebrew seals (DIRINGER, Seals Nos. 17, 19-21, 23, 27, 29-31, 33-7, and several others ; REIFENBERG, Nos. 20-6) has no decoration. Such seals, with writing only, are typically Judaean.

The inscription, surrounded by an oval line and divided into two lines separated by a double line, reads :

> *lgdlyhw*   '(belonging) to Gedaliah
> [']*shr 'lhbyt*   who is over the household'

The title 'who is over the household', meaning major-domo or chief steward, is a well known O.T. term (e.g. 1 Kings iv.6 ; 2 Kings xviii.18). The person mentioned has been identified, with more or less probability, with Gedaliah, son of Ahikam, son of Shaphan (2 Kings xxv.22-5 ; Jer. xxxix.14, xl.5-xli.8, xliii.6), whom Nebuchadrezzar had appointed governor of Judaea after the conquest of Jerusalem. His headquarters was at Mizpah, where seal No. 11 (see above) was discovered.

The Gedaliah seal impression and four other impressions found at Lachish show, on the reverse, marks of the papyrus documents to which they were affixed. That five of these tiny impressions have been recovered at one archæological site testifies to a fairly common use of papyrus rolls in ancient Israel.

It may be added that another clay seal impression from a papyrus roll, found in 1931 at Khirbet et-Tubeiqah (ancient Beth-zur), bears the inscription *lg'lyhw bn hmlk* '(belonging) to Gealyahu, son of the king'. A name Gealyah, though it does not occur in the O.T., is philologically possible ; indeed, it may be parallel with the O.T. name Igal (1 Chr. iii.22). It has been suggested that this person, a descendant of King Jehoiakim, is to be identified with Gealyahu of the seal impression. On the other hand, there is the possibility of error in the seal impression or of a mistake in its reproduction, in which case the name could be Gedalyahu, Gedaliah, and could refer to the same person as is referred to in the seal impression of Gedaliah 'who is over the household'.

V   THE SEAL IMPRESSION OF ELIAKIM

A very interesting round seal impression, found in three copies, two at Tell Beit Mirsim (ancient Kiryath-sepher), and one at 'Ain Shems, perhaps the ancient Beth-shemesh, bears the following inscription in two lines, separated by the usual double line (there is no decoration) :

l'lyqm	'(belonging) to Eliakim
n'rywkn	boy of Jokin'

The term *na'ar* 'boy' may be regarded in some instances, as in the present one, as parallel with *'ebed* (see under No. 1). It has such a meaning in several O.T. passages, e.g. Gen. xxxvii.2 ; 2 Kings iv.2, v.20 ; 1 Sam. ii.13, etc. There is no doubt that, as in the *'ebed*-seals, the word *na'ar* refers to a high official. Elyaqim, or Eliakim, is an O.T. name ; it was borne by three persons— by the chief steward ('he who is over the household') of King Hezekiah (2 Kings xviii.18ff. ; Is. xxii.20ff.) ; by the son of King Josiah, who later became Jehoiakim (2 Kings xxiii.34 ; 2 Chr. xxxvi.4) ; and by a priest mentioned in Neh. xii.41.

The name Yokin is probably an abbreviation of the name Yoyakin or Yehoyakin, i.e. Jehoiachin, the name of the last king of Judah (Ezek. i.2 ; 2 Kings xxiv.6ff. ; Jer. lii.31 ; 2 Chr. xxxvi.8f., etc.). It has been suggested that the whole inscription might be translated thus—'Eliakim steward of Jehoiachin', i.e. administrator of the personal or crown property of the latter.

VI   THE SEAL OF JOTHAM
(Plate 13)

The seals hitherto discussed would seem to have belonged to persons connected with kings of Israel or Judah. A seal discovered in 1940 at Tell el-Kheleifeh (ancient Ezion-geber) has been attributed to a king of Judah. It is encased in a beautiful copper ring. The engraved face of the seal, surrounded by an oval line, pictures a ram walking, preceded by a very rough figure of a man (?). Above the animal there is the inscription. It consists of four letters as follows :

lytm   '(belonging) to Jotham' (?)

The owner of the seal has been identified with King Jotham (*c.* 742-735), mentioned in several O.T. passages (2 Kings xv.30ff. ; Is. i.1, vii.1 ; Hos. i.1 ; 1 Chr. iii.12, etc.). This attribution is by no means certain, but it is highly probable, both on grounds of chronology and of the location of the find. We know from 2 Chr. xxvi that under Jotham's father, Azariah, Judah was very prosperous ; that Azariah 'built Elath and restored it to Judah ' ; and that he conducted successful campaigns against the desert dwellers to the east. However, the problem of the identification of the person referred to on the seal is still open ; even the reading—whether it should be Jotham or Jathom—is uncertain.

VII SEALS WITH FLORAL DECORATIONS

There are also some seals with floral decoration. Two elegantly engraved signets, which were found in Jerusalem, are preserved in the Western Asiatic Department of the State Museums at Berlin (VA 32 and 33). On VA 32, the inscription in two lines, separated by the usual double line, is surrounded by an oval line. All round this oval line there is a rather unusual decoration of pomegranates. This fruit, called in Hebrew *rimmōn*, is often mentioned in the O.T. (Deut. viii.8 ; Joel i.12 ; Songs viii.2, etc.). Pomegranates figure in the ornamentation of the priestly robes (Exod. xxviii.33, etc.) and in the carvings of the Temple (1 Kings vii.18, etc.), and their beauty is alluded to in Song iv.3, 13, etc.

The inscription reads thus :

lhnnyhw   '(belonging) to Hananiah
bn'zryhw   son (of) Azariah'

Both names occur in the O.T. (e.g. Jer. xxviii.1 ; 2 Kings xv.6, 8). Curiously enough, VA 33 presents many features analogous to those of VA 32. It too contains an inscription in two lines separated by a double line ; the engraved face is surrounded by an oval line ; the name of the owner is the same, but not the patronymic ; and it is very elegantly engraved. Its floral decoration is, however, different. It is divided into three zones, the upper one, separated from the rest by a double line, containing a seven-leaved palmette. A nearly identical decoration is found on a fragment which belonged to a stone decorative frieze of the synagogue at Chorazin (Khirbet Kerazeh), to the north of the Sea of Gennesaret, though the seal is probably nine hundred years older than the synagogue.

The inscription reads :

lhnnyhw	'(Belonging) to Hananiah
bn'kbr	son of Achbor'

Of particular interest is the name Achbor 'mouse' (2 Kings xxii.12), names of animals being rare in inscriptions.

Bibliography

BADE, W. F. 'The Seal of Jaazaniah', *Z.A.W.* N.F. x (1933) 150-6.

COOK, S. A. *The Religion of Ancient Palestine in the Light of Archæology* (Schweich Lectures 1925), 1930, 56-66.

DIRINGER, D. *Le Iscrizioni Antico-Ebraiche Palestinesi*, 1934, 159-261, 344f., *et passim* (Plates XIX-XXII).

DRIVER, G. R., 'Hebrew Seals', *P.E.Q.*, 1955, 183.

GALLING, K. 'Beschriftete Bildsiegel des ersten Jahrtausends v. Chr. vornehmlich aus Syrien und Palaestina', *Z.D.P.V.* lxiv (1941) 121-202.

—— *Biblisches Reallexicon*, 1937, 482-90.

GLUECK, N. 'The Third Season of Excavation at Tell el-Kheleifeh', *B.A.S.O.R.* No. 79 (1940) 13-15 (on the seal of Jotham).

HOOKE, S. H. 'An Israelite Seal from Tell ed-Duweir', *P.E.F.Q.S.*, 1934, 97f.

—— 'A Scarab and Sealing from Tell Duweir', *P.E.F.Q.S.*, 1935, 196f.

MAY, H. G. 'Three Hebrew Seals and the Status of Exiled Jehoiakin', *A.J.S.L.* lvi (1939) 146ff.

MOSCATI, S. 'I Sigilli nell' Antico Testamento', *Biblica* xxx (1949) 314-38.

—— *L'Epigrafia Ebraica Antica 1935-1950*, 1951, 47-71.

REIFENBERG, A. *Ancient Hebrew Seals*, 1950.

DE VAUX, R. 'Le Sceau de Godolias, Maître du Palais', *R.B.* xlv (1936) 96-102.

D. DIRINGER

Weights

THE difficulties of classifying Early Hebrew weights are many and great. In the first place, Palestine in O.T. times had so many systems of weights during her long history, and the archæological and chronological data connected with the finds are so uncertain, that any classification based on a metrological system alone must be regarded as provisional. Moreover, a glance at the weights which have been found makes it evident that the standards of the ancient Hebrews were far from exact. This is what anyone acquainted with Palestine in the period before the Mandate would expect. The peasants continued to use stones as weights, selecting one that was approximately of the weight they desired, and in cities odd scraps of old iron were used for weights.

The weights discovered in various archæological sites of Palestine confirm that the situation was no better in ancient times. Although the inscriptions must have been intended as an assurance of the accuracy of the weights, there are no two Early Hebrew specimens bearing the same inscription which have exactly the same weight. Where weights and measures were so different, the words of Amos (viii.5) 'making the ephah small, and the shekel great' gain an added significance, and we can better understand those O.T. passages (Lev. xix.33f. ; Deut. xxv.13ff., etc.) which show that 'divers' weights were employed, both 'just' and 'unjust'. We can also understand why 'false balances' are denounced (Prov. xi.1, xx.23).

The two weights most often mentioned in the O.T. are the talent (Hebrew *kikkār*) and the shekel (Hebrew *sheqel*). While inscribed talents—which doubtless would have been used only in the case of very large consignments—could hardly be expected to be found, there is no satisfactory explanation why, amongst the several inscribed Early Hebrew weights, only one, and a rather doubtful one, should bear the inscription *sheqel*. Notwithstanding, the inscribed Early Hebrew weights are of the greatest interest for the student of the O.T.

Twenty-nine inscribed Early Hebrew weights have been discovered in Palestine. Nearly half of them bear the inscription *netseph* (Pl. 13).   The weight may have been the 'common' shekel, although etymologically the term seems to indicate 'a half' (perhaps of the 'heavy' shekel).   The *netseph* series covers the whole scale between 9.28 and 10.515 grammes, the average being 9.84 grammes.   One of these weights is inscribed *reba' netseph* and weighs 2.54 grammes ; it shows that there also existed fractions at least of this unit of weight.   Seven weights bear the inscription *pīm* ; the series covers the scale between 7.18 and 8.59 grammes, the average being 7.762 grammes.   Seven are inscribed *beqa'* ; they cover the scale between 5.8 (or even perhaps 5.66) grammes and 6.65 grammes, and their average is 6.11 or 6.05 grammes. This shows that the difference between the heaviest and the lightest specimens of the same series is much greater than the difference between the lightest *netseph* and the heaviest *pīm*, or between the lightest *pīm* and the heaviest *beqa'*.   Moreover, it would be a mistake to assume that the differences in the same series are only variations of the average value, because this would not explain the weights which are heavier than the average. Another explanation, as unsatisfactory as the former, is that many had one set of weights which they used when buying (those which were above the average standard), and another set which they used when selling (those under the average standard).

The answer, of course, is that the Early Hebrew system of weights was much more complicated than has been supposed. It may be assumed that there were independent systems which probably varied according to region and/or according to the goods for sale, just as nowadays the chemist, the grocer, and the jeweller use different standards.   Also, these standards varied locally in Palestine before the Mandate.

I   BRONZE TURTLE-SHAPED WEIGHTS

A small weight of bronze, now dark green, made in the form of a turtle, contains on top the word *shql* (?), but only the *sh* is quite clear and the *q* more or less probable ; on the bottom there are two words *plg rb't*, which have been explained, not quite satisfactorily, as 'half of a fourth', i.e. 'an eighth' (of a shekel). The weight is 2.63 grammes.   If the decipherment and interpretation of the inscription is correct, the metrological value of the shekel in question would be (8×2.63) 21.04 grammes.

This weight comes from the region of Ashkelon, and is preserved in the collection of the late Prof. A. REIFENBERG, at Jerusalem. It is interesting to note that another bronze weight made in the form of a turtle, and found near Samaria, bears the inscription *chōmesh* 'one fifth'. It weighs 2.499 grammes, and if the inscription refers to a shekel, it would fix its weight at 12.495 grammes.

II THE 'BEQA'' WEIGHT
(Plate 13)

The seven weights bearing the inscription *bqʿ* ('beqa'') have already been mentioned   The Hebrew word comes from a root which means 'to cleave, split'. This word occurs twice in the Pentateuch, in Gen. xxiv.22 and Exod. xxxviii.26. According to the former passage, the *beqaʿ* was used for weighing gold, and according to the latter passage it was the poll-tax and was 'half a shekel, after the shekel of the sanctuary'. In view of this and of the inscribed weights which have been recovered, it must be assumed that the metrological value of the 'shekel of the sanctuary' was 11.6 or 11.32 to 13.3 grammes.

Three of the *beqa*'s come from Tell ed-Duweir (Lachish), one apparently from Jerusalem, one from Gezer, one from Khirbet et-Tubeiqah (Beth-zur), and one from Ras Salāh, near Shafāt, about two miles north of Jerusalem. The inscriptions are of particular interest as in several of them the letters have unusual shapes.

III THE 'PĪM' WEIGHT
(Plate 13)

Of the seven *pīm* weights, two were discovered at Tell ed-Duweir, one apparently in Jerusalem, one at Silwān, near Jerusalem, and one in each of the excavations at Gezer, Khirbet et-Tubeiqah and Tell en-Nasbeh (probably Mizpah).

The word *pīm* is puzzling. Various interpretations have been suggested, for example, that it may be an abbreviation of (*le-*)*phī m*(*ishqāl*), 'according to the standard weight', or of *pī*(*shena*)*yim*, 'two fractions', i.e. fraction divided into two, i.e. 'half', or else that it may be related to the Sumerian term *shanabi* and the Akkadian *shinipu*, meaning $4/6 = 2/3$ (as in Akkadian *shinā* means 2, *pū* may mean $1/3$, and the Canaanite *pīm* or *payim* would mean

2/3). Be this as it may, it is generally agreed that *pīm* was originally a unit of the metrological value of 2/3 of a higher unit, probably of the 'common' shekel, which thus would have the metrological value of 10.7777 to 12.2 grammes.

The main interest from the O.T. point of view of the inscription *pīm* lies in the fact that this word appears in 1 Sam. xiii.21, and that the discovery of these weights has explained a Hebrew passage which has puzzled all translators. In verse 21 the A.V. has : 'Yet they had a file. . . .' (margin 'a file with mouths'). The R.V. has 'they had a file' (margin 'or when the edges . . . were blunt') ; and the Revisers added 'the Hebrew text is obscure'. The discovery of the *pīm* weight has cleared up the obscurity. The passage 1 Sam. xiii.20f. should accordingly be rendered as follows : 'But all the Israelites went down to the Philistines, to sharpen every man his ploughshare, and his axe, and his adze, and his hoe, and the charge was a *pīm* (or *payim*) for the plough-shares, and for the axes and for the three-tined forks, and for the adzes, and for the setting of the goads' (cp. the Revised Standard Version). The *pīm* here expresses the charge, just as the shekel and the *beqaʿ* do elsewhere.

Whereas the majority of the inscribed weights are of stone and have the shape of a truncated cone, the Jerusalem *pīm* is in bronze and is cubic in form. Moreover, apart from the inscription *pīm* it bears, on another side, the inscription

lzkry	'(belonging) to Zecharya—
hw/y'r	hu/(son of) Jair'

Bibliography

BENZINGER, I. *Hebräische Archäologie*, third ed., 1927, 195ff.

DIRINGER, D. *Le Iscrizioni Antico-Ebraiche Palestinesi*, 1934, 263-90 (Plates XXIII-XXIV).

GALLING, K. *Biblisches Reallexicon*, 1937, 186f.

MOSCATI, S. *L'Epigrafia Ebraica Antica 1935-1950*, 1951, 99-105 (Plates XXIV-XXV).

SPEISER, E. A. 'Of Shoes and Shekels (1 Samuel 12:3 ; 13:21)', *B.A.S.O.R.* No. 77 (1940) 18 ff. (on *pīm*).

D. DIRINGER

The Seal of Shema'

The Seal of Jaazaniah

The Seal Impression of Gedaliah : *(left)* Obverse *(right)* Reverse, showing
marks of the papyrus to which the seal was affixed

The Seal of Jotham and Seal Impression

Netseph Weight

Pim Weights

Beqa' Weights

Plate 13

Yehūd Coin : (*left*) Obverse (*right*) Reverse

Hezekiah Coin

Coin of John Hyrcanus	Coin of Alexander Jannaeus
(135–104 B.C.)	(103–76 B.C.)
(*left*) Obverse (*right*) Reverse	(*left*) Obverse (*right*) Reverse

Plate 14

Coins

(Plate 14)

Coins may be described as minted pieces of metal designed to be used as authorised media of exchange. They usually bear stamped impressions on both faces : some have portraits of human beings, animals or birds, with or without emblems, while others have emblems only. Inscriptions indicate the issuing authority and the values represented by the coins. The invention of coinage by the Greeks early in the seventh century B.C. is the culmination of the search for a convenient and permanent system of exchange. The simplest and most primitive method of transacting business was barter, that is, the exchange of commodities. An advance was made by the introduction of the use of pieces of precious metal of specified weight to represent commercial values and to circulate as recognised media of exchange. Both systems apparently persisted till the invention of coinage.

In the O.T. there are many references to the employment of money in the transaction of business and in the payment of ecclesiastical and other dues, but coins do not appear in O.T. narratives till post-exilic times. The Hebrew word *keseph*, which has the general meaning 'silver', was used also to denote 'money', while a nominal form of the verb *shāqal*, meaning 'weighed', namely *shekel* (or, more accurately transliterated, *sheqel*), became the designation of the standard unit of money as well as of weight. This monetary unit was a piece of silver (though later gold was also used) of a specific weight : money was not counted but weighed. Abraham weighed out four hundred silver shekels 'current money with the merchant' in payment for the cave of Machpelah (Gen. xxiii.16), and Jeremiah weighed out the purchase money for the field of Hanamel (Jer. xxxii.9). In monarchical times commodities, as well as weighed money, were used in payment of dues. The ostraca (potsherds bearing inscriptions) which were discovered on the site of the ancient city of Samaria have been identified, from their written contents, as being chits relating to the payment of taxes in kind to the central government. Subdivisions of the shekel were the half-shekel, also known as *beqa*' (Exod. xxxviii.26), a third of a shekel (Neh. x.33), and a quarter-shekel (1 Sam. ix.8). Multiples of the shekel were the *māneh* = 50 shekels, and the *kikkār* (or talent) = 60 *mānehs*. When coins appeared in post-exilic Judah, the terms used for weighed money were carried over to denote values of minted money.

Coins appear to have been in wide circulation among the Greeks during the sixth century B.C. The Persians evidently learned the art of minting coins from the Greeks, either following upon the defeat of Croesus by Cyrus (546 B.C.), or through earlier contacts. During the reign of Darius I (522-486 B.C.) Persian gold coins, called *darics* and imitating Greek designs, were circulating throughout the Persian empire. As an expression of their enlightened policy towards their dependencies, the Persians permitted these subject territories to mint silver coins. It is through the Persians that we gain our first contact with coins used by the Jews. In the Ezra-Nehemiah memoirs lists are given of the sums of money subscribed for the restoration of the Temple (Ezra ii.69 ; Neh. vii.70ff.), and the unit of coinage mentioned is the *darkemōn* or *'adarkōn*. This coin has been identified as the Persian gold daric, and the earlier identification with the Greek drachma has generally been abandoned. It was but natural that the money in the possession of the Jews should be the coined money which was current in the Persian empire. The reference to this currency may be regarded as proof that the accounts given in these memoirs were written at a time close to the events which they describe.

Jewish post-exilic coins have been found in several places in Palestine. According to A. REIFENBERG, the earliest Jewish coin known belongs to the latter part of the fifth century B.C. This coin, which was found at Hebron, has a Hebrew inscription on it, and yet it seems to conform, in the themes it portrays, to the type of Greek coin current in this century. The inscription, written in the Early Hebrew script, is the word *beqa*' which, as already noted, is the term used for the half-shekel. On the obverse there is a portrait of a bearded male head, and on the reverse a female head wearing a necklace ; both portraits suggest pagan themes. Whereas the darics mentioned above are Persian coins in circulation amongst the Jews, the *beqa*' coin is Jewish, apparently minted in Judah. The authority to mint coins implies

that some wide measure of local autonomy was enjoyed by the
people of Judah.   If REIFENBERG's dating is correct, we may
conclude that, since the coin belongs to the period of Nehemiah
and Ezra or to a slightly later period, the degree of autonomy
granted to the small dependency of Judah by the Persians was
greater than might be supposed from the memoirs of these two
leaders.   However, the stamping of human portraits on Jewish
coins requires some explanation in view of the prohibition against
this practice laid down in Exod. xx.4.   The fact that human
figures are depicted on the wall paintings of the synagogue of
Dura Europos (third century A.D.) and on the mosaic floor of
the synagogue at Beth Alpha (sixth century A.D.) makes their
appearance on Jewish coins less surprising.   It may be that the
prohibition was understood to apply to the making of human
and animal representations for the purpose of worship, but, where
the probabilities of worship were precluded by the very nature
of the object, the prohibition did not apply.   The imitation
of pagan themes of portraiture on Jewish coins, suggesting some
alignment with current secular culture, might also indicate some
limitations on their political independence.   The themes represented on the later Maccabaean coinage (see below) display a
sharp contrast to the earlier ones by their clear assertion of
independence and their rejection of Hellenistic culture.

Jewish coins of the fourth century B.C. again follow the prevailing Greek patterns, with a human bearded head (with head-
dress or helmet) on the one face, and an owl (the emblem of the
Greek goddess Athena) on the other ; on one coin the reverse
has a full male figure (possibly divine) holding a hawk.   The
inscription consists of the three letters *YHD*, written in the
Early Hebrew script, and is to be read *Yehūd*.   (It is to be noted
that the corresponding inscription on the Greek coins consists of
the first three letters of the name of the goddess Athena.)   The
word *Yehūd*, first read correctly by E. L. SUKENIK—before him
it was commonly read *Yahu*, a divine name—is the Aramaic
form of the Hebrew word *Yehūdāh*, that is, Judah, and is found
in the Aramaic portions of the O.T. (e.g. Dan. v.13 ; Ezra v.1, 8)
as the official name of the Judaean province of the Persian empire.
The appearance of the name of the Judaean province on these
coins may be regarded as evidence that the autonomy which the
Judaeans enjoyed in this century (according to SUKENIK, before

the conquest by Alexander the Great) was greater than that which was accorded to them in the previous century. A similar type of coin, found at Beth-zur, which has no trace of the impression on the obverse, has a longer inscription alongside the owl impression on the reverse. W. F. ALBRIGHT, who assigns this coin to the fourth century B.C., reads the inscription as 'Hezekiah'. From a reference in Josephus he identifies this person as the High Priest who was a friend of Ptolemy I. ALBRIGHT concludes that the stamping of the High Priest's name on coins indicates the almost royal status of a priestly dynasty which exercised wide authority within its own territory

The next series of Jewish coins which have come to light are Maccabaean. These appeared some years after the successful revolt against Antiochus IV, who had attempted the forcible Hellenisation of the Jews. Though, according to 1 Macc. xv.6, Antiochus VII issued a decree according to the High Priest Simon the right to mint coins, it may be that it was not Simon, but his son John Hyrcanus, who was the first to issue coins. REIFENBERG, however, assigns to Simon a series of coins which other scholars assign to the first revolt between A.D. 66 and 70. The *lūlāb* (palm branch), *'ethrōg* (citrus), baskets of fruit, and a chalice, are the emblems impressed on them, and the inscriptions, written in the Early Hebrew script, read, on the obverse, 'the year four—one half', or 'one quarter' (i.e. of a shekel), and, on the reverse, 'of the redemption of Zion'. If these coins are early Maccabaean, they reflect a spirit of proud independence and an utter rejection of Hellenism. The year of liberation marks a new era and the symbols portrayed are unmistakably Jewish. If, however, the first Maccabaean coins were issued by John Hyrcanus, the same conclusions may be inferred, for the inscription on them reads 'Yehochanan the High Priest and the Community of Jews', while the symbols used are mainly double cornucopiæ, or horns from which fruit and flowers emerge, the emblem of peace and plenty. The script is, once again, Early Hebrew.

Since the Early Hebrew script is found on coins of the fifth and fourth centuries B.C. and on Maccabaean coinage, it has been concluded that this ancient script had not been completely ousted by the Aramaic square script. The ancient script evidently persisted during these centuries, though probably to a very reduced degree, and the Maccabees gave it prominence on their coins as a demonstration of independence. In other words, they did not revive a script which had already fallen completely out of use and was forgotten ; they made use of a script which still lingered on (on this subject see D. DIRINGER, in *Essays and Studies presented to Stanley Arthur Cook*, ed. D. WINTON THOMAS, 1950, especially 41ff.).

From this brief survey it will be evident how much may be gleaned from a study of coins used by the post-exilic Jews. Existing knowledge may be confirmed, modified or supplemented by this external source of information.

Bibliography

BENZINGER, I.   *Hebräische Archäologie*, third ed., 1927, 197-204.

COOKE, G. A.   *A Text-Book of North-Semitic Inscriptions*, 1903, 352-9.

GALLING, K.   *Biblisches Reallexicon*, 1937, 387ff.

KANAEL, B.   'The Historical Background of the Coins "Year Four . . . of the Redemption of Zion" ', *B.A.S.O.R.* No. 129 (1953) 18ff.

LOEWE, R.   'The Earliest Biblical Allusion to Coined Money ?', *P.E.Q.*, 1955, 141-50.

REIFENBERG, A.   *Ancient Jewish Coins*, second revised ed., 1947.

ROMANOFF, P.   'Jewish Symbols on Ancient Jewish Coins', *J.Q.R.* xxxiv (1943-1944) 161-77, 299-312, 425-40.

SELLERS, O. R. and ALBRIGHT, W. F.   'The First Campaign of Excavation at Beth-Zur', *B.A.S.O.R.* No. 43 (1931) 10.

SUKENIK, E. L.   'The Oldest Coins of Judaea', *J.P.O.S.* xiv (1934) 178-82.

——— 'More about the Oldest Coins of Judaea', *J.P.O.S.* xv (1935) 341ff.

J. WEINGREEN

Aramaic Documents

The Milqart Stele

(Plate 15)

THERE are three royal inscriptions on the steles from the ninth century B.C., the famous Moabite stone, the Kilamuwa stele (from North Syria), and the Milqart stele. Written in Aramaic at the base of the figure in bas-relief of the god to whom it is dedicated (Milqart), the Milqart stele is the earliest inscribed monument bearing the name of a king of Damascus—Ben-hadad I, son of Tabrimmon, son of Hezion, the contemporary of Asa and Baasha (1 Kings xv.18). Apart from the evidence of this stone and the Zakir stele, we are entirely dependent on the O.T. records for the century and a half of Israel's struggle with Syria. Experts on the form of the letters assign the inscription to the middle of the ninth century B.C.

The stele was discovered at a village some five miles north of Aleppo among Roman ruins. As there was no trace on the site of earlier occupation, the stele appears to have been brought to Aleppo in Roman times. It has been suggested that it may have come from a shrine of the god Milqart in the vicinity of Aleppo. If this is so, then the presence of a stele set up by a king of Syria near Aleppo is interesting evidence of the extent and expansion of the Syrian empire in the middle of the ninth century B.C. The stone may, however, have been brought to Aleppo from Syria, even Damascus.

The text of the inscription was first published by MAURICE DUNAND, the excavator of Byblos, in 1941, and translated and edited in the following year by W. F. ALBRIGHT.

Text

The monument which Bar-hadad, son of Tab-Rammon son of Hadyan, King of Aram, set up for his Lord Milqart : (the stele) which he vowed to him, and he hearkened to his voice.

Notes

The text is somewhat defaced and several letters are obscured where the proper names Tab-Rammon and Hadyan are found, but these names do not appear to be in any doubt. The opening line has an exact parallel in the Zakir stele.

Bar-hadad. There do not seem to be sufficient grounds for departing from the Aramaic form *Bar* in favour of the Assyrian pronunciation of it as *Bir*. There are three Bar-hadads generally supposed to be mentioned in the books of Kings, the Ben-hadad I of 1 Kings xv.18 and this stele, Ben-hadad II of 1 Kings xx.1, and Ben-hadad III, the contemporary of Elisha (2 Kings xiii. 24). It has been thought that the first two passages refer to one and the same person. The main objections to this theory are : (i) according to the numbers given in Kings for the reigns of Israelite kings from Baasha to Jehu, Ben-hadad I (the Ben-hadad of both 1 Kings xv.18 and xx.1) must then have reigned at least fifty years. (ii) According to 1 Kings xx.34 Ben-hadad promised Ahab 'The cities which my father took from thy father I will restore ; and thou shalt make streets for thee in Damascus, as my father made in Samaria'. This is most naturally interpreted if the reference is to the father of the speaker, an earlier Ben-hadad.

W. F. ALBRIGHT argues for the view that the Ben-hadads of 1 Kings xv and xx are one and the same person ; 'father' in xx.34 he explains as 'predecessor' ; the chronology of Kings cannot be relied on, must be corrected in the light of the statements in Chronicles, and the length of Ben-hadad I's reign accordingly reduced to some thirty-six years, though he may have ruled for a good forty, like David, Solomon, Asa, and probably Hazael. This theory is held to be confirmed by the Milqart stele—not by any fresh light its contents shed on the history (it simply establishes, what we have no reason to doubt, the existence of Ben-hadad, son of Tabrimmon), but by the character of its script which, ALBRIGHT thinks, takes us down to the middle of the century, *c.* 850 B.C. The case cannot be held to be proven, but it has been more convincingly argued than by earlier defenders of the theory.

Milqart. The name of the god, Milk-gart, Milqart, Græco-Roman Melcarth, means literally 'king of the city'. Since the publication of the Ras Shamra poetic texts, it is clear that we are to understand this as meaning 'king of the underworld', thus proving the old explanation erroneous which connected the name with the city of Tyre whose chief deity was Milqart. As ALBRIGHT has shown, the gods of Canaan were 'not figures of local origin, limited to sharply defined areas, but were cosmic deities, precisely like the deities of Mesopotamia and the Ægean'. (*B.A.S.O.R.* No. 87 (1942) 29).

The artistic style of the figure is not, as some have explained, Assyrian, but Syrian ; the figure wears a Syrian loin-cloth.

Plate 15   The Milqart Stele

Bibliography

ALBRIGHT, W. F. 'A Votive Stele Erected by Ben-Hadad I of Damascus to the God Melcarth', *B.A.S.O.R*, No. 87 (1942) 23-9.

—— 'The Near East and Israel', *J.B.L.* lix (1940) 102-10.

DUNAND, M. 'Stèle Araméenne Dédiée à Melqart', *Bulletin du Musée de Beyrouth* iii (1941) 65-76.

KRAELING, E. G. *Aram and Israel*, 1918, 46ff.

MOWINCKEL, S. 'Die Vorderasiatischen Königs-und Fürsteninschriften', in H. GUNKEL, *Studien zur Religion und Literatur des Alten und Neuen Testaments*, 1923, 278-322.

OLMSTEAD, A. T. *History of Palestine and Syria*, 1931 (especially chs. xxiiiff.).

M. BLACK

The Zakir Stele

LIKE the Milqart inscription, the inscription of Zakir, king of Hamath and Lu'ash, has been cut, in bas-relief, on the base of the figure of the god to whom the stele was dedicated (the Akkadian weather-god 'Ilwēr). The complete stele has not survived : all that remains are four broken pieces of the lower half of the stele, fortunately preserving the bulk of the text of the inscription, but at places badly defaced. The limbs of the god below the knee, with the feet destroyed, but still showing the bottom of a long embroidered garment, are still visible. The original stele is estimated to have been some 210 cm. in height.

The stele was found in 1907 in Afis, twenty-five miles south-west of Aleppo, by H. POGNON, for many years French consul in Aleppo. POGNON published the text of the inscription in 1907-08 along with other inscriptions in Assyrian, Pehlevi, Hebrew and Syriac (the Zakir inscription is in Old Aramaic), but the place of the discovery was kept a close secret till several years afterwards. Its eventual disclosure proved to be important, since the name Aphis occurs in the text, and the modern Afis is situated in the area where the events recorded in the inscription took place. It was almost certainly the site of the shrine of the god 'Ilwēr where the stele was originally erected.

The stele commemorates a victory of Zakir over Ben-hadad (in its Aramaic form Bar-hadad), son of Hazael, king of Syria, and his allies, at Hazrak, the Assyrian Hatarikka and the Hadrach of Zech. ix.1, where it is mentioned along with Hamath (verse 2) as a city of some importance on the northern boundaries of Syria.

Bar-hadad, son of Hazael, supplies our most important clue for the period and dating of the inscription : he can only be the Ben-hadad, son of Hazael, mentioned in 2 Kings xiii.24, the contemporary of Joash of Israel and the prophet Elisha. The events commemorated in the stele must, therefore, have been contemporaneous with the events of 2 Kings xiii. A date *c.* 755 B.C. is generally accepted.

Who was Zakir, and where did his kingdom of Lu'ash lie?

An answer to the second question will help us to answer the first.

To begin with what is known. Hamath is familiar from the O.T. as an important city on the northernmost frontiers of Syria ; its king, Urhuleni, is mentioned in the Nimrod obelisk as one of the conquered kings in the great Assyrian victory at Qarqar on the Orontes in 854 B.C. Hazrak or Hadrach, is also, as we have seen, known both from the O.T. and Assyrian sources. It was situated somewhere, perhaps about midway, between Arpad and Hamath ; the most likely site is the great tell some thirteen miles north-east of Afis.

The main problem of the stele has been the identification of Lu'ash. Among the alternatives proposed (see the Notes) the best seems to be the equation of Lu'ash with the land of Nuhashshe of the Amarna letters, a territory lying between Aleppo and Hamath. Hazrak lies within this area and was no doubt its capital. The stele not only commemorates Zakir's victory at Hazrak (with the help of his patron deity Ba'al-shemain), but it also goes out of its way to recall that it was in Hazrak that Zakir was made king (with the help of the same deity) ; as he is described in the opening lines as 'King of Hamath and Lu'ash' we are almost bound to infer that Hazrak was the capital of Lu'ash as Hamath was of the kingdom or *territorium* of Hamath. A separate coronation would take place in each capital.

Zakir was thus king of both Hamath and Lu'ash, two adjacent territories resembling Judah and Israel, but under the one ruler, stretching from Hamath in the south towards Aleppo in the north. If Aphis marked the northernmost boundary, it stretched to within twenty-five miles of Aleppo. Zakir may have been a usurper (there is a significant omission of the name of his father) : more probably, as we shall see, he was a puppet-king of the Assyrian empire.

The next problem of the stele is to explain how Zakir, apparently 'the son of a nobody', had come to this position of power over two kingdoms, to be eventually in a position to defeat the might of Syria and her allies. There is no mistaking from the stele that Ben-hadad had gathered considerable forces to crush Zakir : a confederacy of more than ten kingdoms, mostly from the region round the mouth of the Orontes and the Amarus mountains, but including Cilicia, or the ancient Kue, united under Ben-hadad, to lay siege to Zakir in Hazrak. It has been suggested that it was Ben-hadad's last campaign and that he perished in the siege.

Explanations which attribute the defeat of Syria and her powerful allies to natural phenomena such as earthquake are unconvincing, besides being without foundation in any records. The whole problem is illumined for us by the mention of several of Ben-hadad's confederate states as among the peoples of the Mediterranean sea-board (including Syria and Israel) so igno-miniously defeated by Shalmaneser III of Assyria in the great carnage of Qarqar, when the Assyrian monarch boasted in the famous black obelisk of 854 B.C., that 'he had dammed the Orontes with their dead'. Among these opponents of Assyria at Qarqar we find record, as we have already seen, of the presence of Urhuleni, king of Hamath. Now, two or three generations later, we find Zakir, king of Hamath, opposing Syria and a similar confederacy. Only one explanation fits the facts, as LIDZBARSKI suggested: Zakir was a puppet-king of Assyria, the 'son of a nobody' from 'Anah on the Euphrates; Hamath and Lu'ash were satellite states of Assyria and Hazrak an outpost of the empire.

There is evidence in Assyrian annals of the importance of the province and city of Hazrak for the Assyrians, but there is no mention on the stele that Hazrak had been relieved by Assyrian forces. That seems, however, the most natural explanation, and Assyrian chroniclers report an expedition against Damascus in 773 B.C., the last full year of Shalmaneser's reign. Hazrak may have been relieved in the course of this expedition to Damascus. Alternatively, as LIDZBARSKI has suggested, Shal-maneser's death was the signal for an organised but abortive uprising of the northern tribes, led by Ben-hadad of Syria, to reduce Hazrak and conquer the outpost states of Hamath and Lu'ash.

How is this fresh knowledge to be related to O.T. history? The O.T. story of Israel's dealings with Syria at this time is one of peculiar interest since it contains the weird, dying prophecy of the prophet Elisha of the impending defeat of Syria by Israel, at a stage when Israel's fortunes vis-à-vis the Syrian power had reached their nadir of humiliation. Under Jehoahaz, Israel had suffered the most crushing defeat, including the loss of some of her cities at the hands of Hazael. Jehoahaz's successor Joash went in desperation to the death-bed of Elisha (2 Kings xiii.14ff.) :

'Now Elisha was fallen sick of his sickness whereof he died: and Joash the king of Israel came down unto him, and wept over him, and said, My father, my father, the chariots of Israel and the horsemen thereof! And Elisha said unto him, Take bow and arrows: and he took unto him bow and arrows. And he said to the king of Israel, Put thine hand upon the bow: and he put his hand *upon it*. And Elisha laid his hands upon the king's hands. And he said, Open the window eastward: and he opened it. Then Elisha said, Shoot: and he shot. And he said, The Lord's arrow of victory, even the arrow of victory over Syria: for thou shalt smite the Syrians in Aphek, till thou have consumed them. And he said, Take the arrows: and he took them. And he said unto the king of Israel, Smite upon the ground: and he smote thrice, and stayed. And the man of God was wroth with him, and said, Thou shouldest have smitten five or six times; then hadst thou smitten Syria till thou hadst consumed it: whereas now thou shalt smite Syria but thrice.'

The sequel is described in verses 20-4:

'Then Elisha died and they buried him . . . And Hazael king of Syria oppressed Israel all the days of Jehoahaz. But the Lord was gracious unto them, and had compassion on them, and had respect unto them, because of his covenant with Abraham, Isaac and Jacob, and would not destroy them, neither cast he them from his presence as yet. And Hazael king of Syria died; and Ben-hadad his son reigned in his stead. And Jehoash the son of Jehoahaz took again out of the hand of Ben-hadad the son of Hazael the cities which he had taken out of the hand of Jehoahaz by war. Three times did Joash smite him, and recovered the cities of Israel.'

The O.T. narrative does not furnish us with any details about Joash's defeat of Ben-hadad, nor does it sketch in the wider political background. With the help of the Zakir inscription we are now in a position to do so, as with other meagrely narrated events of the O.T., from a source outside its pages.

The O.T. historian attributes the defeat of Syria to the goodness of Yahweh, but does not reveal what form this providential deliverance took. From the Zakir text we become aware of an important historical factor, hitherto unknown, which must have contributed largely to the Syrian defeat, if it was not more than a contributing cause, since the Zakir victory may have removed Ben-hadad himself. At any rate, during his reign and probably towards its close, Ben-hadad found himself engaged on two fronts, with Israel and the south and with Zakir, and all that lay behind him, in the north. As events proved, he was defeated on both fronts, and the Syrian empire contracted at both north and south. Israel owed her victory partly at any rate to the continuing power and pressure westwards of the Assyrian empire, that was destined, in the same century, to swallow her up.

Text

(a) FRONT

The monument which Zakir, King of Hamath and Lu'ash erected to 'Ilwēr [in this temple (shrine)?].

I, Zakir, King of Hamath and Lu'ash, am a man of 'Anah.

Ba'al-shemain [exalted me?] and stood by me and Ba'al-shemain made me king in

Hazrak. Bar-hadad, son of Hazael, King of Syria, united against me . . .

5 . . . ten kings: there were Bar-hadad and his army; Bargash and his army; [the King]

of Kue and his army; the King of 'Umk and his army; the King of Gurg[um]

and his army; the King of Sam'al and his army; the King of Miliz and his army; . . .

. . . . .seven kings

there were and their armies. All these kings laid siege to Hazrak.

10 They built a wall higher than the wall of Hazrak; they dug a fosse deeper than its fosse.

Then I lifted up my hands to Ba'al-shemain and Ba'al-shemain answered me. [An answer came from?]

Ba'al-shemain to me through seers and foretellers. [Thus spoke to me]

Ba'al-shemain: 'Fear not, for I have made thee king, and I will stand by thee, and I will save thee from all the kings [who]

15 have laid siege against thee.' [Ba'al-shemain] spoke to me: '[I will destroy?]

all the kings who have laid [siege against thee] . . .
. . . and this wall which they have raised up . . .
. . . .

(b) LEFT SIDE

. . . .
[and brought destruction ?] for chariot and horse.
. . . . . while his king was in it. I . . .
[rebuilt ?] Hazrak, and added
5 to it (?) all the surrounding district (?)
                    (all its holy places ?)
. . . . and set up (or, filled it with . . .)
. . . [and I built]
these fortifications (?) on every side (?).
I built temples for the gods in all my
0 [land ?] ; and I built . . .
. . . and Aphis (?)
. . . the temple [of 'Ilwēr]
. . and set up before ['Ilwēr]
this monument, and I wrote
5 thereon the inscription of my hands . . .
Whoever shall remove the inscription
of the hands of Zakir, King of Hamath and
Lu'ash, from this monument ; and whoever
shall remove this monument
0 before 'Ilwēr ; or shall steal it away from
its place ; or whoever shall send against it
. . . .
. . . . [him will destroy ?]
                    Ba'al-shemain and 'Il-
wēr, and Shamsh and Shahr
5 . . . . and the gods of heaven,
and the gods of earth, and Ba'al-[shemain]
. . . .
. . . . his roots and
. . . .

(c) RIGHT SIDE

. . the name of Zakir and the name . . .

Notes

(*a*) Lines 1f. *Zakir*. The pronunciation of *Zkr*, whether Zakar, Zakir, etc., is uncertain. As he is given no ancestors, he was possibly a usurper, or a puppet-king of the Assyrian empire.

King of Hamath and Lu'ash. Hamath is well known in the O.T. as one of the ancient border cities of northern Syria of considerable importance ; the noun also described the territory of the 'city-state' (e.g. 2 Kings xxiii.33). Lu'ash has been identified (*a*) with the region known as Luhuti in Assyrian annals, a country lying west of the Orontes and north of Phœnicia, (*b*) with the Nuhashshe of the Tell el-Amarna tablets. The latter do not help to locate its position (they do show that it contained several cities or 'city-states'), but other sources point to the region south of Aleppo as the area in question. The contents of the stele support this latter identification. Hazrak, the scene of the victory commemorated on the stele, lies in this area, and the coalition of kings allied with the king of Damascus against Zakir comes from regions around the north of Hazrak. The stele was actually found in this area, south of Aleppo.

Hazrak was almost certainly the capital of Lu'ash : Hamath and Lu'ash were two neighbouring territories related in much the same way, both politically and geographically, as Judah and Israel. Hamath was the capital of the country of the same name ; in relation to the twin states (Hamath and Lu'ash) it probably occupied a position similar to Jerusalem in Judah and Israel ; Hazrak corresponded to Samaria in Israel. Zakir was king of both cities and countries, and the monument goes on to recall (line 4) his enthronement at Hazrak as king of Lu'ash some time preceding the events commemorated in the stele.

'Ilwēr. The monument is dedicated to 'Ilwēr, now commonly identified as the Akkadian weather-god. Earlier writers transliterated the word Alōr, and regarded the name as that of a local deity, otherwise unknown (cp. GRESS-MANN, 443).

'Anah seems more likely to have been a place name than an adjective ('a humble man') ; it has been identified with a place 'Anah on the Euphrates. This would strengthen the view that Zakir was a usurper ; it might even suggest that he had been appointed to both kingdoms by the Assyrians, and was himself a native of Assyria. The name could also, however, be read as *'akko* (the middle letter is uncertain) and identified with a place of this name in Phœnicia.

Lines 3f. *Ba'al-shemain*. The 'Baal of heaven' or 'Lord of (the) heaven(s)' appears throughout the text in the rôle of Zakir's patron divinity. Ba'al-shemain may have been a local deity, perhaps even the god of Zakir's home town 'Anah. The 'Baal of heaven' would seem to have been taken over by the Semitic peoples from the Hittites. The new text enables us to trace the cult at least a century earlier than it has hitherto been known to exist, and in a country at one time Hittite.

Hazrak. The town is named in Zech. ix.1. The context of Zech. ix.1 shows that the place is the same one. The name is also suspected to have been originally present in Num. xxxiv.7 and Ezek. xlvii.5. The Assyrian name is Hatarikka. Its occurrence side by side with Damascus and Hamath in the O.T. text and the important part it plays in Assyrian annals (cp. NOTH, 131) indicate a place and town of some size and significance. It lay probably about midway between Arpad and Hamath (see L. H. GROLLENBERG, *Atlas of the Bible*, Map. 18).

How are we to relate the statement in lines 3 and 4 about Zakir's enthronement in Hazrak with his earlier title 'King of Hamath and Lu'ash'? It might appear, at first, that Zakir, king of Hamath and Lu'ash, was stating here that he had *in addition* obtained Hazrak by annexation and had been crowned king there. But the context does not support this interpretation. As NOTH has argued, the enthronement of Zakir described in lines 3f. lay in the past, and one would expect such a position to be reflected in the opening titles of the king. The solution is that Hazrak was the capital city of Lu'ash. Zakir thinks fit, in a stele commemorating his triumph, with Ba'al-shemain's help, over his enemies in Hazrak, to recall that it was in this very city Ba'al-shemain had exalted him to the throne of Lu'ash (possibly not so long ago).

Lines 5-7. *Bar-hadad* is the Aramaic form of the Hebrew name Ben-hadad ; it appears to have been traditional in the royal house of Syria. This is Ben-hadad III (or II), the son of Hazael and a contemporary of Jehoahaz and Joash of Israel (cp. especially 2 Kings xiii.3, 24). In view of the form *Bir-idri* in cuneiform inscriptions and the Greek form in the LXX, it has been suggested that the name ought to be read as Bar(Ben)-hadar. The number of Ben-hadad's allies was more than 10, but not more than 18 (the first half of the numeral, the second being 10, can only have been a 2, 3, 6, 7, or 8, making 12, 13, 16, 17, 18 possible numbers). As only seven appear to have taken part in the siege (line 8), perhaps 12 or 13 was the original figure.

Kue and *'Umk* are territories in the neighbourhood of Antioch, the first corresponding to the later Cilicia, the second to the modern el-'Amk in the Amarus mountains.

Gurgum appears to have been situated in the same area, in the western half of the Amarus range.

Sam'al lay at the north of the gulf of Alexandretta and at the foot of the Amarus.

Miliz is Milid, later Melitene, the north-eastern half of the Amarus.

The coalition consisted of states (in reality no doubt local tribes) all located in the same general area. Qarqar, where Shalmaneser III had, according to his obelisk of *c.* 854 B.C., 'dammed the Orontes with their dead', lies south of Hamath. But in this obelisk, among the twelve allied kings at Qarqar (including Hadadezer of Damascus, Irhuleni of Hamath and Ahab of Israel) we find mention made of Melid, Gurgum and Bitgusi (Bidgash instead of Bargash in line 5?).

Too long a period intervenes for this to be anything but a long delayed reaction to Qarqar, but, as the other Assyrian obelisks on Shalmaneser's campaigns in the west show, western penetration by Assyrian forces was continuous to nearly the end of the century. The present confederation represents a powerfully organised opposition to this constant pressure.

It is very significant that by the time of Ben-hadad, Zakir, king of Hamath (successor at several removes of the defeated Urhuleni), was an enemy of the new confederacy. We are bound to conclude that Zakir was an Assyrian puppet-king.

Line 12. The system of court prophets in Israel has a long history behind it.

(*b*) Lines 1-13. The inscription on the left side is in a somewhat ruinous condition, but not incapable of supplying us with a general idea of its contents. In line 3 the account of the conquest of Zakir's foes is completed, and in lines 3-13 the king describes (like Mesha in the Moabite stone) building undertaken by him in the town after the raising of the siege, the building or restoration of shrines and the erection of the stele. Lines 16ff. detail penalties for the removal of the inscription on the stele.

Line 11. *Aphis('ps)* can be clearly read in the text. The modern Afis is the name of the place, situated forty kilometres south-west of Aleppo, where the stele was found. In view of the statements in *b* lines 9f., 13f., and *a* line 1, it would appear (i) that Aphis was one of the shrines built (or rebuilt) in Zakir's domain after the enemy had been driven off, (ii) that it was here, where the memorial was found in the twentieth century A.D., that it was set up in the ninth century B.C. We can only venture a guess why a site was chosen at this distance from the main scene of Zakir's victory ; it may have marked the northernmost boundary of Lu'ash. NOTH (p. 138, note 3) draws attention to the name *el-'is* for the region lying beneath the great tell north-east of Afhis, and wonders if this is the ancient Lu'ash.

Line 24. *Shamsh, Shahr,* are the sun-god and moon-god respectively.

Bibliography

ALBRIGHT, W. F.   'The Near East and Israel', *J.B.L.* lix (1940) 102-10.

GRESSMANN, H.   *Altorientalische Texte zum Alten Testament,* second ed., 1926, 443ff.

KRAELING, E. G.   *Aram and Israel,* 1918, 46ff.

LIDZBARSKI, M.   *Ephemeris für Semitische Epigraphik,* III, 1909, 1-11.

MOWINCKEL, S.   'Die Vorderasiatischen Königs—und Fürsteninschriften', in H. GUNKEL, *Studien zur Religion und Literatur des Alten und Neuen Testaments,* 1923, 278-322.

NOTH, M.   'La'asch und Hazrak', *Z.D.P.V.* lii (1929) 124-41.

OLMSTEAD, A. T.   *History of Palestine and Syria,* 1931 (especially chs. xxiiiff.).

POGNON, H.   *Inscriptions Sémitiques de la Syrie, de la Mésopotamie et de la Région de Mossoul,* 1907-1908.

ROSENTHAL, F., in *A.N.E.T.,* 501f.

M. BLACK

A Letter from Saqqarah

IN a pottery jar unearthed in 1942 in Egypt at Saqqarah, the necropolis of Memphis, there was found a part of a letter, written on papyrus, from a king called Adon to Pharaoh. The fragment, now in the Cairo Museum, was published with introduction, commentary and photograph in 1948 by A. DUPONT-SOMMER. A re-edited text and annotated translation, differing in details from those of the first editor, were produced by H. L. GINSBERG. The document contains nine half-lines of Aramaic, the left half of the sheet having disappeared. In several places damage to the papyrus makes for uncertainty of reading, and in the fifth line, the most mutilated, only one word can be deciphered. The script is similar to, but older than, that used in the Aramaic documents from Elephantine, and the letter is regarded as possibly the earliest Aramaic papyrus known.

Text

To Lord of Kings, Pharaoh, thy servant Adon, king of
  [X. May Y, the lord of]
heaven and earth, and Ba'al-shemain, [the great] god, [make the
  throne of Lord of Kings,]
Pharaoh, enduring like the days of heaven. That [I have written
  to my lord is to inform thee that the troops]
of the king of Babylon have come. They have reached Aphek
  and . . .
5 . . . . they have taken . . . . .
For Lord of Kings, Pharaoh, knows that [thy] servant [cannot
  stand alone against the king of Babylon. May it therefore
  please him]
to send an army to rescue me. Do not abandon [me. For thy
  servant is loyal to my lord]
and thy servant has safeguarded his property, and this region [is
  my lord's possession. But if the king of Babylon takes it, he
  will set up]
9 a governor in the land and . . . .

Notes

The conjectural restorations in square brackets in the text largely follow GINSBERG.

Line 1. As in the letter in Ezra vii.12, mention of the addressee and sender comes first. *Lord of Kings*. The Aramaic word for lord, *mār*, is found in Maranatha in 1 Cor. xvi.22. The title used here occurs in Dan. ii.47 in Nebuchadrezzar's confession of Daniel's God. Both Seleucids and Ptolemies bore it. Vocalising the consonants differently, others render 'Lord of Kingdoms', which, it is claimed, is the true form of the Ptolemaic title. Some ancient versions interpret 'kings' as 'kingdoms' in Dan. vii.17. Here the title has been referred to Pharaoh as Ruler of Upper and Lower Egypt ; another view is that it does not have reference to the dual monarchy, but to the Assyrian arrangement whereby Egypt was governed by twelve kings. *Pharaoh* is an Egyptian title meaning 'Great House', and so it referred originally not to the ruler but to the palace. The first certain example of its reference to the king is in a letter to Amenophis IV (Akhenaten, *c.* 1370 B.C.). Later a proper name was added, e.g. Pharaoh-necoh (Necho ; 2 Kings xxiii.29). *servant* here means 'vassal', as in 2 Sam. x.19. *Adon*, another word meaning 'lord', is found as the first element in such names as those of the Canaanite Adonizedek (Josh. x.1) and the Hebrew Adonijah (1 Kings i.5). It occurs also in Assyrian and Ugaritic documents. Presumably here it is an abridged form, a deity's name being dropped. The name of Adon's kingdom has disappeared. Clearly it was somewhere between Egypt and Babylonia, for the historical situation and the proper names in the letter point to this area. Adon may have been the ruler of Ammon, or Moab, or Edom, for we do not possess the names of all the kings of those lands, but the evidence, scanty though it is, seems to indicate rather a Philistine or a Phœnician city. To some extent the choice depends on the historical reconstruction of the events to which the letter is related. Here may be noted one piece of independent evidence which has been adduced. Clay tablets published in 1939 mention as living in Babylon in 592 B.C. two sons of Aga', the king of Ashkelon, as well as a considerable number of captives from this city. It is suggested that those princes were hostages for the loyalty of Aga', who is regarded as a Babylonian vassal raised to the throne when Adon, the vassal of Egypt, was deposed not long after he sent his plea for help to Pharaoh. The suggested connection between Aga' and Adon's kingdom, however, still lacks substantiation.

Line 2. Before the words *heaven and earth* must have stood the name of a god or goddess. The Aramaic word for 'earth' here differs slightly from the word used in Ezra and Daniel, but it occurs in this form in Jer. x.11 where this phrase occurs. This Aramaic word is the first part of the name of the angel Araqiel (1 Enoch vi.7, viii.3). In the O.T. God is called the maker of heaven and earth (e.g. Ps. cxlvi.5f.). *Ba'al-shemain* 'lord of heaven', is the common title of Ba'al among both Aramaeans and Canaanites. It is found on a Byblos inscription which has been dated 1100 B.C. Philo of Byblos identifies Ba'al with Zeus Olympios : 'Baalsamen, who among the Phœnicians is Lord of Heaven, among the Greeks Zeus'. It has been conjectured that the words translated 'the abomination that maketh desolate' (Dan. xi.31) may be an intentional and contemptuous disfigurement of this title. In Dan. v.23 God is called 'Lord (*mār*) of heaven'. Many foreign deities were well known in Egypt, for it was the Egyptian practice to identify the gods of other nations with their own and to domesticate these gods in Egypt. Baʿal-shemain was regarded as the counterpart of the god Seth. In the time of Akhenaten there was a prophet of Baʿal in Memphis, and from the late Eighteenth Dynasty the egyptianised Baʿal had his own priesthood.

Line 3. *like the days of heaven*, i.e. perpetually. The phrase occurs in Deut. xi.21 ; Ps. lxxxix.29 ; Ecclus. xlv.15. Presumably the introduction, which ends here, is to be reconstructed as expressing the hope that the gods mentioned will sustain the throne (cp. Ps. lxxxix.29) of Pharaoh for ever.

Line 4. *of the king of Babylon have come*. The subject of the verb was on the now missing part of the previous line. From the context it must have been a word meaning 'forces'. As in 2 Kings xx.18, the name of the king did not require to be mentioned. The king of Babylon who has come with his troops and now threatens Adon's state must belong to the Neo-Babylonian Dynasty, and only in the reign of Nebuchadrezzar (604-562 B.C.) have historical situations been found which might give rise to such a plea as is found in the letter. It is true that an event which Josephus reports, and which treats of Nabopolassar, the father of Nebuchadrezzar, sending in 605 B.C. a military force under the command of Nebuchadrezzar to quell a rebellious governor, has been linked with the letter. The rebellious governor is identified with the governor mentioned in the last line of the papyrus, which is read '(they have punished) the governor with death'. But the interpretation is very doubtful, and the historical reconstruction more than questionable, for Jer. xlvi.2 implies that in 605 B.C. the dominant power in the area was Egypt and not Babylon, while the letter itself is apparently written by a vassal of Egypt seeking assistance from his overlord, rather than a rebel making common cause with his master's enemy.

More defensible is the theory which regards the letter as a footnote to 2 Kings xxiiif. On this view Adon was writing to Pharaoh Necho II in face of the threatening advance of the forces of Nebuchadrezzar in 603-2 B.C. Nebuchadrezzar had defeated Necho at Carchemish in 605 B.C., but owing to the death of Nabopolassar he had not followed up his victory immediately. Now he was free to eradicate all remaining traces of Egyptian sway in Asia. Jehoiakim, king of Judah, submitted, but Adon, it appears, did not.

Another possible reconstruction connects Adon with events in the time of Zedekiah, when Pharaoh Apries, the Hophra of the O.T. (cp. Jer. xliv.30), invaded Phœnicia and incited Judah to rebel. Judah fell to Nebuchadrezzar in July 587 B.C., and the letter is to be dated about that time. Adon, on this view, was a ruler in Phœnicia, though he is unlikely to have resisted the Babylonian armies for thirteen years as did his neighbour, the king of Tyre.
They have reached. The writing here is difficult, but very probably the translation represents the text. *Aphek*. The identification of this place is uncertain, because there were at least four towns of the name in O.T. times. One was in Sharon, one in the territory of Asher, one east of Jordan, and one in Phœnicia.

The name was not unknown to the Egyptians, e.g. it figures in an Egyptian list of cities under their rule, and in the account of the Asiatic campaign of Amenhotep II it is recorded that he captured Aphek—'it came out in surrender to the great victory of Pharaoh'. Of the various Apheks, that which is the modern Rās el-ʿAin is held to fit best into this account. It is ten miles north of Lydda, and it is regarded by some as the Aphek of our letter. It accords with the hypothesis that Adon was king of Ashkelon in Philistia. If, however, he ruled in Phœnicia, the Aphek in that district would be the town which the Babylonians have reached.

Line 5. *they have taken*. No doubt this line referred to cities captured by the Babylonians.

Line 6. The missing part of this line must have contained a verb of wishing or requesting.

Line 7. *rescue*. Though the reading is not quite certain, the word is probably from the same root as the word which is regularly used in O.T. Hebrew of delivering from enemies. The appeal is reminiscent of the entreaties addressed to Pharaoh in the Tell el-Amarna letters, when rulers in Palestine were beseeching their Egyptian overlord for help. Neither Isaiah (xx, xxx.1-7, xxxi.1ff., xxxvi.6) nor Jeremiah (xxxvii.6ff.) had any illusions about the help likely to be afforded by Egypt, 'this bruised reed . . . whereon if a man lean, it will go into his hand, and pierce it' (Is. xxxvi.6). It is improbable that Adon's experience was much different.

Line 8. In place of 'and thy servant has safeguarded his property' a translation 'and thy servant remembers his kindness' has been suggested. Whichever is correct, Adon is setting forth the grounds of his expectation of help. *region* renders a word which, if correctly read, means 'island, sea-district'. This is how Isaiah refers to his land (xx.6).

Line 9. *governor*. The word, borrowed from the Assyrian and found in the Hebrew and Aramaic portions of the O.T., is used of governors in the Babylonian and Persian empires (cp. Jer. li.57 ; Hag. i.1 ; Ezra v.3, 14). *land*. The word so translated does not occur in the O.T., but it is found in Akkadian and in the Aramaic version of the story of Ahikar with this meaning. Some regard the line as a prognostication of the fate which will befall Adon's kingdom ; the translation '(they have punished) the governor with death' (see note on line 4) describes what has happened elsewhere, probably in another of Pharaoh's vassal states. The interpretation of the rest of the line is even more uncertain. The words that follow have been translated 'and the secretary they have changed', but others leave them untranslated. No exposition of the history underlying it could be based on a reading so uncertain, and this serves to illustrate the limitations of the papyrus.

The mutilation of the fragment with the consequent disappearance of vital details such as the name of Adon's kingdom, the absence of any date or certain means of dating the document with precision, the uncertainty of the identification of the persons and place named, together with the possibility of alternative interpretations, make the reconstruction of the historical background of the letter precarious. On the other hand, the usefulness of the document, though limited, is definite. Its chief value is that, with other documents, such as the Lachish ostraca (see p. 212ff.) and the tablets from Babylon which throw light on Jehoiachin's captivity (see p. 84ff.), this letter helps to fill in the background against which we have to see the prophet Jeremiah and his contemporaries. Thus the fact that Aramaic is the language of this letter sent from a ruler in one continent to a king in another is an illustration of the use of Aramaic in international diplomacy already in the Jeremian period. It also serves as a footnote to 2 Kings xviii.26, and, in general, its ideas and vocabulary, echoing so often the usage of the O.T., contribute to our better understanding of the text of the O.T.

Bibliography

BEA, A. 'Epistula Aramaica saeculo VII exeunte ad Pharaonem scripta', *Biblica* xxx (1949) 514ff.

BRIGHT, J. 'A New Letter in Aramaic, written to a Pharaoh of Egypt', *B.A.* xii (1949) 46-52.

DUPONT-SOMMER, A. 'Un papyrus araméen d'époque saïte découvert à Saqqarah', *Semitica* i (1948) 43-68.

GINSBERG, H. L. 'An Aramaic Contemporary of the Lachish Letters', *B.A.S.O.R.* No. 111 (1948) 24-7.

THOMAS, D. WINTON. 'The Age of Jeremiah in the Light of Recent Archæological Discovery', *P.E.Q.*, 1950, 8-13.

W. D. MCHARDY

Papyri from Elephantine

In the early years of this century some papyri, bearing writing in Aramaic, were purchased in Assuān, in Egypt, and later more became known, and it was learned that they came from Elephantine, an island in the Nile opposite Assuān. The first collection was published in 1906, and the second partly in 1908 and then completely in 1911. Since the Second World War a further collection of papyri from the same place became known. These had been purchased as long ago as 1893, and had lain unread for more than half a century. These, too, have now been published. Some are in an almost perfect state of preservation, while others are broken, leaving gaps in the text.

All of these papyri came from a Jewish military colony in Elephantine, and many of them bear dates running from the year 495 B.C. to the end of the fifth century. A number of them are doubly dated, giving the precise day by both the Egyptian and the Babylonian calendar. Some are legal documents, such as marriage settlements and records of lawsuits, or deeds recording the transfer of property. From their study we can learn a good deal about the life of the community, and we can reconstruct a plan of a part of the town in which the Jews lived.

The language in which these texts are written is of great interest and importance, because it is a form of the Aramaic language somewhat older than that in which parts of the books of Ezra and Daniel are written. For, unlike all the other books of the Old Testament—save one verse of Jeremiah—these two books are not wholly in Hebrew, but partly in Hebrew and partly in Aramaic. In Jer. x.11, the one verse in Aramaic in that book, the word for 'earth' is written in two different spellings, of which the one is an older form than the other, and it was formerly thought curious that they should stand side by side. In the papyri we frequently find the same thing, with this and other words, showing that there was a time when newer and older usages were both current.

We can only speculate how the colony came into Egypt. It must have existed there long before the Persian conquest in

525 B.C., as may be seen below from the letter to Bagoas. In the fifth century it had a military character, and was integrated into the Persian defences of the country.

We learn from many of the texts that there was in Elephantine a temple of Yahu, which is a variation of the name Yahweh, and even a subscription list has been preserved. The worship does not seem to have been very pure, since other deities appear to have been worshipped alongside Yahu, and the subscription list shows the apportionment of the gifts to Yahu, to Ishum-bethel and to Anath-bethel. In other texts we find references also to Anath-yahu and Herem-bethel. Anath was an old Canaanite goddess, whose name survives in the name of Jeremiah's home town, Anathoth, and Anath-yahu may have been a goddess worshipped beside Yahweh. With this we may compare the references to the Queen of Heaven in the book of Jeremiah (vii.18, xliv.17). It is perhaps significant that in the letter to Jerusalem, translated below, there is no reference to any deity save Yahu.

That a Jewish temple stood in Elephantine in the fifth century came as a surprise. For the law of Deuteronomy, which Josiah had put into force in 621 B.C., prohibited any altar save one, which was naturally interpreted as the Jerusalem altar. It is clear from the O.T. that Josiah's reform was not lasting, and the suppressed practices crept back before the fall of Jerusalem in 586 B.C. But in the fifth century B.C. the legitimacy of a single sanctuary, at least in Judaea, seems to have been accepted without question. Yet the Elephantine community does not appear to have regarded this as affecting their temple, so that when it was destroyed they appealed to the Jerusalem authorities to use influence on their behalf for its rebuilding. It has sometimes been thought that they may not have heard of the Deuteronomic law, but since they were in touch with the Jerusalem priests this seems unlikely, and it is more probable that they did not think this law applied to them. For a small province like Judaea a single sanctuary might suffice, but if the Elephantine temple was already built before the law of the single sanctuary had become fully recognised in Judaea, it is not surprising that the Elephantine Jews should cling to it, since it afforded them the opportunity of practising their religion more completely than they could otherwise have done. It should also be remembered that in the second

century B.C. one of the Jerusalem high priestly family built a
temple at Leontopolis, in Egypt.

Amongst the texts are some which have a bearing on the
religious practice of the colony, and which tell us of the above-
mentioned destruction of the temple by a mixed mob, at the
instigation of the Egyptian priests, and of efforts made by the
community to secure authority to rebuild it.   Four of these texts
are translated below.   All of them belong to the documents
found early in the century, and published nearly fifty years ago.

I   THE SO-CALLED PASSOVER PAPYRUS

This letter was sent to the Jewish garrison in Elephantine in the
fifth year of Darius II, i.e. in 419 B.C.   The text is much broken,
and while some of the gaps might be restored with probability,
the only restorations here given (in square brackets) are certain.
It concerns the observance of a festival in the month of Nisan,
running from the fourteenth to the twenty-first day, and since
leaven is prohibited, it must be the feast of Unleavened Bread.
The order for the fourteenth day was probably, therefore, to
keep the Passover, since Passover preceded the days of Unleavened
Bread.   The word Passover, however, has not survived, and there
are some scholars who are doubtful if it ever stood there.

It would appear that the Elephantine colony had not observed
this spring festival hitherto, and the reason for this can only be
surmised.   The law of Deuteronomy, which first became public
in 621 B.C. and was put into effect by Josiah, limited the observance of the Passover to Jerusalem (Deut. xvi.5f.).   It may be that
the colony did not observe the festival for this reason, though the
very existence of its temple was equally an infringement of the
law of Deut. xii.5.   Another suggestion is that the slaughter of
lambs would be an offence to Egyptian sentiment (see the following letter), and it was for this reason that it had not been observed.
But this presupposes that the document refers to the Passover.

What is more surprising is that the order comes on the authority of the Persian king.   We find in the book of Ezra documents
written in the name of the king and dealing with Jewish religious
matters, and it was formerly held that these were probably
spurious.   Since the finding of this letter, it has been recognised

that that view is improbable.   In the present case the king was doubtless approached through the proper channels by the Jewish authorities, and if the view is correct that it was fear of offending the Egyptians which had prevented the observance of the feast heretofore, this would explain why royal authority was felt to be necessary.

Text

[To] my [brethren

Yedo]niah and his colleagues the [J]ewish gar[rison], your brother Hanan[iah].   The welfare of my brethren may the gods [seek . .].

Now this year, the fifth year of King Darius, an order was sent from the king to Arsa[mes, saying,

'. . . . . Jew]ish [garrison].'   Now therefore do you count four-
5 [teen days of the month Nisan and ke]ep . . ., and from the fifteenth day until the twenty-first day of [Nisan

. . . . .].   Be ritually clean and take heed.   [Do] n[o] work

[. . . . no]r drink . . ., and anything whatever [in] which the[re is] leaven

[do not eat . . . from] sunset until the twenty-first day of Nis[an

. . . . . do not br]ing [it] into your houses, but seal [it] up between [these] day[s].

10 [. . . . . ki]ng.

[To] my brethren Yedoniah and his colleagues the Jewish garrison, your brother Hanan[iah].

Notes

Line 1.   The restoration of this line and the beginning of the next is made certain by the address at the end.

Lines 2f.   *Yedoniah* was a priest, and the following letter shows that he was the head of the Jewish colony in 407 B.C.   Hence the Darius of this letter must be Darius II.   *Hananiah* was apparently a Jew, since his name was compounded with Yahweh (cp. 'your brother' in line 11).   He was an important official under Arsames, whose coming to Egypt is mentioned in another letter.   Presumably Hananiah uses the plural 'the gods' as a stereotyped formula.

Line 3.   *Arsames* was the governor of Egypt for many years and related to the Persian royal house.

Line 5.   It is probable that the text read 'keep the Passover', though, as has been said above, there are some scholars who do not share this view.

Line 7. The text may have read 'drink no beer'. It does not refer to wine, which was drunk at Passover, and which was not forbidden during the days of Unleavened Bread, but probably to beer, which was made from fermented grain. This appears to have been a specially Egyptian drink, and the prohibition was necessary for the Jews living in Egypt, but is not mentioned in the O.T. in this connection.

II PETITION TO BAGOAS, GOVERNOR OF JUDAEA

(Plate 16)

This letter describes how the Elephantine temple was destroyed by the Egyptians in the year 410 B.C., and how the Jewish leaders had first appealed to the Persian governor in Jerusalem and the Temple authorities there, begging their intervention to secure permission for the rebuilding of the destroyed temple. Another papyrus, which was bought separately in 1898 or 1899 and published in 1903, refers to the attack on the Jews in the fourteenth year of Darius. It was apparently addressed to a Persian official in Egypt, but his name has not survived. It begins by referring to the loyalty of the Jewish garrison, which had not rebelled when Egyptian regiments had rebelled, and complains that, after Arsames had left Egypt, the priests of Khnub had bribed Widrang to connive at the attack, and that in the course of the attack the well which supplied the garrison with water had been stopped up. The part of the letter which refers to the temple of Yahu is much broken, but it is probable that it ends with a request for authority for the rebuilding. It may be that the appeal to Jerusalem was made because of the lack of response to this one. If Arsames were still at court at this time, it is possible that the acting governor was unwilling to take the responsibility of a decision in his absence. The lost appeal to Jerusalem had met with no response either, and so in 407 B.C. the Jews in Elephantine wrote this letter to the Persian governor, Bagoas, and simultaneously appealed to the Persian authorities in Samaria for their help. It is perhaps significant that this appeal was no longer addressed to the priestly authorities in Jerusalem, and it may be that the Elephantine Jews had reason to think that they were not sympathetic.

In the middle of the fifth century Sanballat, the governor of Samaria, had been the bitter enemy of Nehemiah. That he was a worshipper of Yahweh is indicated by the names of his sons, Delaiah and Shelemiah, both of which are compounded with Yahweh, and by the fact that his daughter had married the son of the Jerusalem High Priest (Neh. xiii.28). But when the Elephantine Jews appealed simultaneously to Jerusalem and Samaria, it would seem that either they did not know of the strained relations between the two cities, or that relations had improved since the time of Nehemiah. Later they certainly became again embittered until the complete breach was made. This continued down to the N.T. times, and is referred to in John. iv.9.

This letter is important because it shows clearly that if the Elephantine Jews knew of the law of the single sanctuary, they did not think it applied to them. It is also important because of its bearing on the vexed question of the relative order of Nehemiah and Ezra. From the reading of the books of Ezra and Nehemiah it would appear that Ezra preceded Nehemiah, the one coming in the seventh year and the other in the twentieth year of Artaxerxes. Nehemiah was contemporary with Sanballat in his heyday, but Sanballat appears now to have been old, since the affairs of the province were administered by his sons. Hence his heyday must have been in the middle of the century, and Nehemiah must have belonged to the time of Artaxerxes I. But Ezra was contemporary with the priest Johanan (Ezra x.6, Jehohanan and Johanan being variant forms of the same name). Johanan is mentioned in this letter as in office in 407 B.C., towards the end of the reign of Darius II. As he was the grandson of Eliashib, (cp. Neh. xii.22 ; in Ezra x.6 he is called the son of Eliashib, but son often stands for grandson in Hebrew), who was contemporary with Nehemiah (Neh. iii.1), it is probable that he had not long been High Priest in 407 B.C., and he may have continued in office into the reign of Artaxerxes II, and Ezra may have belonged to that reign. This view was already advanced before the discovery of the papyri, but it finds some support from this document.

It may be wondered why the letter was found in Egypt, if it was addressed to Bagoas in Jerusalem. Two copies of this letter were found in Elephantine, of which the second is more broken than this one, the ends of the lines being missing, and there are some small differences between them. It is therefore probable that two drafts of the letter were made before the final copy was despatched, and that these were preserved for record purposes.

Text

To our lord Bagoas, governor of Judaea, your servants Yedoniah and his colleagues, the priests who are in the fortress of Elephantine.   The welfare

of your lordship may the God of Heaven seek abundantly at all times, and give you favour before King Darius

and the court circles a thousand times more than at present, and may He grant you long life and may you be happy and prosperous at all times.

Now your servant Yedoniah and his colleagues depose as follows : In the month of Tammuz in the fourteenth year of King Darius when Arsames

5 departed and went to the King, the priests of the god Khnub in the fortress of Elephantine combined with Widrang, who was governor here,

saying : 'Let the temple of the God Yahu in the fortress of Elephantine be done away with.'   Then Widrang, that

scoundrel, sent a letter to his son Nephayan, who was in command of the garrison in the fortress of Elephantine, saying: 'Let the temple which is in Elephantine,

the fortress, be destroyed.'   Thereupon Nephayan led the Egyptians with the other troops.   They came to the fortress of Elephantine with their weapons,

entered that temple, razed it to the ground, and broke the stone pillars which were there.   Moreover five gateways

10 of stone, built with hewn blocks of stone, which were in that temple, they destroyed, and their doors were set up, and the hinges

of those doors were of bronze, and the roof of cedar wood, all of it, with the rest of the timber-work and other things which were there,

was entirely burned with fire, and the basins of gold and silver and everything whatsoever that was in that temple they took

and made their own.   Our fathers built this temple in the fortress of Elephantine in the days of the Kings of Egypt, and when Cambyses entered Egypt

Plate 16   Petition to Bagoas, Governor of Judaea : Elephantine Papyrus .

he found that temple already built, and though all the temples
of the Egyptian gods were destroyed, no one did any harm
to that temple.

15 When this was done we, with our wives and children, put on
sackcloth and fasted and prayed to Yahu, the Lord of
Heaven,

who let us see our desire upon that hound Widrang. The anklet
was torn from his legs, and all the wealth he had acquired
was lost, and all the men

who had sought to do harm to that temple were all killed, and
we saw our desire upon them. Further, before this, at the
time when this evil

was done to us, we sent a letter to your lordship and to the High
Priest Johanan and his colleagues the priests in Jerusalem
and to Ostanes, the brother

of 'Anani, and the leaders of the Jews. They have not sent any
letter to us. Moreover from the month of Tammuz in the
fourteenth year of King Darius

20 until this day we have worn sackcloth and fasted. Our wives are
made as widows, we do not anoint ourselves with oil,

and we drink no wine. Also from then till the present day, in
the seventeenth year of King Darius, meal-offering and
inc[en]se and burnt-offering

have not been offered in this temple. Now your servants Yedoniah
and his colleagues and the Jews, all citizens of Elephantine,
say :

'If it seems good to your lordship, take thought for that temple to
rebuild it, since they do not permit us to rebuild it. Look
upon your well wishers and friends here in Egypt. Let a
letter be sent from you to them concerning this temple of the
God Yahu

25 that it be rebuilt in the fortress of Elephantine as it was built
before, and let meal-offering, incense and burnt-offering be
offered

upon the altar of the God Yahu in your name, and we will pray
for you continually, we, our wives, and our children and all
the Jews

who are here, if it is so arranged that this temple be rebuilt, and it
shall be a merit to you before Yahu, the God of

Heaven, greater than that of a man who offers Him a burnt-
offering and sacrifices worth as much as a thousand talents
of silver.' Now concerning gold, concerning this
we have sent and given instructions. Further we have set out the
whole matter in a letter sent in our name to Delaiah and
Shelemaiah, the sons of Sanballat the governor of Samaria.
30 Also Arsames knew nothing of all this that was done to us. Dated
the twentieth of Marchesvan in the seventeenth year of King
Darius

Notes

Line 3. The meaning in this context of the word rendered *prosperous* can only
be guessed. It comes from a root meaning 'strong' or 'fit', and may have the
meaning 'healthy' here.

Lines 4f. It is clear that *Arsames* was absent from Egypt at the time of the
attack on the temple of the Jews. It is possible that his absence gave the
opportunity for the attack.

Line 5. *Khnub*. This is the name of an Egyptian god, which is usually spelled
Khnum. It has the latter form in some others of the papyri. There was a
temple of this god in close proximity to the temple of Yahu in Elephantine,
separated from it, indeed, by only a street. As the symbol of this god was the
ram, some probability is given to the view that the sacrifice of Passover lambs
would be an offence to his devotees. *Widrang* is shown by another papyrus
to have been the head of the garrison in Syene. He is here given a Persian
official title *fratarak*, which appears to be of higher rank.

Line 10. *set up*. The meaning here is obscure. The literal rendering is
'were raised', and the renderings 'were lifted off' and 'were left standing'
have been suggested,—or even 'were leaned against the wall' to burn them.

Line 11. *timber work*. In Ezra v.3, 9 this word is rendered in the R.V. by
'wall', but this meaning will not fit here. The meaning has been variously conjectured as 'furniture', 'panelling' or 'beams'. It is clear that it was something
which could be burned.

Line 13. *in the days of the Kings of Egypt*, i.e. before the Persian conquest under
Cambyses, in 525 B.C.

Line 16. *hound*. The word is normally rendered 'dogs' and made the subject of
the next sentence : 'The dogs tore the anklet' ; but the verb is not likely to
have had 'dogs' as its subject, and it is more probably an opprobrious de-
nominative word meaning 'son of a dog'. The subject of the next verb is then
the indefinite 'they', and the sentence means that Widrang was demoted, and
the symbol of his rank was torn from him.

Line 18. *Johanan* is mentioned in Neh. xii.22f. We learn from Josephus that
some time after this, in the reign of Artaxerxes, he was on bad terms with
Bagoas, who thought to remove him from office and replace him by his brother
Jeshua. But Johanan killed his brother in the Temple. Possibly Bagoas and

Johanan were already on bad terms, and that was why the answer came in the name of Bagoas only.

Line 28. *concerning gold.* This probably refers to a present sent to Bagoas to weight the request for his help.

Line 29. *Delaiah and Shelemaiah, the sons of Sanballat.* The letter was probably sent to the sons of Sanballat, since their father was now old. He was a contemporary of Nehemiah when he came to Jerusalem nearly forty years before this time, and it is probable that though he still had the title of governor, the actual administration was in the hands of his sons. The O.T. does not tell us that Sanballat had the title of governor, which we learn here, but it had been conjectured before the finding of the papyri that he must have had that position.

III REPLY TO THE FOREGOING LETTER

No direct reply to the foregoing letter has survived, but it would appear from the memorandum below that a verbal answer was sent to the Persian governor, Arsames. Presumably a verbal reply was sent, either directly or indirectly, also to the Jews in Elephantine. The authority of Arsames would be required for the rebuilding, and the Jewish colony had appealed to the Persian authorities in Jerusalem and Samaria to exert their influence on their behalf. This they did through the messenger who carried the memorandum. The brevity of its terms does not mean that it was curtly communicated to Arsames, or that Bagoas was of higher authority than Arsames. The letter had stated that the destruction of the temple had taken place while Arsames was absent from Egypt, but he had now returned.

It is to be noted that, though the rebuilding of the temple was supported, no mention is made of burnt-offering, but only of meal-offering and incense. That this was deliberate and significant is made almost certain by the letter that follows. In consequence many scholars have concluded that the destruction of the temple by the Egyptians may have been due to religious passions which were stirred up by Widrang, owing to the introduction of the sacrifice of lambs—perhaps consequent upon the receipt of the 'Passover' Papyrus. The Egyptians did, however, sacrifice some animals. An alternative suggestion is that it was to avoid offending the religious susceptibilities of Arsames that animal sacrifices were not mentioned. As a Zoroastrian he would hold that fire was profaned by contact with dead bodies. Against

this it is to be noted that in the rescript of Artaxerxes, which Ezra
carried (Ezra vii.7), there was no difficulty about the mention of
sacrifices.

Text

Memorandum of what Bagoas and Delaiah said
to me : Let it be a memorandum to you in Egypt to
   say
to Arsames concerning the altar-house of the God of
Heaven, which was built in the fortress of Elephantine
5 long ago, before Cambyses,
which that scoundrel Widrang destroyed
in the fourteenth year of King Darius,
that it be rebuilt in its place as it was before,
and that meal-offering and incense be offered upon
10 that altar as was formerly
done.

Notes

Lines 3f. *the God of Heaven.* It is to be noted that the name Yahu does not
figure in the reply.

Line 5f. Emphasis is laid in the reply, as in the letter, on the antiquity of the
temple, and on the fact that it was already there in the days of Egyptian
independence. It was not, therefore, the fruit of Persian policy, and the
Egyptians could not claim that its existence was an affront to them. Its
destruction is ascribed to *Widrang*, and no reference is made to the Egyptian
priests. But in the text cited in the introduction to the foregoing letter,
apparently written to a Persian official in Egypt, the initiative was ascribed
to the Egyptian priests, who bribed Widrang.

Line 8. *in its place.* It may be that there was some Egyptian desire that it
should not be tolerated in the vicinity of the temple of Khnub, and the emphasis
on its being rebuilt on the same spot was to counter this.

IV FURTHER LETTER ABOUT THE TEMPLE

This letter is apparently connected with the preceding documents, but it contains no address. It makes it clear that the
Elephantine colony had to bribe those whose influence or help
it invoked. The letter to Bagoas had mentioned a verbal message
concerning a bribe, and it has been thought that this letter was
sent along with the other. This seems improbable, as in that case
there would have been no need to refer to a verbal message there.

Moreover, the verbal message refers to gold, whereas this letter refers to silver and barley only. Further, the letter to Bagoas asked for authority to offer animal sacrifices, as well as meal-offerings and incense, whereas this already recognises animal sacrifices as not permitted. It is therefore probable that it was addressed to some Egyptian official, perhaps Arsames, at some time after the delivery of the message in the preceding memorandum.

Whether the temple was ever rebuilt we have no means of knowing. But within a few years the Persian control of Egypt came to an end, and the Jewish colony disappears from view. It has commonly been held that the Persian rule in Egypt came to an end in 404 B.C. when Amyrtaeus set up a new independent Egyptian kingdom. But one of the papyri in the latest collection to be published is dated in the fourth year of Artaxerxes II, showing that for the first few years of his reign Amyrtaeus did not control the whole country, and Persian rule was still recognised in Elephantine. But soon after this papyrus was written Cyrus, the younger brother of Artaxerxes II, revolted. This revolt is familiar to us because Cyrus had some Greek mercenaries on his side, and Xenophon has told in his *Anabasis* the story of their return home after the collapse of the revolt. But this revolt doubtless gave Amyrtaeus his opportunity to extend his hold on Egypt. With the collapse of Persian power, the Jewish garrison was doubtless soon eliminated, and we hear no more of it. What happened to the Jews we can only speculate. They may have continued to live in Egypt, either at Elephantine or elsewhere, but the priests of the neighbouring temple of Khnub would doubtless have been successful in suppressing the worship of Yahu, which they so much hated.

It has been said above that some scholars have thought that Ezra belonged to the reign of Artaxerxes II, and that he came to Jerusalem in 397 B.C. The suggestion has been made that the king was influenced by political considerations in sending Ezra on his mission. The collapse of Egyptian power in Egypt inclined the king to a policy which would rally Jewish sentiment to his side, and which would tend to strengthen his position in what was now the frontier province of his empire.

Text

Your servants Yedoniah, the son of G[emariah] by
    name, one,
Ma'uzi, the son of Nathan, by name, one,
Shemaiah, the son of Haggai, by name, one,
Hosea, the son of Yathom, by name, one,
5 Hosea, the son of Nathun, by name, one : five persons
    in all,
Syenians who [ow]n [proper]ty in the fortress of
    Elephantine,
say as follows : 'If your lordship is [favour]able
and the temple of Yahu ou[r] God [is rebuilt]
in the fortress of Elephantine as it was form[erly
    built],
10 but sheep and oxen and goats are [no]t offered there,
but incense and meal-offering . . . .
and your lordship iss[ues] an edict [to this effect],
we will pay to your Lordship's house the sum of
    . . . in si[lver . . .]
a thous[and] ardabs of barley.'

Notes

Line 6. Syene was on the mainland, opposite Elephantine, and is the modern
Assuān.

Line 11. It is thought that the missing words may have included drink-
offerings, but there can be no certainty. In view of the preceding line it cannot
have been the ordinary word for sacrifice, which follows meal-offering and
incense in line 25 of the letter to Bagoas.

Line 14. The *ardab* was a Persian and Egyptian dry measure, representing
about a month's allowance of barley for a single person. A thousand ardabs
would therefore be a substantial quantity.

Bibliography

Cook, S. A. 'The Significance of the Elephantine Papyri for the History of
Hebrew Religion', in *A.J.T.* xix (1915) 346-82. (Of the innumerable
articles written on the papyri, this is singled out for mention because it is
solely concerned with their importance for the student of the O.T.)

Cowley, A. *Aramaic Papyri of the Fifth Century B.C.*, 1923. (This contains all
the texts published by Sayce and Cowley in 1906 and by Sachau in

1908 and 1911, together with the papyrus published by EUTING in 1903. The Aramaic is given, together with introduction and full notes. The texts translated above are Nos. 21, 30, 32, 33, in this edition.)

GINSBERG, H. L., in *A.N.E.T.*, 491f. (This great collection of texts contains translations, with very brief notes, but without introduction, of the papyri translated above, and one or two others.)

KRAELING, E. G. *The Brooklyn Museum Aramaic Papyri*, 1953. (This contains the texts which first came to light in 1947. There are facsimiles and a full edition of the texts, with notes, and a fine introduction dealing with the various aspects of their significance.)

VINCENT, A. *La Religion des Judéo-Araméens d'Éléphantine*, 1937. (This is the fullest discussion of the religious significance of the papyri so far published.)

H. H. ROWLEY

The Words of Ahikar

THE proverbs and similitudes attributed to the sage Ahikar are contained within the framework of a tale of ingratitude and its due reward in which Ahikar is the hero. The antiquity of the story is evident from a fragmentary Aramaic version of it preserved amongst the Elephantine papyri of the fifth century B.C. Its provenance is Assyria, and it purports to tell of events which took place during the reign of Sennacherib, though, in the form in which it has been transmitted, the story can hardly have been composed earlier than the middle of the seventh century B.C. Its diffusion in the ancient world was wide. Some portions, at least, of the history and of the parables were known to the Jewish community in Elephantine ; fuller versions of the story are extant in Syriac, Arabic, Armenian and Slavonic ; and, in varying degrees, the words and acts of Ahikar are echoed over a wide range of languages and literatures. The story of Ahikar finds, for instance, a place in the supplementary chapters to the Arabian Nights ; its influence on the story about the Greek Æsop is so marked as to presuppose direct dependence on the part of the latter ; it was known, according to Clement of Alexandria, to the Greek philosopher Democritus, and the Koran too knows of it. It is not surprising, therefore, that the Bible, both O.T. and N.T., and the Apocrypha, should reveal some close associations with this widely current cycle of Assyrian folk-lore and wisdom. The apocryphal book of Tobit, which has a very close affinity with the story of Ahikar, does in fact mention the sage by name (i.21f., ii.10, xi.18, xiv.10).

Except where otherwise stated, the selection from the proverbs and similitudes here presented is translated from the Syriac version contained in the seventeenth-century manuscript preserved in the University Library, Cambridge (Camb. Add. 2020), for they can be more fully studied in this version than in the much older fragmentary Aramaic version.

Points of contact between Ahikar and the O.T. range from similarities in thought and expression to cases of apparent identity. It is with the later books of the O.T. notably Psalms,

Proverbs, and Ecclesiastes, that these occur, and they certainly cannot all be accidental. In two instances (see below XII and XVII) we have the plainest evidence of older and more primitive versions of sayings in Ahikar than their counterparts in the book of Proverbs. The date when the Syriac version of Ahikar was made is not known, but it is not likely to have been before the early centuries of the Christian era. That this and other subsequent versions have been influenced by local religious, social, or geographical considerations no doubt accounts for some of the variations in detail in the story and sayings. But there is no evidence of borrowing by Ahikar from the O.T., and where there are signs of direct or indirect dependence of the one upon the other, there is always the strong presumption that this lies on the side of the O.T. and not *vice versa*. There are also many cases where similarity is of a general character only, and where the precise nature of the connection is not apparent. But in such cases, as elsewhere, it can at least be seen that Ahikar bears witness to a class of Wisdom literature familiar to the compilers of some of the later books of the O.T., and upon which they drew freely in the development of their themes.

Text

I. My son, it is better to move stones with a wise man than to drink wine with a fool.

II. My son, pour out thy wine upon the graves of the righteous, and do not drink it with iniquitous men.

III. My son, with a wise man thou wilt not become depraved, and with a depraved man thou wilt not become wise.

IV. My son, be a companion to a wise man and thou shalt become wise like him, but be not companion to a clamorous and talkative man lest thou be numbered with him.

V. My son, while thou hast shoes on thy feet, tread down the thorns and make a path for thy sons and for thy sons' sons.

VI. My son, the son of the rich man ate a snake, and they said, For his healing he ate it; and the son of the poor man ate it, and they said, For his hunger he ate it.

VII. My son, envy not the prosperity of thine enemy, and rejoice not at his adversity.

VIII. My son, draw not near to a woman that is a whisperer, nor to one whose voice is loud.

IX. My son, go not after the beauty of a woman, nor lust for her in thy heart; for the beauty of a woman is her discretion, and her adornment the word of her mouth.

X. My son, if thine enemy meet thee with evil, do thou meet him with wisdom.

XI. My son, the wicked falleth and riseth not; but the just man is not moved, for God is with him.

XII. My son, withhold not thy son from stripes; because stripes for a youth are like manure for a garden, and like a bond for an ass (or any other creature), and like a rope on the foot of an ass.

[*Elephantine Papyrus*] Withhold not thy son from the rod, if thou canst not keep. . . . If I smite thee, my son, thou wilt not die, and if I leave thee to thine own heart. . . .

XIII. My son, subdue thy son while he is yet a boy, before he become stronger than thee and rebel against thee, and thou be put to shame in all his corrupt doing.

XIV. My son, just as a tree is fair in its branches and in its fruit, and like a mountain that is bosky with trees, so is a man fair in his wife and in his sons; and the man who hath not brethren, nor wife, nor sons, is despised and contemptible before his enemies, and resembles a tree by the wayside, from which every passer-by taketh, and every wild beast shaketh down its foliage.

XV. My son, smite a man with a wise word that it may be in his heart like a fever in summer; for if thou shouldest smite a fool with many rods, he will not perceive it.

XVI. My son, I have carried salt and removed lead, and I have not seen anything more burdensome than that a man should have to pay back when he did not borrow.

XVII. My son, I have carried iron and removed stones, and they were not more burdensome upon me than when a man dwells in the house of his father-in-law.

[*Elephantine Papyrus*] I have lifted sand and carried salt, and there is nothing that is heavier than. . . . I have lifted chaff and taken up crumbs, and there is nothing which is lighter than a sojourner.

XVIII. My son, teach hunger and thirst to thy son, that according as his eye sees he may govern his house.

XIX. My son, better is a friend that is near than a brother that is far away, and better is a good name than much beauty ; because a good name standeth for ever, and beauty grows old and becomes corrupted.

XX. My son, better is death than life to the man that hath no rest ; and better (i.e. more beneficial) is the sound of lamentation in the ears of a fool than singing and joy.

XXI. My son, rejoice not over thine enemy when he dieth.

XXII. My son, when thou seest a man who is older than thee, rise up before him.

XXIII. My son, if water should stand up without (being banked up with) earth, and the sparrow fly without wings, and the raven become white as snow, and the bitter become sweet as honey, then may the fool become wise.

XXIV. My son, if thou art a priest of a god, be thou ware of him and enter his presence in purity, and from his presence do not depart.

XXV. My son, him that God prospers, do thou also honour.

XXVI. My son, strive not with a man in his day, nor stand against a river in its flood.

XXVII. My son, if thou desirest to be wise, restrain thy mouth from falsehood, and thy hand from theft, and thou shalt become wise.

XXVIII. My son, in the espousal of a woman have no part ; for if it go ill with her, she will curse thee ; and if it go well with her, she will not remember thee.

XXIX. My son, he that is agreeable in his dress is agreeable also in his speech, and he that is despicable in his dress is despicable also in his speech.

XXX. My son, let not thine eyes look upon a woman that is beautiful, and be not inquisitive into beauty that does not belong to thee ; for many have perished through the beauty of a woman, and her love has been like a fire that burneth.

XXXI. My son, let the wise man strike thee with many words, and let not the fool anoint thee with perfumed oil.

XXXII. My son, let not thy foot run after thy friend, lest he be surfeited with thee and hate thee.

XXXIII. My son, put not a gold ring on thy finger when thou hast nothing, lest fools make mock of thee.

XXXIV. My son, I taught thee that there is a God, and thou

risest up against good servants, and beatest those that did not trangress, and just as God has preserved me alive on account of my integrity, so hath he destroyed thee for thy works.

xxxv. My son, they set the head of an ass in a dish upon the table, and it rolled off and fell in the dust. And they say, He was angry with himself, for he has not accepted honour.

xxxvi. My son, thou hast verified the proverb which is current : Call him whom thou hast begotten thy son, and him whom thou hast purchased call thy slave.

xxxvii. My son, true is the proverb which is current : Take thy sister's son beneath thy arm and dash him against a stone. But God is he that hath preserved me alive, and he will judge between us.

xxxviii. To him that doeth good, what is good shall be recompensed, and to him that doeth evil, what is evil shall be repaid. And he that diggeth a pit for his neighbour filleth it with his own body.

Notes

ii. The primitive practice of making libations or other offerings for the dead receives approval in Tob. iv.17, where the wording is similar, and also in Ecclus. vii.33, xxx.18. It is mentioned in Jer. xvi.7 and Ezek. xxiv.17. Deut. xxvi.14 by implication condemns it. Cp. also Bar. vi.32.

iv. The same idea is expressed in Prov. xiii.20.

vii. Prov. xxiv.17 is closely similar. Cp. also xvii.5 and Ps.xxxv. 15, 19.

ix. Cp. proverb xxx. The theme is generally current throughout the Wisdom Literature. For the injunction not to look upon *the beauty of a woman*, cp. Ecclus. ix.8 and the Testaments of the Twelve Patriarchs (Test. of Reuben iii.10, iv.1 ; Test. of Judah xvii.1 ; Test. of Issachar iv.4). In the book of Proverbs, however, the emphasis is different. Here it is not the beauty of a woman which is the stumbling-block causing the inquisitive to err, but rather the 'foolish woman' (Prov. ix.13) or the 'strange woman' herself (Prov. ii.16, v.3, vi.24, vii.5), who, by her words, rather than by her outward appearance, leads foolish men astray and is to be avoided (Prov. v.8). In Prov. xxxi.10-31 the abiding quality of a woman is shown to rest in her practical and moral propensities, whereas 'Favour is deceitful, and beauty is vain' (verse 30). The thought expressed in the second half of Ahikar's saying appears to have been taken up by the O.T. sages and developed (see especially verses 17, 25f.).

xi. Prov. xxiv.16 is closely similar, and in part Ps. xxxvii.24.

xii. Cp. proverb xiii. The close similarity between the Elephantine text and

Prov. xxiii.13f. provides a strong presupposition of dependence on the part of the latter upon Ahikar, either directly or indirectly. For variations of the same adage, cp. Prov. xiii.24, xix.18, xxii.15, xxix.15, 17.

xiv. Ps. cxxvii.5 expresses the same thought.

xv. Cp. proverb xxiii. There are some points of close similarity in Prov. xvii.10 and xxiii.35, and it is quite possible that in each case some form, or forms, of this saying of Ahikar has been drawn upon.

xvi, xvii. The Elephantine text supplies us with proof of the antiquity of these sayings, and the versions of them which occur in Ecclus. xxii.14f. and Prov. xxvii.3 are manifestly connected with Ahikar, and in all probability are directly derived from this source.

xix, xx. For xixa, cp. Prov. xviii.24b ; for xixb, xx, cp. Eccles. vii.1f. In both cases Ahikar may have been the source.

xxi. Cp. proverb vii.

xxiii. Cp. proverb xv.

xxvi. Cp. Ecclus. iv.26b, where a similar idea is expressed.

xxx. Cp. proverb ix. Ecclus. ix.8 is closely parallel.

xxxi. Cp. Ps. cxli.5.

xxxii. Cp. Prov. xxv.17. (See D. WINTON THOMAS, *J.T.S.* xxxviii (1937) 402).

xxxvii. Cp. Ps. cxxxvii.9.

xxxviii. Cp. Prov. xxvi.27, xxviii.10 ; Eccles. x.8 ; Ps. cxli.10.

Bibliography

BAUMGARTNER, W. 'The Wisdom Literature', in *The Old Testament and Modern Study*, ed. H. H. ROWLEY, 1951, 210-37.

CHARLES, R. H. *Apocrypha and Pseudepigrapha of the Old Testament*, II, 1913, 715-84.

CONYBEARE, F. C., RENDEL HARRIS, J., and LEWIS, A. S. *The Story of Ahikar from the Aramaic, Syriac, Arabic, Armenian, Ethiopic, Old Turkish, Greek and Slavonic Versions*, second ed., 1913.

COWLEY, A. *Aramaic Papyri of the Fifth Century B.C.*, 1923, 204-48.

GINSBERG, H. L., in *A.N.E.T.*, 427-30.

A. E. GOODMAN

Indexes

I. General Index

Aaron 215
Ab 206
Ab (month) 76, 79
Abdiheba (king of Jerusalem) xviii, xx, 38-44 *pass.*
Abdili'tu 66
Abibaal, Abi-ba'al 74, 206f.
Abiel 207
Abiezer 205
Abijah 207
Abilakka 55, 57
Abimelech 126
Abimelek 205
Abiyan 206
Abraham 156, 195, 245
Absalom 121
Abydenus 71
Achaeans 137
Achbor 41, 213, 226
Acre 52
Acrostic poem 97
Adad (storm-god, Hadad) 21f., 45, 47, 52, 72
Adad-'idri (Hadadezer) 47f.
Adad-nirari III xviii, 50f.
Adaiah 42
Adar (month) 72, 80, 81, 82
'Adarkon 232 (cp. daric)
Adda (Adad, Hadad) 45
Addaya 39, 42
Adennu 47
Adon xx, 251-4; identity of his kingdom 252
Adonai 115
Adonijah 252
Adonizedek 252
Adoption, law of 33
Adrammelech 70
Adultery, law of 31f., 36
Adunu-ba ali 47
Aesop 270
Afis 242f., 250
Aga' 252
Agade 93
Agriculture 202
Ah 206
Ahab xviii, xix, 48, 122, 195, 198, 204, 206, 240, 249 (Ahabbu (met) Sir'-ilaia 48); contribution to army at Qarqar 47
Ahaz xviii, 221 (cp. Jehoahaz); tribute to Assyria 53, 57

Ahaz (name in Samaria ostraca) 207
Ahikam 223
Ahikar 270; Words (Story) of xxii, 107, 254, 270-5; and Old Testament 270f.; and Proverbs 271, 274f.; and Tobit 270; versions 270
Ahimelech 40
Ahi-millei 74
Ahimiti 61
Ahinoam 205
Ahiyahu 214, 215
Ahlab 68 (cp. Mahalliba)
Ahura-Mazda 94
Aiamurru 66
Aijalon 40, 42
'Ain Shems 224
Akhenaten 38, 143-50 *pass.*, 252, 253 (Akhenaton); religious policy 142f.; sun-worship 44
Akhetaten 143
Akkad 82, 89-93 *pass.*
Akkadians 14f.
Akkadian language xvii, 27, 38, 111; letters 38; naming of weapons 15; pantheon 17; translation of Sumerian texts 111
Akku 66
Akzib 66
Aleppo 47, 56, 239, 242f., 248, 250
Alexander the Great 234
Alexandretta 249
Allabria 51
Ator 248
Am 206
Amanus (= anti-Lebanon) 88
Amarna *see* Tell el-Amarna
Amarus mountains 243, 249
Amenemope 173f., 180; teaching of xxii, 149, 154, 172-86; and Proverbs 172ff.; and other books of Old Testament 174, 178
Amenhotep II 149, 254
— III (Amenophis) 38, 88, 137, 142
— IV (Akhenaton) 38, 44 142f.
Ammon 47, 57, 252
Ammonite(s) 27, 140
Amon (sun-god) 44
Amon-Re 143f., 149, 152f.
Amorite-land 51f.
Amos 107, 227

279

II Index of Biblical References